Revolutionizing Expectations

Revolutionizing Expectations

Women's Organizations, Feminism, and American Politics, 1965–1980

MELISSA ESTES BLAIR

The University of Georgia Press *Athens and London*

Athens, Georgia 30602
www.ugapress.org

Set in Kepler Std by Graphic Composition, Inc.
Printed and bound by Sheridan Books, Inc.
The paper in this book meets the guidelines for permanence and durability of the Committee on Production Guidelines for Book Longevity of the Council on Library Resources.

Most University of Georgia Press titles are available from popular e-book vendors.

Printed in the United States of America
18 17 16 15 14 P 5 4 3 2 1

Library of Congress Cataloging-in-Publication Data

Blair, Melissa Estes, 1980–
Revolutionizing expectations : women's organizations, feminism, and American politics, 1965–1980 / Melissa Estes Blair.
pages cm
Includes bibliographical references and index.
ISBN 978-0-8203-3979-5 (hardcover : alk. paper) —
ISBN 0-8203-3979-2 (hardcover : alk. paper) —
ISBN 978-0-8203-4713-4 (pbk. : alk. paper) —
ISBN 0-8203-4713-2 (pbk. : alk. paper)
1. Feminism—United States—History—20th century. 2. Women—United States—Societies and clubs—History—20th century. 3. Women—Political activity—United States—History—20th century. I. Title.
HQ1236.5.U6B562 2014
305.420973—dc23
2014005791

British Library Cataloging-in-Publication Data available

To my Mom and Dad, and to Ross
With love and thanks

CONTENTS

ACKNOWLEDGMENTS

I am very grateful to have an opportunity to thank the many, many people who helped, in ways large and small, to bring this book into being. As with any first book, the road was long, and therefore the debts are many. It's impossible for me to thank everyone, but there are many people whom I am pleased to be able to acknowledge here.

Financial support for this project was provided by many institutions. This book began its life as my dissertation. While I was conducting that research, an Annaley Nagel Redd grant from the Charles Redd Center at Brigham Young University helped offset the costs of spending a month in Denver. The Graduate School of Arts & Sciences at the University of Virginia provided several small travel grants to support my other trips. UVA's Corcoran Department of History also supported my dissertation through several years of teaching assistantships and by awarding me a Doris G. Quinn Foundation Fellowship, which allowed me a year off teaching to write the dissertation and finish my PhD promptly. While turning my dissertation into this book, I received additional support from the Sallie Bingham Center for Women's History and Culture at Duke University. The Department of History and Political Science at Warren Wilson College helped cover the expenses of preparing the book's index.

Every history book is a testament to the hard work and helpfulness of archivists, and I was fortunate enough to work with many wonderful women and men at libraries across the country. I thank the staffs of the David M. Rubenstein Rare Books and Manuscripts Library's Sallie Bingham Center at Duke University, the William Henry Smith Memorial Library of the Indiana Historical Society, the Colorado Historical Society, the Special Collections Division of the Auraria Library at the University of Colorado–Denver, and the Schlesinger Library at Harvard. The staff of the Western History and Genealogy Division of the Denver Public Library deserve special mention. They were thrilled to have a graduate student pursuing dissertation research at their library and went out of their way to be helpful and welcoming, often pulling things for me after I had left or making other librarians aware of my work so that I found everything I might need. Working there was a joy, and I hope other historians will look to the very rich archives many public libraries hold to further their own research.

I had a wonderful team of professors and friends at the University of Virginia who helped see me through the ups and downs of graduate school. Professors Brian Balogh, Gary Gallaher, and Chuck McCurdy and fellow graduate students Elizabeth Barrett Blount, Josh Botts, Danielle Carlotti-Smith, Lisa Goff, Amy Jacobs, Victoria Meyer, Rob Rakove, Matt Speiser, and Anne Throckmorton all made my six years in Charlottesville wonderful ones. Erik and Carrie Alexander and Vanessa May and Pat McDonough remain some of my closest friends and have given me wonderful advice about grad school, academia, motherhood, and life in general for a decade now. Vanessa has also read every version of this project many times, and the book is far better for her repeated critiques, questions, and suggestions.

I was incredibly lucky to have the best possible adviser. Every one of Cindy Aron's students speak glowingly of her in our acknowledgments, for good reason. She is the model of what a graduate school adviser should be: a gifted scholar who turned her mind to my work again and again and offered the best feedback anyone could hope for. Cindy is also tremendously kind and an unfailing advocate for her students and their work. We all say this, but she truly is my model of how to balance being a mother, a teacher, and a scholar.

After I left UVA and continued work on this project, I incurred many more debts. I spent a year as a lecturer at the University of Georgia, where I was fortunate to find myself among scholars who took me under their collective wing and helped me make the transition from grad student to professor. I will always be grateful to Shane Hamilton, Ari Levine, Bethany Moreton, and Paul Sutter for their guidance. At Warren Wilson College, I have been fortunate to find in Philip Otterness a department chair who encourages my research agenda at a very teaching-heavy small college and has supported the completion of this book in every way he can. My friends here in Asheville, especially Lucy Lawrence, Chris Kypriotis, Erin Montero, and Jen Mozolic, have provided needed breaks and helped keep me sane.

As I began the final major revision of the manuscript, Michael Estes, Philip Otterness, and Rachel L. Pierce each read a chapter and gave me invaluable feedback. Melanie Beals Goan read two chapters and provided thoughtful critique at every turn. I am grateful to all of them for their work on my behalf. I also wish to thank the reviewers for the University of Georgia Press for their input, which strengthened the book in many ways. Derek Krissoff brought my book to the UGA Press and was always in my corner through some early rough patches. Since his departure Beth Snead and Mick Guisnde-Duffy have ably shepherded me across the finish line.

Finally I have to thank my family. My mother, Babs Weinmann, and my father, Allen Estes, have supported and encouraged my dreams every day of my life. My brother, Michael Estes, is a wonderful sounding board about everything, academic and otherwise, as well as an excellent writer in his own right who eagerly brings a much-needed nonhistorian's eye to my writing. My daughter, Maggie, brings me joy and perspective every day and helps ensure that I don't take myself too seriously. I cannot imagine a better partner than my husband, Ross. His own career has taken a backseat to mine so that I could take a tenure-track job, finish this book, have a child, and not completely lose my mind. His support has made it possible for me to accomplish all that I have; this book would not exist without him. Most importantly, he has made me laugh every single day of the decade we've spent together. Dedicating this book to him is but a small fraction of the thanks he is owed.

Revolutionizing Expectations

INTRODUCTION

In April 1970, women from all over the country gathered in Houston for the Young Women's Christian Association's (YWCA) twenty-fifth national convention. The organization's triennial conventions brought members together to vote on the group's broadest priorities for the coming three years. The list of priorities adopted in 1970 moved the YWCA toward more aggressive tactics, as well as a rethinking of the organization's public image. Members were urged to think about questions such as "What is outworn in institutions today, especially in our YWCA?" and "What barriers must be broken now to free human beings to achieve the freedom we ask for them in our treatises and prayers?" In answering these questions and establishing the group's direction in the new decade, the YWCA committed itself to feminism. Members pledged that chapters would work to "revolutionize society's expectations of women" as well as members' self-perceptions in order to raise women "from second rate citizenship."[1] YWCA members returned to their homes encouraged to do everything they could to transform their organization into a group that led the way in bringing about feminist change throughout the country.

This book examines the role that organizations such as the YWCA played in the women's movement of the 1960s and 1970s. In cities and towns throughout the country, women's organizations that predated the feminist movement of those decades became vital channels for feminist ideas and activism.[2] In two of the three cities examined here—Denver, Colorado, and Indianapolis, Indiana—existing women's groups worked alongside local chapters of the National Organization for Women (NOW). In Durham, North Carolina, NOW struggled to gain a foothold, as did any other explicitly feminist group, and existing women's organizations were the heart and soul of feminism in that city. Exploring the feminist work of women's groups at the local level gives us a fuller understanding of what feminist action looked like, where it happened, and who undertook it during one of the most important periods of changes for women in American history.

This broadening of perspective on the women's movement is necessary, in part, because of the dominance of radical feminism in the scholarship about the movement. The earliest studies of the movement, such as Jo Freeman's *The Politics of Women's Liberation* and Sara Evans's *Personal Politics*, were published in the second half of the 1970s while the movement was still flourishing and by authors who were active in the movement's radical branch. By recording their own experiences and those of their peers, these scholars and others who followed them contributed enormously to our understanding of how the women's movement looked from the inside. Such an insider perspective, however, continues to dominate historians' work on the subject even as scholars who did not participate have begun writing about it.[3] The majority of the literature of the women's movement has focused on the efforts of the movement's theorists and nationally recognized leaders, most of whom lived in New York or a handful of other very large cities. By the late 1990s, the cumulative effect of many works of scholarship that examined similar subjects was the creation of an implicit definition of who a 1960s or 1970s feminist was. She was a woman living in New York, Boston, Chicago, San Francisco, or Washington, D.C. She was white and middle class, and her age could be accurately guessed by her organizational affiliation. If a child of the baby boom, she was a member of a small women's liberation or radical feminist group. If somewhat older, she was more likely to join NOW.[4]

Academic works appearing since the late 1990s have collectively eliminated the impressions that the women's movement consisted solely of white, middle-class women and that the ideas of feminism appealed only to such women. Books have described the role of media in the movement, the relationship between women of color and feminism, and coalition work undertaken by white and African American feminists.[5] Historians Anne Enke, Judith Ezekiel, and Stephanie Gilmore have explored, as I do, the course of the movement in cities far from its intellectual home in the Northeast, telling pieces of the feminist histories of cities as diverse as Dayton, Detroit, Memphis, and Milwaukee.[6] *Revolutionizing Expectations* complements Gilmore's 2012 monograph *Groundswell* in many ways, as she examines the work of local NOW chapters in southern (Memphis), midwestern (Columbus), and western (San Francisco) cities. I also consider the work of NOW on the local level in Indianapolis and Denver, where the organization had active chapters. But by incorporating other organizations into my story, I am able not only to expand our understanding of what the women's movement looked like on the local level but also to broaden our notions of who feminists were and how they pursued feminist change in their communities.

These newer works have continued to share one thing in common with the older studies: all but one examine radical feminists.[7] There are good reasons for this focus. As historian Anne Valk has argued, radical feminists were "a cutting edge that helped introduce new styles of activism and ideas about women's oppression."[8] Radical feminists were, by and large, the movement's leading theorists and led the way in discussing the multiple sources and types of oppression women faced in late twentieth-century American society.[9] They also were the women to most consistently link women's oppression to the macro structures of American society, such as capitalism.[10] They were the intellectuals and theorists of the movement. In trying to understand feminism, studying the women who created its theories and beliefs is a logical place to begin.

However, such women were not the only feminists, especially in the 1970s. As the women's movement spread, a much wider range of women, with far more diverse political backgrounds and beliefs, were drawn to the movement's ideas. This book tells the story of women who did not identify as radical feminists, and some who did not self-identify as feminists at all. It looks at the work of liberal women's groups and their members in spreading the messages of the women's movements, implementing feminist programs, and lobbying for feminist laws. These women's organizations did work with more-radical and explicitly feminist groups, especially in Indianapolis. But in Denver, Durham, and Indianapolis, as in most smaller cities around the country, the ideas of the radicals were spread by women's organizations and leaders whose activism on women's issues predated radical feminism. Focusing on the role of local feminist activism outside explicitly feminist groups reveals that feminist ideas were advanced in Denver, Durham, and Indianapolis in much the same way that other hot-button political issues of the day were: either through the national media or through the networks of women that made up existing women's groups such as the YWCA and the League of Women Voters (LWV). The feminist activism of women's organizations that predated the women's movement meant that feminist ideas came to Denver and Durham and Indianapolis not only as ideas promoted by the movement's intellectual leaders on television but also from neighbors, coworkers, and fellow church congregants telling their fellow citizens that the treatment of women in the United States and their local communities both could and should be changed.

Not all of the women engaged in these projects, however, would have described themselves as feminists. Although deeply involved in feminist action, many were put off by media depictions of feminists as aggressive women who wanted to radically alter gender roles in American society.[11] Looking beyond those women who identified as feminists enables me to study a wider range of people engaged in feminist action, revealing a larger and more complex grassroots feminist movement. Indeed, the existing scholarship's focus on women who identified as feminists has greatly narrowed our understanding of what feminist action looked like at the height of the women's movement.[12] The effect of this limited focus has been to imply that the only feminist activists during the women's movement were to be found in newly formed organizations.[13] When looking at local feminist activists in the 1970s, scholars have retained a focus on those women who identified as feminists. However, scholars of periods in which there was no thriving, explicitly feminist movement have done much to uncover feminist work in those years by looking in perhaps unexpected places such as labor unions.[14] Similarly broadening our focus in the 1970s reveals thousands of grassroots feminists whose activism was vital to changing ideas about gender roles and passing feminist legislation, but whose activism has gone unheralded.

I chose Denver, Durham, and Indianapolis as the locations in which to examine local feminism for several reasons. In 1965 they were all medium-sized cities (Denver's rapid growth was just beginning at that time). Archival records of women's organizations in all three cities gave me access to the voices and experiences of a broad cross section of each city's women—not only the middle-class white women who tended to populate League of Women Voters chapters, but the racially and class-diverse members of YWCAs, women who pursued civic work through religious organizations like the National Council of Jewish Women and Churchwomen United, and women of color who worked through racially specific groups like the National Council of Negro Women. Most important, however, was the fact that they were cities in different parts of the country. Each town had a different racial mix, a different economic base, and different political leanings. Women's groups were adept at designing programs that were sensitive to those local conditions and were able to bring about change on many contentious issues by working within local norms. In spite of this sensitivity to local conditions, however, women's groups played a similar role in local politics in all three cities. By studying cities in different parts of the country and finding similar experiences in each, I can tell a national story. The role that women's organizations played in Denver, Durham, and Indianapolis was one that they undoubtedly played in many other cities throughout the country. Their common experiences, then, tell us much about the course of feminism throughout the United States and how some of the core ideas of the women's movement came to be widely accepted by the end of the 1970s.

While this book is, at its heart, a study of local feminist activism, that narrative is embedded within a broader exploration of the role of women's organizations in local politics. The actions of the women in these groups compelled this structure, because feminism was never the only issue with which they were engaged. Well before the emergence of the women's movement, women's organizations were active participants in local politics. In the mid-1960s, League of Women Voters chapters, YWCAs, and other women's organizations were leading voices in local discussions about the environment, antipoverty programs, and school integration. As feminism came to the fore, they retained those previous commitments, folding feminist work into a broad liberal agenda. In all three cities, for example, women's organizations played central roles in implementing school integration plans ordered by federal judges in the early 1970s while simultaneously lobbying for ratification of the Equal Rights Amendment. Their activism on nonfeminist issues was crucial to women's groups' success as feminist actors. Community members were used to the organizations' participation in and leadership of public discussions of politics. Leaders of women's organizations were regularly among the voices explaining to the public how contentious national issues affected their communities and would be implemented in their towns, and they had influence within their cities.

Although women's organizations were not the only avenues through which women engaged in local politics in the 1960s and 1970s, only single-sex organizations are examined here, for several reasons. It was in these groups that women had control over every aspect of activism, from choosing tactics to prioritizing issues and then carrying out action. A focus on women's organizations also illuminates how women saw their position as activists in their communities, where they considered women's action to be appropriate, and when they chose specifically gendered forms of activism. Uncovering the work of these groups highlights the vital role that women's organizations played in local politics in the 1960s and 1970s.

Because they were single-sex groups involved in a wide range of issues, the development of organized antifeminism in the 1970s presented a particular challenge for women's organizations. Groups that conducted feminist work alongside other projects faced the possibility of having all their work discredited by STOP ERA and other conservative organizations that overtly only disagreed with their feminist positions. This ability of antifeminist groups to discredit entire agendas of women's organizations, however, not only threatened the groups' feminist work; it also imperiled their political standing more broadly. Throughout the post–World War II period, local politicians had turned to mainstream women's groups to get a sense of what "women" in their community thought about a particular issue. The League of Women Voters, with its staunch adherence to principles of nonpartisanship and emphasis on providing what members described as "factual" information about hotly contested topics, was particularly prominent in this regard.[15] The emergence of antifeminism in the form of Phyllis Schlafly's STOP ERA organization gave the lie once and for all to the notion that all women felt the same way about issues. Antifeminism, therefore, represented a threat not only to mainstream women's groups' feminist commitments but to their role in local politics more broadly. If women disagreed about political issues, what service did established women's groups like the League provide to civic leaders that was different from other interest groups, whose numbers had increased dramatically over the course of the 1970s?

In the last years of the 1970s, therefore, women's organizations faced serious decisions about their future. Some groups attempted to take a step back and return to the nonpartisan, multi-issue tactics of earlier years. But other groups had, by the late 1970s, become thoroughly feminist organizations and felt they could not back down in the face of serious threats to the feminist gains that many of them had helped secure in their community. These groups, in effect, "doubled down" on feminism, increasing their activism on those issues and letting other areas of interest slide. Their persistence was in itself a sign of the women's movement's accomplishments. Members of the groups that maintained their feminist commitments simply could not imagine returning to a worldview or ways of operating that were not shaped by feminist beliefs. The change in perspective created by the women's movement could not be undone.

This book moves from a collective discussion of all three cities to an individual focus on each and then back to the collective lens. Chapter 1 outlines the political activism of women's groups before the rise of the women's movement. Documenting the actions that these organizations took on the controversial political issues of the 1960s, specifically civil rights and poverty, highlights the central role that women's organizations played in local politics in that era. Women's groups—especially but not exclusively the League of Women Voters—played two major roles in their communities with regard to these topics. First, they served as sources that local politicians could tap to "take the temperature" of the community and see how certain segments of the local population felt about an issue or project. Second, they provided essential womanpower for implementing projects, whether those projects were designed by local politicians or mandated by federal programs, such as the neighborhood councils established to implement War on Poverty initiatives. The centrality of women's organizations in both of these roles meant that both the groups' authority within the community and their organizational capacity for action were well established before the women's movement emerged and primed these groups to become channels of feminism.

Chapters 2, 3, and 4 each focus on a single city. Chapter 2 documents the vital role played by women's organizations, especially the YWCA, in providing feminist services in Durham, a city where one activist remembers NOW being considered "too radical" by locals throughout the 1970s.[16] Because of their established presence in the community, women's groups were able to provide a range of feminist programs and services—some of them typically associated with radical feminism—without raising the alarm bells of more conservative residents of their southern town. Also, because feminist action flowed through existing women's organizations that had publicly committed themselves to racial integration in the 1960s, the women's movement in Durham was an integrated effort to a much higher degree than some previous studies suggest was possible.[17] African American women were involved in establishing many of the early feminist services and programs at the Durham YWCA, and the city's African American community appears to have supported many of feminism's goals.

Chapter 3 examines the course of feminism in Indianapolis. Indianapolis was home to a thriving radical feminist group, Indianapolis Women's Liberation (IWL), in the early 1970s, and that group merged with the large local NOW chapter in 1974. Indianapolis, then, had the potential to become a city with an extensive radical feminist community, similar to the one discovered in Dayton, Ohio, by historian Judith Ezekiel in her book *Feminism in the Heartland.* But the landscapes in which IWL and Indianapolis NOW were operating were quite different from that of their Ohio peers for one major reason: Indiana was a battleground state in the effort to ratify the Equal Rights Amendment (ERA), which passed Congress in 1972 but saw ratifications by state legislatures stall after 1974. This chapter, therefore, traces the efforts of both existing women's groups and explicitly feminist organizations as they worked together, sometimes quite tensely, to secure ratification of the amendment. They achieved that goal in 1977, making Indiana the last state to ratify. Focusing on Indianapolis women's groups' work on ERA ratification uncovers the decisions that were made, the prioritization of issues, and the compromises that some feminists felt were necessary to wrest ratification out of a state legislature never regarded by national ERA leaders as particularly likely to ratify.[18] But the ERA was not the sole issue through which women's groups or explicitly feminist organizations engaged with the women's movement. Documenting the complex nature of feminist action that was somewhat concealed by the ERA fight, chapter 3 paints a picture of a robust, multifaceted, and ultimately quite effective feminist community in a conservative midwestern town.

Chapter 4 turns to Denver, where a similar mix of existing and new women's groups engaged in a wide range of feminist action throughout the 1970s. The context feminists encountered in Denver, however, could not have been more different from that in Indianapolis. Both the Denver city and the Colorado state governments proved remarkably open to many of feminism's legal and legislative goals throughout the first half of the 1970s. The feminist community that emerged in Denver, therefore, operated within a more welcoming space. This different context led to a different mix of feminist groups than existed in the other two cities studied here. The Denver League of Women Voters, for example, engaged in very little feminist work, unlike chapters in Indianapolis and Durham, where the LWV was a key ERA supporter. The comfort that many feminist activists in Denver likely felt led to a less robust grassroots network of feminist groups—the local NOW chapter undertook much of the activism in the city, and the Colorado Commission on the Status of Women served as the kind of state-level clearinghouse that women's organizations provided in the other two locations. In the end, however, this amenable atmosphere proved to have one serious drawback. When conservative activists began to challenge feminist programs and laws, there was no strong group outside the government where feminists could rally. The tremendous amount of support feminists encountered in the first half of the 1970s in Denver rendered them somewhat flat-footed when they faced challengers late in the decade.

Chapter 5 takes a broader focus and considers the reactions and decisions made by liberal women's organizations in all three cities once antifeminist activists gained visibility in each town. It documents the dismay that many women activists felt at what they understood to be not only different policies that these conservative activists were pursuing but, perhaps even more startlingly, the different tactics they were using to achieve those goals. Over and over again, feminists—especially those who came to feminism through existing women's groups—decried what they described as the use of "emotion" by conservative activists. Chapter 5 documents the varied choices that liberal women's groups made in the face of these rapid changes and shows that while some groups were a bit more successful than others, by 1980 no liberal women's organization maintained the same position and sway in local politics that it had held just five years earlier.

The women's movement brought sweeping changes to every corner of the United States. By 1980 ideas about what women could and should be doing had expanded dramatically, rape crisis centers were proliferating, attitudes toward domestic violence were beginning to shift, and women's legal status had made major gains in becoming the same as men's. Feminists did not achieve all their objectives, but they accomplished a tremendous amount. Focusing on cities that were not the birthplaces of feminism and on the feminist activism of women who chose not to join NOW or other women's liberation groups but who were, nonetheless, feminists helps explain the rapid, transformational accomplishments of the women's movement.

CHAPTER ONE

Women's Grassroots Political Activism in the 1960s

In May 1964, President Lyndon Johnson declared a national War on Poverty, stating that the federal government would work for "an end of poverty and racial injustice" and toward creating a society that "serves not only the needs of the body and the demands of commerce but the desire for beauty and hunger for community."[1] A major part of the War on Poverty was the creation of community organizations that would bring poor men and women more fully into the decision-making process around programs that helped them and engage them more deeply with government at the local, state, and national levels.[2] In the spring of 1966, the Indianapolis League of Women Voters became one of the leading organizations in the city helping to implement the War on Poverty plans. The group held a workshop for CAAP (Community Action against Poverty) neighborhood workers on "Who's In Charge Here," a League program that explained the many jurisdictions and departments of the city, county, and township governments in greater Indianapolis.[3] The League also supervised elections of neighborhood representatives to the CAAP council and organized a workshop in January 1967 to teach mothers receiving welfare how to lobby state legislators.[4] These programs represented the primary way that the Indianapolis League engaged with the War on Poverty. The chapter merged its commitment to encouraging citizen participation in government, a longtime focus of League work, with War on Poverty directives to bring low-income people into active engagement with the city and state government.[5] League members went into their city's poor neighborhoods and tried to help the people living there interact effectively with their government, demonstrating through that work the group's commitment to the goals of the War on Poverty.

This chapter examines the activism of local women's groups like the Indianapolis LWV on poverty and welfare and school desegregation from the mid-1960s through the early 1970s.[6] These were far from the only areas in which women were active. Environmentalism and foreign policy were also frequent topics of public forums, programs, and lobbying by women's groups—especially the League—in these years.[7] This chapter focuses on poverty and school desegregation because these were the issues to which members of many organizations were most devoted in all three cities. They were also the most complex and controversial sets of problems faced by all three cities in the years before the emergence of the women's movement. And in all three cities, politicians and community members knew of women's groups' long histories of successful activism and believed those groups were well positioned to offer advice and develop programming regarding some of the biggest problems facing each community.

In the 1960s, women's organizations continued to play an important role in the lives of middle-class women, much as they had since the organizations' founding in the late nineteenth century. Groups like the League of Women Voters, the YWCA, and the American Association of University Women (AAUW) provided women with spaces that were women-only, where they could freely discuss their personal lives, the political and social problems of the day, and the interactions between those seemingly different types of issues.[8] As scholar Anne Ruggles Gere has argued, women's organizations, from their founding, had "political as well as personal dimensions."[9] By the middle of the twentieth century, those political dimensions had made many women's clubs central players in local politics, with members speaking before city council meetings and on local television news programs on behalf of their groups. Women's clubs also connected their members to peers throughout the nation, creating "common ground" among women across the country.[10] All these factors made women's club members central figures in local politics.

The two women's organizations that are at the heart of this book are the League of Women Voters and the YWCA. The history of these two groups structured their activism in the late twentieth century, decades after the groups were founded. The League of Women Voters was formed in 1920, when the National American Women's Suffrage Association (NAWSA) renamed and repositioned itself for the postsuffrage era. The League's founding mission was "training for citizenship, improved legislation, efficient government, and international cooperation."[11] Early on, members established strict nonpartisanship as the group's policy: it would never endorse candidates for office nor lobby for a position using partisan arguments. The organization was also devoted to providing "objective facts," and to ensure that the group's position on issues was based on fact rather than opinion, an elaborate decision-making structure was established. Once an issue was selected for discussion, "units" of fifteen or so women gathered in one another's homes and studied agenda items for several months. After multiple meetings on an issue, each unit agreed on a consensus position. Only if a majority of the chapter members concurred on a consensus position could action be taken or public statements be made in the League's name.[12] These policies and practices were still firmly entrenched in the 1960s and 1970s. The number of women in the League chapters studied here ranged from three hundred to six hundred during the 1960s, with all three chapters gaining members throughout most of that decade.[13]

The YWCA's structure was less rigid, but its history was no less important in attracting members and shaping their responses to the dramatic social and political changes of the 1960s. While the League existed to promote political participation and lobby for legislation, the YWCA was created in 1866 to provide social and educational services and develop leadership skills in women.[14] It was an organization dedicated to assisting those in need of help, especially women and girls, and meeting the needs of all women in the community as best it could. While there was a national board that issued broad statements of goals, local associations retained a great deal of autonomy in building their programs. As a result of these factors, the YWCA was a more flexible organization than the League at the national and especially at the local level. This flexibility enabled YWCAs around the country to respond, in many cases, more promptly and more creatively than the League to the most controversial issues of the day. This purpose, however, also makes determining the size of a particular YWCA and the scope of its influence difficult. Each chapter studied here had only a few hundred members but annually served over a thousand women and girls through its programs.

While groups like the Durham YWCA and the Denver LWV were branches of these national organizations, they were first and foremost local organizations. Studying their work on school integration and antipoverty reveals groups of women who thought hard about the best way to approach these sensitive issues in their communities. They were very aware of their local context and made decisions about the tactics to use, the level of publicity to seek, and other factors based on their analysis of local feelings about the topic and the local political climate. This pattern of careful attention to local context bore fruit in the late 1960s and early 1970s, enabling women's organizations to implement effective programs that addressed controversial issues. That experience, in turn, influenced the choices that women's groups made when they engaged with the women's movement.

By exploring women's groups' reactions to and interactions with the

War on Poverty and school integration in Durham, Indianapolis, and Denver, this chapter introduces readers to the organizations and cities that are main characters of the book. Stories of facilitating community-action committee elections and writing editorials about school integration illuminate the tactics that women's groups used in their political work in the 1960s. Groups' activist histories and tactical preferences remained part of each group's identity when they began exploring feminist ideas around 1970. The political climate of each city that was built by the fights over school integration and antipoverty work formed the context in which feminist action would take place. Telling the story of those battles and debates, therefore, establishes the landscape that feminism encountered as the women's movement spread in the 1970s and demonstrates how, for many women's groups, the kinds of activism undertaken in the 1960s strongly foreshadowed their sympathy for and engagement with feminism.

Durham

By the mid-1960s, the demographic makeup of Durham, North Carolina, was being altered by a series of economic changes. By 1940 Duke University, which had been in Durham since 1892, was evolving from a regional institution into a nationally recognized school with a strong academic reputation, enrolling 3,700 students for the 1940–41 year and growing rapidly from there.[15] The growth of Duke, along with the Research Triangle development, which began construction just southeast of Durham in the late 1950s, pulled an enormous number of highly educated nonsoutherners to the area throughout the postwar era, a migration that peaked in the 1970s and 1980s.[16] This influx of newcomers, however, was not unknown to Durham. As a New South boomtown in the 1880s and 1890s, it had a long history of incorporating nonnative residents. As historian Leslie Brown has stated about the first decades of the twentieth century, and as was equally true in the middle of the century, "almost everyone in Durham came from someplace else."[17]

After World War II, Durham was also home to a sizable middle-class African American community, centered around North Carolina Mutual Life Insurance Company (the largest black-owned life insurance company in the country), the historically black North Carolina College, and Lincoln Hospital and its nurses' training school.[18] Mutual Life Insurance executives and NCC professors were joined in the city by numerous African American employees of the city's tobacco factories. The presence of a large black middle class did nothing, however, to diminish the city's Jim Crow regime.

Civic leaders in the city took pains to preserve the moderate, middle-class reputation of the city that attracted northern investment while also maintaining racially segregated schools and discouraging demonstrations in opposition to segregated accommodations.[19]

Durham's women's organizations were involved in some of the most controversial political topics of the postwar era. But unlike their sister chapters in other cities, all of Durham's groups seem to have been deeply concerned about maintaining respectability in the community. The caution with which women's groups proceeded in the 1960s highlights the importance of place and local context. Daily life in Durham had been rocked since the mid-1950s by the deconstruction of the Jim Crow regime, a process that was still under way in the second half of the 1960s. Durham was a deeply divided community racially and politically in the 1960s; in the 1968 presidential election Democrat Hubert Humphrey, Republican Richard Nixon, and conservative States' Rights candidate George Wallace each earned roughly one-third of the county's vote.[20] In the face of such a sharp division of opinion, members of the YWCA and the League limited the amount of public, vocal support their groups gave to controversial issues such as school integration. Despite the presence of a large number of nonsouthern white residents, Durham remained a town very attached to a traditional southern identity in the 1960s. That community identity made women's organizations seeking progressive social change move cautiously and quietly in pursuing their goals.

By 1965 Durham's women's groups had achieved various levels of progress in integrating their memberships. Nationally, the League of Women Voters and the American Association of University Women were both predominantly white organizations in the mid-1960s, and YWCA chapters were, at that time, at various points along the road toward unifying their historically segregated black and white chapters. In Durham, as historian Christina Greene has noted, middle-class and professional African American women had achieved modest levels of integration in the memberships of both the local League of Women Voters and AAUW chapters by the early 1960s.[21] The number of black women joining the League grew slowly but steadily throughout the 1960s, and by 1969 the chapter had several dozen black members and was actively recruiting more.[22] However, "recruiting negro members" had first been suggested as a way to boost membership in 1963; that half a decade passed before the suggestion was acted on is a good indication of the pace of racial change within the League chapter.[23] Progress toward an integrated membership began earlier at Durham's YWCA, due to a 1946 directive from the national office that all chapters had to begin integrating their black and white branches.[24] Throughout the 1950s and 1960s, black and white women in Durham's YWCA had very different ideas about how quickly things were moving and how much progress had truly been made.[25] In 1962 African American members of the group were happy with the progress that had been made "in the area of human relations and civil rights."[26] By the end of the decade, the majority of the YWCA's classes for children and teenagers were operating on an integrated basis, and in 1970 Rose Butler Browne, an African American woman, was elected president of the chapter.[27] As Durham's two largest women's groups worked on antipoverty and school integration issues in the 1960s, then, both organizations were taking steps toward serving as racially inclusive spaces for Durham women.

In spite of Brown's election, however, at the end of the 1960s many felt that the YWCA still had far to go to achieve racial equality within the group. In 1969 the chapter reported to the national office that there was "deliberate, planned inclusion of women and girls from different social, ethnic and economic backgrounds" in the organization's membership.[28] But roughly two years later, a report to the national office stated that "little [had been] attempted" to concretely bridge "gaps between the racial, ethnic, and socio-economic groups."[29] The continuing tension over integrating Durham's schools was cited as one reason for this lack of progress on an issue that the national YWCA had first ordered chapters to address almost twenty-five years earlier. The report also noted that due to "community patterns" of race relations, the historically African American Tubman branch had retained its own board of directors and budget, in spite of moves made in the late 1950s and early 1960s to merge the Tubman and Central branches.[30] Even where integrated memberships created the public appearance of progress on integration, there was still much to accomplish as Durham's women's organizations moved into the 1970s.

As they continued to address and negotiate internal issues of race, Durham's women's clubs also had to consider their relationship to and interaction with the newly declared War on Poverty. In Durham a community group called Operation Breakthrough (OBT) was created to organize and administer War on Poverty programs. Many women's groups in the city became important allies of OBT.[31] The Durham League first began to work with the War on Poverty in 1965 when the group met with OBT's director of public information.[32] The League announced volunteer opportunities with the program and heard reports on its progress for several years. But even at the height of the War on Poverty in the mid-1960s, the group was never entirely comfortable with the large-scale assault on poverty embodied by the federal initiative. In January 1967, the League reminded members that the chapter's support of the War on Poverty as a national program did not automatically translate into approval of "any specific program in [their] community."[33] Two months later, as part of a study on welfare programs and services on the state level, the Durham League reached consensus only on two issues: a plan to begin a "homemaker service" that sent older women into the homes of low-income women to teach them domestic skills and a proposal to increase the pay and decrease the case load of Department of Welfare caseworkers. More support for legal aid and greater publicity for the local welfare department were studied, but no consensus was reached on those issues, suggesting a lack of member support for all but the most modest programs designed to battle poverty.[34]

The following year, the Durham League appeared to assume a somewhat more forceful position on poverty and its connections with civil rights. The January 1968 general meeting featured a panel discussion of community members addressing what individuals could do to facilitate equal opportunity for all Durham residents. The LWV newsletter article announcing the panel discussed antipoverty work in the context of race, featuring a quote from Charles Watts, the retiring head of OBT, in which he stated, "[The slow pace of change is due to] a suspicion of motives of anyone who is not just like you either as to race, religion, or economic advantage. All of Durham's efforts are diluted because of this problem."[35] The author of the newsletter article called this quote "disturbing" and urged members to come to the panel discussion—where Watts would be one of the featured speakers—ready to, "in the spirit of January remove with the shovel of honest inquiry some of the drifts of ignorance which hamper[ed] *all* the citizens of Durham."[36] In spite of such heartfelt rhetoric, however, the League did not increase its active participation in OBT programs or other War on Poverty projects. A year later, the newsletter was once again merely announcing volunteer opportunities with the group.[37]

Although some members of the group seem to have felt strongly about the issue, the Durham League never became deeply involved in antipoverty or welfare work, despite the fact that by the early 1970s these issues were near the top of the agenda of the national LWV office.[38] In the early 1970s, the Durham League did little regarding antipoverty work beyond making members aware of the national office's positions and encouraging letter writing when bills came up for consideration in Congress or the state legislature.[39]

Part of the League's reluctance may have derived from the fact that antipoverty programs were quite controversial in the city in the last years of the decade, for two separate but related reasons. The head of Operation

Breakthrough was Howard Fuller, a young African American man who was hired by OBT in 1965 and who, by 1968, was both the public face of OBT and a leading black power figure in North Carolina.[40] By the late sixties, Fuller was publicly describing his job as one of "stir[ring] people out of apathy."[41] In the fall of 1969, Fuller's brainchild, Malcolm X Liberation University (MXLU), opened in downtown Durham with a curriculum based on black power, pan-African, and anticolonial theories. As historian Devin Fergus has noted, upper- and middle-class residents of Durham, including many middle-class black individuals, were "unreceptive" to the new school, so unreceptive that Fuller moved MXLU from Durham to Greensboro, North Carolina, a year later.[42] As a middle-class organization with politics that were liberal but far from radical, the Durham LWV likely distanced itself from local War on Poverty efforts because they were tied to Fuller.

Members of the Durham League greatly valued their group's position as a source of objective and dispassionate information on government issues, as did most League members nationwide. Their desire to retain that reputation made the group shy away from many controversial issues, and by the last years of the 1960s, the War on Poverty was deeply controversial in Durham. The city's representative in Congress, Democrat Nick Galifinakis, spelled out the reasons for the controversy as he understood them in a letter to the League president in late 1967:

> The accusation is that the community action programs have in fact ignored the needs of the total community while concentrating on the desires of our poorer citizens. . . . I believe that the poor need a voice, Mrs. Smith. But I also believe that we can never succeed unless that voice is engaged in conversation. . . . I am afraid one of the main examples of this lack of communication exists in our own city of Durham. The board of Operation Breakthrough was originally made up of representatives of every segment of our community—government, business, and the poor. Certain of this representation dropped off the board and this is when the programs began to drift away from the support of the community.[43]

It is unknown what exactly led the men and women who left the OBT board to leave the organization. Howard Fuller's presence was likely a factor, given his radical politics. But for many reasons, OBT was a controversial group by the late 1960s.[44] By distancing itself from such an organization, the League retained its reputation as a group above partisanship and controversy. As chapter 2 will explore, retaining that reputation paid dividends in the 1970s as the League lobbied for ratification of the Equal

Rights Amendment without having that advocacy depicted as radical, an appearance that North Carolina's ERA advocates prized.

In contrast to the local LWV, the Durham YWCA saw itself as laying the groundwork for the success of the War on Poverty. Nationally, the YWCA had a long history of designing programs for lower-income women, and the Durham chapter encouraged its members in the 1960s to volunteer with Operation Breakthrough and other War on Poverty initiatives, as the League did.[45] But the YWCA moved beyond these efforts, entering poor neighborhoods and designing social and educational programs for their residents. YWCA members believed that they, as a group of women, had a special role to play in helping women and girls find their way and be successful in society. Focusing specifically on poor women and girls as a parallel project to War on Poverty initiatives was in many ways merely an extension of work that the YWCA had always done. The group's membership, which more accurately reflected the racial makeup of the city than did the LWV's, and the organization's longer presence in Durham's black neighborhoods may also have eased its transition into work alongside OBT.

At the Durham association's 1965 annual meeting, the president of the board of directors commented, "The Great Society is promoted in part by helping citizens understand each other," and noted that the YWCA had been working toward such understanding by encouraging members to get to know people outside their racial and socioeconomic group.[46] As the 1960s progressed, the Durham YWCA moved beyond simply creating the kind of interpersonal understanding necessary to a successful War on Poverty and began to design its own neighborhood-based programs to serve poor people. In 1966 the Durham chapter reported to the national office that "real progress" had been made in its programs "geared towards the culturally deprived," both through cooperation with War on Poverty programs and through the YWCA's own recently expanded program of outreach to women living in public housing.[47] Establishing programs in public housing complexes was a common way for YWCAs to work with low-income women. When the organization expanded those programs—which consisted of regular meetings offering a mix of arts and crafts and home economics classes and discussions of current events, with free child care provided—into African American public housing complexes, it reported to the national office that the participants were "taking responsibility in the YWCA and other groups," an obvious source of pride for YWCA leaders.[48] When the YWCA issued its report, a lawsuit brought by Joyce Thorpe, a public housing resident, was working its way through the court system. The case had garnered much local publicity and in 1969 led to a Supreme Court ruling that for the first time gave public housing tenants rights with regard to eviction.[49] Although Thorpe did not participate in the YWCA programs, in its report the YWCA appeared to be taking at least some of the credit for inspiring Thorpe's actions. The organization saw her persistence in pursuing the case as proof that its projects had succeeded in encouraging, if not directly developing, the leadership potential of low-income women.

The nature of the Durham League and the YWCA's work on behalf of low-income women highlights the differences between the two groups' styles of activism. The League worked almost exclusively on finding strictly political solutions to the problems of poverty by writing letters to elected officials and keeping abreast of OBT's programs. The League also valued maintaining its dispassionate, detached reputation, and allying too closely with OBT and its controversial leader, Howard Fuller, could have jeopardized that reputation. The Durham League moved very cautiously in the mid-1960s. For example, in 1967 the board of directors decided that it was in the group's interest to have its own "observer" at all Operation Breakthrough meetings in order to "keep informed on the progress of Breakthrough."[50] The group was worried about its image and reputation and wanted to be sure that the information it had on a controversial group like OBT came from a source that understood the League's concerns.

YWCA leaders, although more likely to work alongside OBT on neighborhood projects, also shied away from linking their group too publicly with Fuller's. The YWCA had always focused its actions at the neighborhood level, creating programs to broaden the horizons of low-income women and girls. The neighborhood focus of the YWCA's work was inherently less public than the League's method of pressuring elected officials, and YWCA members did not push to gain greater recognition for their efforts. There was little coverage of the chapter's antipoverty work in the *Carolina Times*, the city's African American newspaper, and no evidence that this lack of coverage concerned YWCA leaders. Even though the organization was sympathetic to OBT and frequently worked with low-income women, the group still relied on financial support from middle-class men and women, both white and black, many of whom were wary of Howard Fuller. Cooperating more visibly with OBT could have jeopardized that support.

Among the most visible advocates of increasing programs and opportunities for Durham's poor in the mid-1960s were the city's African American women's groups.[51] In 1964 the national president of the historically black sorority Delta Sigma Theta called on the sorority's members to begin paying as much attention to poverty as they did to employment, education, and racial discrimination.[52] This and other similar statements were extensively publicized in the *Carolina Times*, and the Durham Delta chapter urged support of the group's national initiatives. Delta was not the only sorority to shift its attentions in this direction in the mid-1960s. In a 1965 article celebrating the fifty-sixth anniversary of Alpha Kappa Alpha, another historically black sorority, the head of the Durham alumnae chapter informed the readers of the *Carolina Times* that the "days of extravagant spending on lavish entertainment" had passed. The group was instead committing itself to work for "Freedom Now" in whatever way it could.[53] The chapter acknowledged its life membership in the NAACP and also stressed the role that the sorority played in preparing undergraduate women for leadership. In announcing this change, the chapter stated that young women so prepared could then help lead the civil rights struggle, which the group described as requiring "the interest, enthusiasm, and efforts" of all black women.[54] Such an explicit civil rights agenda was a major shift in focus for a group primarily known in the city for its annual debutante ball.[55] By the second half of the 1960s, Durham's black women's organizations were committed to publicly encouraging discussion of and action on issues of poverty, alongside civil rights concerns.

The city's black women's clubs were also involved in meeting another pressing challenge in Durham in the late 1960s: the fact that virtually all black children in Durham still attended segregated schools. In the wake of the *Brown v. Board* decision, North Carolina had adopted the Pearsall Plan, a program under which token integration was achieved by African American parents petitioning the school board to allow their children to go to previously all-white schools. The Pearsall Plan was in effect throughout the 1960s, and no historically white school in North Carolina had more than a handful of African American students until the plan was rejected by a federal court in 1970. The Durham City Council did its part throughout the 1960s to ensure that nothing more than token integration ever occurred in Durham. Council members made effective use of a gerrymandering scheme through which parts of the county could be annexed into the city but designated "city-out." "City-out" areas of town received city utilities and other services and paid city taxes. But children in those areas were permitted to attend the overwhelmingly white county schools. Through this plan, city officials enabled white flight from city schools. By 1970 the Durham City public school system was 55 percent black, and nearly all black children attended schools whose student bodies were overwhelmingly African American.[56] The patina of peace that prevailed in Durham's schools—the token integration of historically white schools had occurred without much public reaction from the white community—masked the pains that the city's white leaders took to prevent true integration of the city or county schools.[57]

Durham's white women's groups did little to encourage school integration before it was explicitly court ordered. From the 1954 *Brown* decision until a federal district judge ordered integration in Durham in 1970, the Durham League of Women Voters regularly discussed school funding, districting, and other issues related to the quality of public education in the city. The group went out of its way, however, to avoid discussing integration directly. In 1958 the Durham League distributed "factual material" to PTAs, newspapers, and other civic clubs regarding a ballot initiative to consolidate the city and county schools but was careful to note that the chapter took "no stand" on the issue of consolidation, and the material the group distributed made no mention of the racial implications of such a move.[58] The next year the North Carolina LWV barred local Leagues across the state from studying school integration.[59]

The North Carolina League's ban on studying school desegregation held for the entire decade of the 1960s. In 1970, in the wake of the Supreme Court's decision in *Green v. New Kent County*, a federal judge ordered actual integration in Durham.[60] Only after this decision did the Durham League begin to formulate an official position on the issue, and over the next year the group passed resolutions declaring its support for any plan that ensured "safe, efficient, effective school integration" and created "an interracial teaching and learning experience for all students."[61] In July 1971, League women participated in a two-week series of open, citywide meetings called "Save Our Schools," also known as the "Durham Charrette." The Planning Committee for the charrette was an integrated group made up of men and women, black and white, middle class and working class. Women were well represented in the Planning Committee and leadership of the group; African American activist Ann Atwater was a cochair.[62] League member Yonina Rosenthal was one of the middle-class white women on the group's Steering Committee. For two weeks, an impressively diverse range of Durham residents—students, teachers, administrators, and city residents, representing every class and race in the city—discussed everything from curriculum and teacher qualifications to the actual details of how students would be assigned to schools.[63] Issues were assigned to small groups, each of which had representatives from every demographic, and the small groups worked through the details of their particular issue, ranging from the place of black history in the curriculum to the role of public schools in sex education.[64] Each small group reported its recommendations to the public at open evening meetings. After the charrette was over, Rosenthal distributed printed copies of its recommendations to the League membership.[65] The structure of the charrette was strikingly similar to that of the League, with a larger group breaking down into small study groups and then returning to the general group with recommendations. The charrette also fit perfectly with the League's preferred method of action: it was an effort to bring people together and overcome prejudice and distrust over political issues through the use of facts and expertise.

While the Durham League took no action on school integration until such integration was court ordered, its members had at least discussed school issues intermittently for the preceding fifteen years. There is no evidence that the city's YWCA did so, nor that the YWCA as an organization supported the charrette. The only mention of school integration in the YWCA's papers was a 1970 report to the national office that cited tension over school integration as a reason why little had been accomplished in combining the white, Central YWCA and the African American branch more fully into one organization.[66] It is likely that individual YWCA members attended the charrette meetings, but as an organization the YWCA did not push for school integration or support a particular plan for its implementation. Partially this lack of involvement was due to the racial tensions still present within the YWCA chapter.[67] But it also stemmed from the YWCA's growing emphasis on keeping a low public profile. By 1971 the group had begun building a multifaceted feminist program that would be the center of Durham's feminist community for the entire decade. Becoming a leading voice for school integration at that time could have threatened the group's public respectability—and therefore its funding—and endangered the potentially more controversial feminist work the group was beginning to conduct.

Durham's mainstream women's organizations were fairly tentative in their interactions with school integration and especially the War on Poverty. Both the League of Women Voters and the YWCA were aware of their position as liberal organizations in a town with deeply divided political opinions. Both groups also strove to remain "respectable" places for southern women to spend time discussing politics and social issues in the company of other women. Both of the city's major women's groups had also, as institutions, made commitments to racial integration. Actual implementation of that integration was slow. But both groups publicly and frequently talked the talk of racial equality, even as they struggled to walk the walk. Such talk—especially in a southern city still in the midst of determining what exactly the civil rights movement meant for the community—was a sign of the deep-seated progressivism of both groups. When the women's movement burst onto the scene, that deeply held ideology primed these groups to become effective channels of feminist action.

Indianapolis

Throughout the post–World War II era, Indianapolis had a reputation as an extremely conservative town. The far-right John Birch Society was founded there in 1958.[68] Politicians at both the city and the state level were known well into the 1960s for their belief in small government and their opposition to the liberal consensus that had dominated American politics since the New Deal.[69] Indianapolis also had a poor record on racial issues, especially school and residential integration. Despite a 1949 Indiana law mandating the desegregation of the state's public schools, Indianapolis schools remained segregated until a federal court demanded integration in 1968. The city and county school boards fought the court order, and Indianapolis schools were not integrated until the early 1980s.[70] In the 1950s, only one neighborhood in the city was integrated, and it developed a strong neighborhood association in order to fight the persistent efforts of blockbusting real estate agents and others who sought to eliminate the island of integration.[71] Two members of the YWCA national staff who visited in 1972 commented on the "ultra conservatism" of Indianapolis.[72]

The city was home, however, to numerous progressive women's groups. The priorities and attitudes of women in two of the city's biggest groups, the YWCA and the LWV, differed markedly from those of women in the same organizations in other cities. The Indianapolis YWCA was far more insular and far less proactive than YWCAs elsewhere. And the city's League chapter was far more likely to move beyond the organization's traditional focus on lobbying and into neighborhood-based work. There are two possible reasons for this divergence. In the late 1950s and early 1960s, the Indianapolis YWCA was in a shambles and nearly forced to close. Suburbanization and "extremely poor staff leadership" were blamed for the problems.[73] These difficulties at the YWCA meant that women in Indianapolis who wanted to join a women's group working effectively for progressive social change (and not wishing to work strictly with women of their own race or faith) had only one option: the League of Women Voters.[74] In other cities, such women chose between the League and the YWCA. The Indianapolis League also seems to have attracted women who in Colorado may have joined politics in a more formal way. As will be discussed in chapter 4, Colorado had a long tradition of women holding public office, and members of the League and other women's organizations cycled in and out of women's groups and formal roles in the government frequently. In Indiana there is no evidence that women had such a role in state elected politics, especially in the 1960s. Since the YWCA was not an effective organization in 1960s Indianapolis, and there was no tradition of women holding office, women with a wider range of interests and backgrounds entered the LWV of Indianapolis than in other cities.

These factors and others created an Indianapolis LWV that was not only committed to racial justice in the community but was also, unlike the Denver and Durham chapters, itself an integrated group. African American women participated not only as members but also as leaders of the group throughout the 1960s. The chapter had an African American president, Nellie Gustafson, from 1964 to 1965 and always had at least one black woman on the board of directors throughout the second half of the decade.[75] In the 1960s, efforts were made to ensure the continued presence of an appreciable number of black members; the League advertised for new members in the city's black newspaper and sent letters to African American ministers, asking them to invite women congregants to join the LWV.[76] The presence of a group of active black members kept the Indianapolis League more attentive to civil rights concerns than either the Denver or the Durham chapters. Along with the local chapters of the NAACP and the National Council of Negro Women, the Indianapolis League cosponsored a large get-out-the-vote rally and voter registration campaign in September 1963.[77] In 1968 the League set up a voter registration booth at the YWCA, taking advantage of the downtown building's proximity to low-income and low-registration neighborhoods.[78]

What such an integrated membership did not do, strikingly, was diminish the League's respectability in the community. One member recalls that the Indianapolis League was "respected," that the group "had a seat at the table," and that "other women's groups sought [them] in coalition."[79] The League, in other words, was an important player in Indianapolis politics and the community more broadly, in spite of being very liberal in comparison to other civic groups in the city. The League's liberalism was particularly apparent in the stance the group took regarding school integration.

A federal judge ordered Indianapolis public schools to integrate in 1968. In the wake of that order, the method of achieving integration and the pace at which such integration should occur were debated throughout the city. Historian Richard Pierce has argued that Indianapolis civic leaders fought school integration with a "ferocity" seldom seen outside the South.[80] Throughout the first half of the 1970s, debates raged about busing, consolidation of the city and county school systems, and other possible methods of achieving racial balance in the city's schools. Women's groups were frequent contributors to these discussions.

The Indianapolis League of Women Voters gradually came to its position of supporting school integration over the course of the 1960s. The group opposed a 1961 school reorganization plan because it did not create "equalized opportunity" for all students. The plan also, in the League's opinion, did not distribute financial resources equitably among the city's schools.[81] The League's major goal in involving itself in the school issue in 1961 was not to bring about school integration but to mediate between the city and county school boards in order to reach a "rational compromise" between the two groups.[82] The compromise that the League supported would have increased integration in the city's schools, but the League did not offer that as the reason for its involvement.[83] Increased integration was not an explicit question examined in the League's 1961 school study, and the group took no formal position on the issue. Because no consensus was reached on integration during the 1961 school study, the chapter did not take a position on the increasing segregation of Indianapolis's high schools in 1965. Several members wanted the League to speak out about the increasing segregation at Shortridge High, but the president, Nellie Gustafson, reminded members that the League could not speak publicly if no study had been undertaken.[84]

As Gustafson's admonition reflects, maintaining the objectivity and nonpartisanship of their League was foremost in group leaders' minds throughout the early 1960s. In April 1961, at the group's annual business meeting, one of the board members noted, "Still another indication of our prestige may be the fact that so far we have escaped being singled out for condemnation by the 'far right,' though this may be a dubious honor."[85] This quote demonstrated the connections that League members saw between nonpartisanship and "prestige" and how highly members of the group prized the latter. However, it also suggests, as did the group's actions, that although the Indianapolis League was officially nonpartisan, it was no friend of the "far right." This was the line that all Leagues straddled in the 1960s and 1970s, as a group that was officially nonpartisan but, in its positions on issues and its actions, was a decidedly liberal organization. Such an identity enabled the League to bring particular strengths and weaknesses to the women's movement in the 1970s.

Wanting to maintain its community position did not mean that the Indianapolis League sat on its hands and did no work on controversial issues, as the Durham League had regarding antipoverty work. The Indianapolis League undertook another school study in 1967, and a year later a federal judge ordered Indianapolis schools to integrate.[86] With that order, the League began not only to support government action to implement the order but also to create a community program to ease integration.[87] In May 1969, the League, along with several other women's groups in the city, sponsored the "Women's Conference on the Crisis in Our Schools." The conference was open to the public and had a general session on integration, as well as more-focused panels that examined teacher preparation, curriculum, and students' concerns.[88] The similarities to the Denver community school panel discussed later in this chapter—and the leading role of women's groups in general, and the League in particular, in both of those efforts—are striking. Throughout the country, women's groups were turned to as leading community organizations that could effectively assist local officials in implementing contentious policies. In May 1971, the League publicly supported both busing and racially sensitive districting as effective ways of integrating the city's schools.[89] The organization continued to push for busing as a solution for three years and issued a statement in 1974 decrying the extraordinary efforts that the city and township school boards were undertaking to avoid that solution.[90] By 1974, however, the League was fighting a largely losing battle in its busing advocacy. In the wake of that year's *Miliken v. Bradley* decision, which made busing between independent city and country school districts unconstitutional, the Indianapolis LWV dropped its strong pro-busing position and incorporated monitoring the progress of the various integration lawsuits into a more general education agenda.[91]

Not until the League of Women Voters first began promoting busing as the solution to the segregation of Indianapolis's schools in 1971 did the YWCA begin to publicly discuss school integration. The YWCA sent a strongly worded memo to the school board in May 1971 arguing that while integration would create "hardship" for everyone involved, the city could not wait for changes in residence patterns to bring about integrated schools. The YWCA therefore urged the school board to "take whatever action [was] deemed necessary including busing of both white and black children."[92] The next year the group sent a similar letter to President Nixon.[93] The board also decided in the fall of 1972 to participate in an Urban League–sponsored workshop on desegregation issues.[94]

After this flurry of activity, however, the chapter ceased working on the problem. Racial tensions within the Indianapolis YWCA were quite high in the early 1970s, and much of the action on school desegregation was pushed by Pree Jones, an African American woman and head of the group's Racial

Justice Committee who worked tirelessly and on many fronts to bring the chapter into compliance with the organization's national imperative to eliminate racism. Jones fought an uphill battle. When the opportunity to work with the Urban League came up in November 1972, for example, Jones had to beat back efforts by several board members to delay making a decision until the board held a "forum" to discuss the issues involved in desegregation. This tactic was often used when board members wished to table an issue. Jones reminded the other women that desegregation had already been voted on by the board and that the board had spoken publicly both in the city and nationally in support of busing. The board agreed to cooperate with the Urban League only after Jones's statement.

Indianapolis's largest women's groups were united—at least publicly—in their support of busing, one of the most controversial solutions to the problem of integrating schools. In antipoverty work, there was less common ground. Each organization undertook its own projects to address the needs of the poor.

The Indianapolis YWCA's relationship with antipoverty work generally—and federally funded War on Poverty projects in particular—was ambivalent, despite the group's location downtown, close to many impoverished neighborhoods. In 1959, in order to comply with the national office's order to integrate white and African American branches, the Indianapolis YWCA closed the city's Phyllis Wheatley branch.[95] The Wheatley branch had run a successful mothers' group in a public housing complex in the late 1950s, but this program was dropped when the Wheatley branch was closed and was not reactivated for several years.[96] When the YWCA reactivated this group and created new ones to serve low-income women and girls, those groups focused almost exclusively on recreation.[97] Unlike in the case of the Durham YWCA, the advent of the War on Poverty did little to alter this focus in the Indianapolis YWCA's work with poor people. Nor did the potential of federal funds for new projects cause the chapter to expand its programming in low-income areas. The neighborhood work of the Durham YWCA expanded, over time, to include job training and other skills-oriented programs. In Indianapolis work with poor women never went beyond the level of social and recreational programming.

In January 1965, the Indianapolis YWCA board agreed to work with War on Poverty programs only where those programs were compatible with the existing projects of the organization and such cooperation was "appropriate."[98] By the following February, the group had six Volunteers in Service to America (VISTAs)—college-educated young people who volunteered for an effort funded by the War on Poverty and conceived of as a "domestic Peace Corps"—working for them.[99] Groups of VISTAs came and went for the next several years, and the YWCA consistently used them to staff existing programs rather than allowing the volunteers to design their own programs, as happened at other YWCAs. VISTAs took over most of the programming for inner-city women and girls, including two of the largest programs, Mothers' Morning Out and Junior Jills, a recreation program for eight- to twelve-year-old girls who were referred to the YWCA by various social service agencies such as the juvenile court.[100] For the Indianapolis YWCA, the VISTA volunteers were free labor to carry out the association's existing neighborhood-based programs.[101] The group also tried to tap into federal War on Poverty money to offset the cost of existing programs in 1966, when the group applied for a grant from the local community action group (CAAP) to operate a summer camp for "disadvantaged" girls that the YWCA had previously run with its own funds.[102] The application was rejected by the local CAAP office. Such repeated attempts to use War on Poverty funds to pay for existing programs demonstrates that unlike other women's groups throughout the country, the Indianapolis YWCA did not see the War on Poverty as an opportunity to expand its work with low-income women or girls. This decision is another example of the conservatism of the Indianapolis YWCA, a conservatism that shaped the city's feminist community in the 1970s.

In contrast to the work of the YWCA, the Indianapolis League of Women Voters worked consistently on poverty issues throughout this period, using not only citywide political pressure but also working at the neighborhood level. Historian Marisa Chappell has explored the "strong commitment" by the LWV nationally to "eradicating poverty" and improving federal welfare programs in the 1970s.[103] The 1960s work of local chapters such as the Indianapolis League likely contributed to the strong position that the organization adopted nationally in the following decade. The Indianapolis chapter worked consistently on poverty issues for over ten years, beginning in 1963, and its work within the frame of antipoverty was wide ranging. The group began studying welfare in 1963 and in November 1964 unanimously concluded that the maximum grants available through Aid to Families with Dependent Children (AFDC) should be increased and that the bureaucracy of public assistance in Marion County needed to be streamlined.[104]

After coming to consensus on these positions, the Indianapolis League pursued the change members sought through a variety of means. The group merged its interest in voter services and government participation with its concerns about poverty by working in low-income neighborhoods and designed programs to help people living there speak on their own behalf. From the mid-1960s into the early 1970s, League members recruited individuals to serve on CAAP neighborhood councils and in other War on Poverty programs and supervised CAAP elections.[105] The organization focused particularly on helping welfare recipients speak on their own behalf for improved benefits and treatment, conducted lobbying workshops for them in 1966, and in 1970 facilitated a meeting between welfare officials and recipients.[106] Not only did League members believe in the value of this work; their expertise in these areas was sought: it was at the request of city officials that the League supervised the CAAP elections and moderated the meeting between welfare recipients and officials. These facts demonstrate the regard that city officials had for the organization's impartiality and its role in city government.

While continuing to enjoy a reputation for objectivity among the city's political leaders, in the second half of the 1960s and into the 1970s much of the League's antipoverty work examined the gendered aspects of welfare. This work especially helps highlight the contours of Indianapolis residents' opinions and political beliefs in the era. Beginning in 1964, the League urged city offices to make birth control information available to interested welfare recipients and also pushed for state legislation that would have enabled families with present but disabled fathers to draw AFDC benefits.[107] At the same meeting where this latter issue was discussed, board members also spent much time discussing the need to dramatically overhaul the types of public housing in Indianapolis and the ways in which such housing was allocated and maintained.[108] One striking aspect of these conversations was that while both AFDC and public housing were seen by the public primarily as African American problems, the League never explicitly mentioned race or civil rights in pushing for action on these issues. Given the racial conservatism of the city, as demonstrated by its tenacious resistance to school integration, the League likely believed that reinforcing the racial stereotypes associated with welfare and public housing would decrease the group's opportunities to improve either of these programs. So it focused instead on the gendered dimensions of welfare. The fact that promoting access to birth control was less controversial than tying welfare rights to race-based civil rights highlights the fault lines of Indianapolis public opinion and suggests one reason why such a conservative city proved relatively open to feminism in the following decade.[109] Such actions also highlight the League's role in pushing city and state officials on potentially controversial issues.

Both the LWV and the YWCA of Indianapolis—the city's two largest women's groups—reacted to the controversial problems they confronted in the 1960s differently than their sister chapters in other cities. The Indianapolis League fully embraced antipoverty work from an early date and took very progressive positions on welfare and school integration issues in the 1970s. The group also moved beyond traditional League political and lobbying work and engaged with low-income people directly, helping them to develop the skills to lobby government officials themselves. The city's YWCA, by contrast, was more reluctant than YWCAs in other cities to take on a wide-ranging program of action. It neither expanded its work with low-income people during the War on Poverty nor worked enthusiastically to bring about school integration. The group was also far more obstinate in its refusal to take more than the most superficial steps toward integrating the chapter's leadership structure or programs than were other YWCAs studied here. In the 1970s, the League was one of the key organizations in pushing for feminist change and, especially, ERA ratification in Indiana. On the ERA and all other feminist issues, the Indianapolis YWCA was virtually silent. The institutional commitment that a group made to racial equality was, in Indianapolis as in Durham, a good indication of how active a presence the group would become in its city's women's movement.

Denver

World War II marked the beginning of a period of far-reaching changes in Denver. The city was home to several new military bases and defense plants during the war, and many of those industries and the people who worked in them stayed on after the war's end.[110] In 1940 approximately 322,400 people lived in the city of Denver. By 1970 the number had swelled to 515,000.[111] As the population increased, so did its diversity. In 1950 just over 15,000 African Americans and nearly 25,000 Hispanics called Denver home. By 1970 those numbers had jumped to 47,000 African Americans and 86,000 Hispanics. The Asian and Native American population also tripled in those years, although the combined total by 1970 was just under 9,500 residents.[112] In its rapid population growth, which was driven largely by migration into the region by young people and families, Denver was similar to other post–World War II western boom towns such as Dallas and Seattle. It also shared with those cities what one scholar has termed a "businessmen's government," which prioritized highway construction, airports, and other building projects to facilitate economic growth over other types of government expenditures.[113] In Denver, policies encouraging business growth above all else began to be questioned in the late 1960s and 1970s as new interests—concerns of minorities, environmental issues, and tension between suburbs and city center—came to dominate local government.[114] Women's groups were among the organizations pushing these new issues to the forefront.

It took most women's groups in Denver some time to turn their attention to the issue of school integration. No city or state law forbade children of different races from attending the same school, as had been the case in Durham and Indianapolis, and most women's groups in Denver did not begin considering the issue until the second half of the 1960s. Unsurprisingly, the first groups to address the issue were organizations of racial minorities. Both women's groups such as the city's Delta Sigma Theta alumni chapter and mixed-sex groups—notably the city's La Raza chapter—began questioning in the mid-1960s whether schools where minority students were the majority were receiving their fair share of funds.[115] La Raza was a community-based civil rights group for Mexican Americans, similar to organizations such as Martin Luther King's Southern Christian Leadership Conference (SCLC) that were formed to fight for civil rights for African Americans.[116] The Denver chapter's 1966 program also stressed the need for "integration without assimilation (ethnic pluralism)."[117] Once minority groups began raising these concerns women's groups throughout the city—especially the League and the AAUW—began to address school integration issues. Their work increased throughout the late 1960s and into the 1970s and culminated with a 1973 U.S. Supreme Court case, *Keyes v. Denver School District No. 1*. The *Keyes* case was the first time the Court declared that cities like Denver, where schools had been segregated by de facto forces rather than by laws, were bound by the *Brown* and *Green* decisions.[118]

In the wake of the *Keyes* decision, Denver and other cities like it were obligated to take affirmative steps to integrate their public schools. Women's groups played a major role in planning and facilitating the integration of Denver's schools, which began with the 1975–76 school year. Throughout the course of the city's integration struggles, women's groups pursued a two-pronged attack. Organizations combined pressure on elected officials using factual material and polling data with neighborhood-based projects that brought citizens together to talk through their concerns about the methods being used to equalize the racial balance in Denver's public schools and the speed at which those changes would occur. Unlike in other cities, none of these tactics was the province of a single organization. Three major women's groups in Denver—the League, the YWCA, and the AAUW—all lobbied the school board and the mayor's office, and League and AAUW members went into their neighborhoods to ease tensions surrounding the enforcement of the Court's decision.[119]

Beginning in 1967, the Denver League of Women Voters played a prominent role in pushing for school integration and facilitating its implementation. In that year, more League members worked on school issues than on any other subject, campaigning for the passage of a bond initiative for the city's schools and pushing the school board to pass an integration resolution.[120] In November 1968, the group endorsed an integration proposal that was before the city school board, although it strongly criticized the plan's proposal not to begin integration until the fourth grade.[121] The League's president also issued a statement to the school board that year, stating, "After long study, [the national LWV] made a national commitment to work for equality of educational opportunity and to support efforts to bring about racial integration of schools. All of Denver, including the Denver League, has talked about this for some time. It is our belief that now is the time for action."[122]

In 1968 the League also undertook two projects that foreshadowed the community-based technique the group would use once the Supreme Court ordered integration of the city's schools. The chapter sponsored "Speak Out on School Integration," an event open to the public that encouraged citizens to gather and discuss their opinions on the integration issue. The group also sent representatives to the Citizens for One Community, an organization formed to push for racially balanced schools in the wake of Martin Luther King Jr.'s assassination.[123] After school integration was ordered, the League formed a citizens' group called People Let's Unite for Schools (PLUS). PLUS sponsored community forums throughout the city, creating space for parents and other concerned citizens to come together and discuss desegregation.[124] The Denver League proudly reported to national League leaders that PLUS was "praised" by the United States Civil Rights Commission for the part it played in the relatively peaceful implementation of integration in Denver.[125] The Denver League was a multifaceted group whose members proved willing not only to push elected officials using "unbiased" facts but also to go into the streets of Denver, meet their neighbors, and bring people together to work toward a solution to a complex and difficult problem. The Denver League, like its sister chapter in Indianapolis, had a wide range of tools in its activist toolbox and made effective use of them all in helping to facilitate school integration.

The Denver YWCA was substantively different from the other YWCAs studied here, primarily because the chapter integrated its membership earlier than other predominantly white organizations like the League.[126] However, that difference did not move the group toward greater engagement with school desegregation than that of the Durham or Indianapolis YWCAs. By 1961 the Denver YWCA was committed, as an institution, to addressing racial inequality. In that year, the group was building a new facility in Denver's largest black neighborhood to replace the Welton branch, which had previously served the African American community. Board members were dedicated to a state-of-the-art facility that would provide integrated programs in the area. They also discussed the need to refer to the new building as the "Northeast YWCA" instead of the "Branch," to eliminate the name given to segregated facilities and indicate the new building's openness to all people.[127] The group also ran an "experimental" integrated program for girls that summer; the effort was seen as so successful that a Denver congressman wrote to congratulate the group on its "splendid work."[128] By 1965 training and encouraging women to make "racial, religious, social, and economic integration" a goal for their activism and their lives were primary aims of the YWCA's largest program for adult women.[129] As was true in the Durham association, not everything was as integrated as it seemed on the surface. African American women's frustrations with the Denver YWCA became public in the early 1970s and will be discussed in more detail in chapter 4.

This history, however, did not lead the YWCA to take a sustained role in the issue of integrated schools in the 1960s. In 1962 the group urged the creation of a commission to study "integration in the schools" and issued recommendations for specific topics of inquiry to that group.[130] After working with the commission, however, the YWCA did not address school integration again until 1968.[131] The YWCA became deeply involved in antipoverty work in the intervening years and also may have felt it could do little to change the racial imbalance in the city's schools, since segregation resulted from residential patterns rather than city or state laws.

When the school board announced its first integration plan in the fall of 1968, the YWCA supported the plan without mentioning the reservations about timing that the League expressed about the same plan. The YWCA simply stated its support for any plan that would satisfy federal law and ensure "quality" education for all students.[132] After that public statement, the YWCA never took up the issue again. School desegregation was not an issue that the YWCA could solve through its own programming, and the chapter apparently chose to let other women's groups take the lead in publicly pressuring city officials. There is no evidence, however, that this lack of effort was due to the same kind of conservatism that marred the Indianapolis YWCA. The Denver association was an active participant in antipoverty programming, unlike the Indianapolis chapter, and had made numerous commitments to integration in its own programming.

A third women's group that addressed school integration was the local American Association of University Women chapter. Much of the chapter's work was channeled through a project called the Green Circle, a program that sent AAUW members and other volunteers into area elementary schools to teach children about diversity. The AAUW began offering Green Circle classes in 1964, two years before La Raza or Delta Sigma Theta began to speak publicly about the problems of racial discrimination in the Denver schools. The program grew rapidly, reaching ten thousand children in five elementary schools in 1967.[133] The organization continued running the program until at least 1973.[134] Its early attention to this issue may be due to the fact that the AAUW was, as an organization, very attuned to education issues. As a group of college-educated women, members may have seen the coverage of school integration in the South and decided to begin laying the groundwork for such integration in Denver. The records of the group unfortunately do not indicate its motivation for beginning the project. In addition to the Green Circle, AAUW members also wrote letters to the school board urging action and publicized their group's support of integration.[135]

Denver's women's organizations were crucial players in facilitating the integration of the city's public schools. The League of Women Voters urged city officials to take steps in that direction several years before action was court ordered, and the AAUW began working with elementary school children at quite an early date to help them get to know children of other races and begin to break down racist beliefs at a young age. These large women's groups were clearly on the pro-integration side of this issue, and they effectively used a variety of tactics to help integrate the city's schools.

While a number of women's organizations came together to work on school desegregation issues in a variety of ways, most of the antipoverty work in the city was undertaken by two of the biggest organizations, the YWCA and the LWV. The Denver YWCA organized its first program specifically for low-income women in 1961 when it began a mothers' group at Stapleton Homes, one of the city's public housing complexes.[136] Two years later, the group applied for grant money to expand the Stapleton Homes program. The association faced criticism over the grant application from Denver's United Fund, which believed that the YWCA was a "character-building organization" and therefore not equipped to deal with the "complex problems" of low-income people.[137] The YWCA bristled at this characterization, although the organization did apply for a grant from the National Institute of Mental Health to pay for a social worker to help staff the program. YWCA leaders were quick to point out, however, that the social worker was being hired to work with the children of the women in the program; YWCA members felt they had all the expertise necessary to work with the women themselves.[138]

With the advent of the War on Poverty in 1964, the group undertook steadily increasing levels of work with low-income people. By 1965 there were two programs for mothers receiving welfare, in addition to the Stapleton Homes project.[139] The following year the first set of VISTAs was assigned to the Denver YWCA; the young volunteers were promptly installed at a public housing complex where the chapter had not previously been active.[140] YWCA members also volunteered with the local Women in Community Service (WICS) program, a national project undertaken by a coalition of smaller women's organizations like the National Council of Jewish Women and Churchwomen United to facilitate members' work on behalf of the War on Poverty.[141] All these programs were designed for a clientele not served by the Denver YWCA before the 1960s, but much of the programming was similar to what the organization had always done for adult women. Most of the projects provided free child care, giving women the opportunity to come together as a group of adults for education and camaraderie. A 1965 program for women receiving welfare, for example, was designed to expose the women and their preschool-aged children to literature and the arts as a way to prepare the children for school.[142] While such programs were appreciated by low-income women whose opportunities for time away from their children were few, they were not projects that altered the fundamentals of the women's lives.[143]

In the mid-1960s, the Denver YWCA moved beyond this focus on recreational activities and began to pressure public officials about welfare laws and programs. The chapter undertook this city-level work far more frequently than other YWCAs. In 1963 the group wrote letters in favor of a bill that made birth control information available to welfare recipients upon request.[144] Two years later, the organization informed the head of the Colorado Coordinating Council of Women's Organizations' legislative chair that the YWCA was interested in working to change the laws regarding residency requirements for public assistance and other Aid to Dependent Children laws.[145] In 1968 the YWCA Public Affairs Committee lobbied the governor, urging him to explore additional funding sources to increase the availability of day care for women in work-training programs and to make AFDC grants equal to "100% of basic minimum budgetary needs."[146] That year the group also began meeting with representatives from the city's Welfare Rights Organization, and the YWCA soon began providing the WRO chapter office space in its building.[147] The National Welfare Rights Organization was only a year old in 1968, having been founded by a male veteran of the civil rights movement and a coalition of welfare recipients across the country to try to improve both the material benefits of public assistance and, more importantly, the requirements placed on women on welfare and the lack of respect with which they were treated.[148] YWCAs around the country frequently provided office space and other resources to the organization.

The Denver LWV pursued similar kinds of lobbying work and coalition work with the Denver WRO. As individuals, many League members volunteered for War on Poverty programs such as Foster Grandparents and Head Start or worked with the WICS program in the city.[149] But most of the work of the Denver League, like that of its sister chapter in Indianapolis, focused on applying legislative pressure and using the organization's interest in government to bring low-income people more fully into the government decision-making processes that affected their lives. Beginning in the mid-1960s, the group conducted numerous voter education classes and other programs designed to encourage political participation by low-income people.[150] When a dispute arose between the Denver urban renewal office and the residents of Auraria, the city's oldest Hispanic neighborhood, which was slated for demolition, League members stepped in to mediate the conflict. In an "Action Briefing" sent to members in the fall of 1971, League leaders reported, "DURA [Denver Urban Renewal Authority] survey of Auraria area [shows that number of] residents in need of relocation is 155 families. ARO [Auraria Residents Organization] survey of area [shows that number of] residents in need of relocation is 235 families," and urged League members to conduct their own "independent door to door survey" to clarify the discrepancy.[151] The briefing also noted that while DURA stated there was an office in the neighborhood to help those being displaced find new housing, "ARO state[d] that the DURA office in Auraria [was] there but never open," and requested, "Could a LWV unit check daily at different hours to see if the office is open and functioning for Auraria residents?"[152] The League's tactics on this issue are a classic example of the group's work. Since 1969 the group had supported clearing the neighborhood so that a community college could be built on the land.[153] But it was also a good-government group that wanted to ensure that the city was fulfilling its responsibilities to the people being displaced by the demolition of their homes, and it sent out "fact-finders" to ascertain whether the city was living up to that obligation. Its actions regarding Auraria reveal the LWV to be a thoroughly middle-class group that believed a community college was of more use to Denver residents than a run-down neighborhood. But it was also a middle-class group that believed poor people should be treated fairly by the government and given the assistance they needed to relocate.

When the national League began a welfare study in the early 1970s, the Denver LWV devised creative ways of engaging members with the issue, developing more community-based programs that encouraged interaction between League members and welfare recipients. In the winter of 1971, the group organized a "Welfare Understanding Day" that was open to the public, in order to make Denver citizens more aware of the problems faced by welfare recipients.[154] The workshop was part of a yearlong effort by the League to "humanize" the public image of welfare recipients.[155] Members were urged to meet with members of the local WRO chapter and to try to live for a week on a welfare budget.[156]

The group's most ambitious project was a "Live-In" weekend, when League members and welfare recipients came together to "discuss myths and fallacies regarding each other" and talk about goals and methods for welfare reform.[157] The goal of these League efforts mirrored a key aim of the National Welfare Rights Organization (NWRO). Humanizing welfare recipients, proving to the public that they were women just like other women and therefore had the same rights as other women, was a major focus of NWRO work. It was particularly important to the African American single mothers who made up the bulk of the NWRO's membership and were only too aware of the ways in which stereotypes about promiscuous, lazy welfare recipients had justified cuts to AFDC benefits for decades.[158] National LWV publications encouraged members to advance the cause of improving welfare's image by publicly questioning negative stereotypes about welfare recipients whenever possible.[159] The Denver LWV embraced the totality of the national League's welfare work in a way that the Durham and Indianapolis chapters did not. The range of projects developed in Denver demonstrates that when members were passionate about an issue, even a hierarchical organization like the League had space for creative, community-based programs that moved beyond a strict focus on pressuring legislators and influenced public opinion about legislation.[160]

Examining the work of Denver's women's groups on school desegregation and poverty shows that, as in Durham and Indianapolis, Denver women tackled some of the most controversial and complex issues of the era through a combination of community programs and traditional political pressure tactics. Both the YWCA and the LWV were committed to action to address the problems facing the poor and racial minorities of their city. As chapter 4 will explore, however, drawing a straight line between these positions of racial progressivism and a group's engagement with the women's movement is not as accurate in Denver as it is in Durham and Indianapolis. The Denver YWCA was an active feminist group, fitting with the pattern found in the other two cities. But the Denver LWV was not. Context mattered: there was less need for grassroots feminist activism from a legislatively oriented group like the League because feminism's legislative and legal goals were accomplished fairly quickly in Denver. But the League's behavior with regard to the Auraria neighborhood hints at another possible reason for the chapter's distance from the women's movement. The

Denver League comes across, more so than the other Leagues studied, as a group deeply convinced of the correctness of its own positions. It believed that it knew best—that a community college was in the best interest of Auraria residents, for instance, even when neighborhood activists were fighting to save their homes. As chapter 4 will document, the Denver LWV's first encounters with feminism were not positive. It seems likely that because the organization's initial impression of feminism was that it was not for the Denver LWV, it simply shut out any further thought or discussion of the issues.

As they worked on a wide range of issues during the 1960s and 1970s, women's organizations in Denver, Durham, and Indianapolis remained vital forces in local politics, as they had been since the earliest days of the twentieth century. They continued to encourage and shape the political involvement of middle-class women, black and white. As feminism brought new ideas about equality and highlighted the problems with traditional gender roles, women's groups were primed to become channels of feminist action. Just as they had done with race and poverty, women's organizations translated the ideas of national feminist leaders into programs and language that resonated with their communities. They mediated between the women's movement and local conditions. The YWCA, the League of Women Voters, and other mainstream women's groups became vital channels for feminism, especially in cities like Durham where new feminist groups such as NOW had difficulty gaining traction. Even in cities where local NOW chapters flourished, mainstream women's groups did not disappear. They worked side by side with NOW to raise awareness and provide women with services and spaces to discuss feminist ideas. Understanding how these organizations worked and what their members believed was the purpose of each is critical to understanding why grassroots feminism took the shape it did. Earlier activism, especially on issues related to race, prepared these mainstream women's groups to serve as channels for feminism. Members were accustomed to working to solve sensitive, wide-ranging, difficult problems through women-only groups. These groups' 1960s activism created activist landscapes in all three cities that both changed and were changed by the women's movement in the following decade.

CHAPTER TWO

Race and Feminism in a Southern City

Durham, North Carolina

In 1973 twenty-two-year-old Connie Winstead graduated from Duke University and decided to drive across the country in order to, in her words, "have an adventure."[1] Winstead took two months to drive from North Carolina to California and eventually connected with a friend from Duke who lived in Berkeley. Winstead stayed in Berkeley, working as a waitress in a restaurant across the street from the University of California campus and volunteering with the Berkeley Women's Health Collective, where she did "problem pregnancy and birth control counseling." After almost a year in Berkeley, Winstead longed for the woods of North Carolina. She once again packed all her belongings into her pale green Datsun sedan and drove back across the country to Durham. When she returned, she wanted to continue working on women's health issues. She found a home for that work at the Women's Health Collective run by the Durham YWCA's Women's Center. She was impressed by the outreach the YWCA did with the community and nearly forty years later took pride in the fact that the YWCA's Women's Health Cooperative "emphasized tolerance and acceptance and presented all choices to women."[2]

The fact that Winstead found the YWCA to be the best venue through which to continue her feminist health work illustrates one of the central facts of the women's movement in Durham. The leadership of the women's movement in the city was provided largely by mainstream women's organizations, particularly the YWCA, a fact that makes Durham quite different from historians' depictions of local feminism.[3] Members of mainstream women's organizations mediated between national ideas and rhetoric and the conditions of their local community. They introduced their neighbors and coworkers to feminist ideas in much the same way that they had helped ease the integration of Durham's schools.

Given the lack of public outcry over programs like the Women's Health Collective, YWCA members and other women working through mainstream women's organizations to bring about feminist change knew their audience in Durham well. Connie Winstead felt that by the end of the 1970s, the women's movement was "widely accepted" in Durham.[4] Similarly, Gilna Nance, who ran the Women's Center from 1974 to 1976, believes that "public opinion progressed closer to the values of the group" of women running the Women's Center as time passed.[5] Winstead and Nance's early twenty-first-century recollections somewhat contradict the archival record. As chapter 5 will discuss, in the very last years of the 1970s the Durham YWCA and its Women's Center faced funding difficulties, which members believed were due to community unhappiness with their feminist work. The oral histories and the YWCA records do agree, however, that prior to 1977 no such backlash was apparent. Working through existing organizations—essentially ensconcing feminism in existing, "respectable" women's spaces—enabled the creation of a vibrant feminist community in Durham and changed many residents' minds about supporting the goals of the women's movement.

The leadership of mainstream women's groups in Durham's feminist community highlights the regional gender norms that feminists in Durham confronted in a southern setting, norms that limited the range of effective tactics for feminist action. Even though a substantial percentage of Durham's population was not southern born, white women activists in the city appear to have confronted the same gender roles and rules that challenged southern suffragists half a century earlier.[6] The ideal of a white "southern lady" remained strong, and white women did not easily take public stands on political issues. The "lady" ideal of white womanhood was a linchpin of the ideology of ruling southerners, tying together beliefs about patriarchy and racial hierarchy in the middle of the twentieth century just as it had done in the antebellum period. Challenges to this identity by white women were seen as threats to the "southern way of life."[7] In the third quarter of the twentieth century, white Durham women conducted virtually all their activism behind the scenes; the exception was their work on the Equal Rights Amendment. The quiet, almost undercover nature of feminist work in Durham highlights a fact that Stephanie Gilmore makes in her work on Memphis: in the South "all feminism was radical."[8] But whereas the members of Memphis NOW whom Gilmore studied openly worked against the region's gender norms, most Durham women undertaking feminist work tried to create feminist change without explicitly challenging the region's gender norms. The need to be seen as "ladies" remained an important part of white women's identity in 1960s and 1970s Durham, perhaps even more so because of the erosion of white supremacy, the other pillar of white southern identity, by the civil rights movement. Feminists in the city, especially those working through the YWCA, did not prioritize undermining that identity.

Middle-class African American women in Durham were also enmeshed in a culture that valued respectability and decorum—a culture that had a similar impact on middle-class black women's public activism as the "lady" ideal had on white women. The middle-class African American women active in civic groups in Durham were firm believers in what historian Evelyn Brooks Higginbotham has termed the "politics of respectability."[9] This idea, which began shaping African American women's activism in the last years of the nineteenth century, held that black women and men had to behave with the utmost decorum and propriety, behave better than most white people, in order to gain respect in their communities and thereby improve the condition of the race.[10] Few African American communities in the country could equal the zeal with which Durham's black middle class embraced the politics of respectability. The city was home to some of the most successful black-owned businesses in the country in the first decades of the twentieth century, leading sociologist E. Franklin Frazier to label the city the "Capital of the Black Middle Class" in 1925.[11] Historian Leslie Brown has described the "hegemony" of the respectability ideal in Durham in the first decades of the twentieth century, arguing that middle-class black women in the city "carried respectability like a sword," using it as a weapon with which to improve their lives.[12] In the 1960s and 1970s, these beliefs were still very much in play, shaping middle-class African American women's responses to and involvement in the civil rights movement as well as the women's movement.[13]

Middle-class women in Durham, both black and white, chose not to directly challenge traditional gender roles and therefore were far less likely to undertake public demonstrations or use other confrontational methods than were feminists in Denver or Indianapolis. When members of a consciousness-raising group from neighboring Chapel Hill sought to increase awareness of sex stereotyping in children's books and education, for example, they did not hold a march or picket a school board meeting. Instead, they sent speakers to the Durham YWCA and the League of Women Voters and wrote letters to the editors of local newspapers.[14] Women in Indianapolis and Denver used similar tactics extensively, but they were not the only options available to feminists in those cities. Occasionally Durham feminists undertook public actions, such as the Women's Workshops sponsored by the YWCA and efforts by members of the League of Women Voters and other organizations to secure ratification of the Equal Rights

Amendment in North Carolina. But beyond ERA work, feminism in Durham remained ensconced in the respectable space of women's organizations.

Yet these restrictions did not eliminate feminist activism in the city. At the YWCA in particular, a multifaceted feminist agenda thrived in the group's Women's Center. The brainchild of YWCA leader Muriel Smith, the Women's Center was begun in 1971 as a space for women's groups to meet and where women could come to find pamphlets and other material on local women's groups. The center rapidly transformed, however, into a site of diverse feminist activities, ranging from providing abortion referrals to offering day- and weekend-long workshops on feminism to area women. The library evolved into a space that gave Durham women access to cutting-edge feminist writing from around the country. And in 1974 the Women's Center expanded even further, beginning to offer meeting space to a lesbian feminist organization and other feminist groups and housing the Health Collective that Connie Winstead ran. While this rapid expansion of scope was occurring at the YWCA, several unsuccessful attempts were made to start a NOW chapter in Durham. Over the course of the 1970s, a NOW chapter began in the city on three separate occasions. The group never met for more than eighteen months before falling apart. The YWCA Women's Center was the heart of feminism in Durham.

The racial makeup of the feminist community in Durham also sets it apart from the movement's national leadership. In Durham, as in other cities that were not intellectual centers of the women's movement, feminist action was undertaken by a racially integrated group of women. Middle-class black and white women worked together on a wide range of feminist projects throughout the 1970s. Most of the predominantly white women's organizations in the city had taken steps to integrate their memberships by the late 1960s. The leadership of those groups in the city's feminist community meant that creating a white-only or black-only feminism would have required intentional separation of women who, in some cases, had been working together for years. The leaders of groups like the YWCA were also sensitive to the fact that African American women may not have the same relationship to feminist ideas as white women and devoted time to exploring the impact of racial difference on feminist ideas and practices.

This chapter begins by exploring the women-centered activism of Durham's middle-class women's groups in the 1960s, examining the ways in which that activism prepared many groups to undertake feminist work once the women's movement burst onto the national scene. Specifically, undertaking women-centered work while working on civil rights and poverty issues, even if the projects were small or peripheral to a group's main focus, laid the groundwork for members of these groups to fold feminist activism into their broader liberal programs. The chapter then examines Durham's feminist community and the work it undertook, arguing that, while using tactics that differed greatly from those of the movement's national leaders, the community did much to improve women's lives in the city. The experiences of Durham's feminists show how extensive feminism's appeal was in the first half of the 1970s. Even in a place where the range of effective actions available to feminists was limited, hundreds of mostly middle-class women, black and white, worked hard to find creative ways to introduce feminist ideas to their neighbors and friends. To the movement's leaders and to many historians of the movement, establishing a feminist library within a YWCA may not have looked like consciousness-raising. But in Durham, where regional gender codes rendered the pickets, marches, and other preferred methods of nationally prominent feminists counterproductive, such a project was an effective way to introduce feminist ideas to the community. Studying grassroots feminism in Durham reveals a racially integrated group of middle-class women who found innovative means of bringing about feminist change in their community without directly challenging the gender norms that were an important part of many southerners' identity.[15]

Women-Centered Activism in Durham's Women's Clubs

Throughout the postwar era, the political involvement of middle-class Durham women flowed through mainstream women's organizations. The city was home to a large YWCA, a well-respected League of Women Voters chapter, and several African American women's groups. As chapter 1 documented, by the middle years of the 1960s most of Durham's large women's clubs were publicly committed to integrating their memberships, a process that was often slow and proceeded unevenly among the different groups. But by the last years of that decade, nearly all of Durham's historically white women's groups had begun actively recruiting African American women. The YWCA ran its classes on an integrated basis and provided leadership opportunities for black women.

Many women's organizations also engaged in what I call women-centered activism throughout the 1960s. Women-centered activism was work that dealt with needs and concerns unique to women but did not do so from a feminist perspective. In many ways this was "pre-feminist" work that familiarized groups with considering issues from the perspective of gender and primed them to be receptive to feminist ideas as they began spreading throughout the nation. Examining the women-centered activism of a sample of the city's women's groups before the emergence of the women's movement sets the stage for understanding the contours of the feminist community that developed in Durham in the early 1970s. It shows that 1960s women's groups were spaces where members valued the groups' identities as women's organizations and the influence of that identity on an organization's activism. These groups were engaged in women-centered activism in the 1960s, even though much of their focus was on issues related to race. In other words, even before the women's movement emerged as a national force, women's organizations had experience blending an institutional awareness of gender and the opportunities and obstacles that a gendered identity created with attention to issues where sex was not overtly perceived as a factor. Their 1960s experiences, then, poised these groups to integrate feminist projects into their activist portfolios in the 1970s.

The Durham organization most focused on women's issues during the 1960s was the YWCA. In undertaking this kind of work, the chapter was in keeping with the national YWCA's history. The national YWCA was created to meet the needs of women and girls.[16] This emphasis on the YWCA as a women's movement became more pointed in the postwar era, when many YWCAs faced pressure from United Funds and other civic funding bodies to consolidate with their town's Young Men's Christian Association (YMCA), consolidations that would have eliminated the women-only space provided by the YWCA.[17] At the 1961 national convention, the organization adopted a resolution stating, "The YWCA has a new awareness of the significance of its own responsibilities as a women's movement. It is faced with a new urgency to help women and girls find meaning in their own lives, develop to the full their capacity for leadership, [and] play an effective and constructive part in the life of today."[18] At the national level, then, the YWCA entered the 1960s focused squarely on the effects of the organization's identity as a women's group.

Although the Durham YWCA did not face pressure to consolidate with the city's YMCA, the chapter followed the national office's attention to their group's gendered identity, and programming for women and girls was a focus throughout the 1960s. Its identity as a women's organization clearly played a role in determining the issues discussed at the YWCA. And concerns about women's identity both within and outside the home were not restricted to the white members of the group. In 1957 the African American Tubman branch distributed a questionnaire to its members titled "Are You Satisfied Being a Woman in Today's World?" The form asked questions such as "What preparations do you wish you had had for your present status?" and inquired if the women were happy in their current situation or would prefer to be single or, if they preferred being married, whether they would prefer to work or stay home, be childless or have children.[19] The Tubman branch's use of the questionnaire shows that middle-class African American women were equally aware of—and perhaps felt equally affected by—the "malaise" that many national magazines were beginning to discover among American housewives in the late 1950s and that Betty Friedan would publicize even more widely in *The Feminine Mystique* in 1963. Unfortunately the results of the questionnaire do not survive, making it impossible to know how satisfied Tubman members were with their positions in life. But the fact that the questionnaire was circulated at all is fascinating. The magazine stories that addressed the stifling nature of being a housewife in the late 1950s were virtually all in white-oriented periodicals such as *Ladies' Home Journal*.[20] In spite of such placements and the fact that the majority of the branch's members were employed outside the home, the leadership of the Tubman branch felt that the malaise of homemaking was a contemporary issue their organization, as a women's organization, should be open to discussing.[21]

In the mid-1960s, the Durham YWCA's women-centered activism began to focus on a study of "sex morality," which the national organization adopted as part of its triennial program platform in 1964. The national board wanted to create programs that taught members about the changing sexual mores of young people, so that the YWCA could continue to work effectively with teenage girls.[22] Members of the Durham YWCA approached issues of sexuality, and especially the issue of changing sexual norms, from a different angle than feminist activists would in the coming years. Feminists claimed a woman's right to her own sexuality and sexual fulfillment. For the women of the Durham YWCA, the issue of sexuality was deeply embedded in their identity as members of a Christian women's organization and the ideal of a woman remaining chaste until marriage.[23] But while members were challenged by the conflict between their desire to continue working with teenage girls and their disapproval of the apparent changes in youthful sexual behavior, YWCA members took their organization's mandate to work with young women and develop their leadership skills seriously. They therefore tried to find nonjudgmental ways to meet the needs of young women. To that end, in 1967 the YWCA began discussing the problems faced by pregnant teenage girls who were barred from the Durham city and county school systems because of their pregnancy.[24] By 1969 the YWCA was working with several other area women's groups and receiving outside funding to run the Cooperative School for Pregnant Teens, which operated on an integrated basis.[25]

Because of their belief in the association's mission to work with teenage girls, the women of the Durham YWCA were willing to honestly confront the problems some of those girls were facing, even when they personally disapproved of the girls' behavior. Group members did not seek to punish young women who transgressed what YWCA members considered proper sexual boundaries. They saw their job as giving those young women the skills and opportunities to have successful, fulfilling lives, even if that meant establishing a school for unwed teenage mothers. Working with the Cooperative School may have also helped soften the ground at the YWCA for feminist analyses by exposing members to young women who were clearly being discriminated against because of their sex. The girls' male partners were not banned from school because they had fathered children, and seeing the material damage done to the girls' futures (were it not for the Cooperative School) likely sensitized members of the YWCA staff to issues of sex discrimination.

While the Durham YWCA took on projects that in hindsight may have laid the foundations for the group's 1970s feminist activism, the city's League of Women Voters shied away from women-centered activism in the 1960s. While the YWCA's history and purpose encouraged women-centered activism, the institutional culture and history of the LWV worked against a close focus on women's issues. The group was devoted to increasing women's understanding of and participation in politics, but that understanding and participation were not, in themselves, gendered. When the group took a position on an issue, it did not do so as a women's group; rather, its positions were couched in terms of engaged citizens.[26] Occasionally, however, the Durham League in the 1960s subtly pushed the boundaries for women. In the spring of 1966, leaders of the Durham League began a discussion with the editors of the *Durham Morning News* that lasted, off and on, for over a decade. That May board of directors member Emily Warner "brought up the problem of [the organization's] relations with the newspaper." Warner noted, "Although our coverage on the Woman's Page is very good, we are hard pressed to get adequate coverage in the City section. Mrs. Lebovitz suggested that a delegation go to the managing editor for a policy statement on what qualifies as news."[27]

The delegation apparently came away from the meeting having learned that the opinions of women on political and economic issues did not qualify. The group battled the newspaper on this issue off and on for a decade. In 1975 League women were still trying to get their positions before a larger audience by getting stories about those positions into the newspaper's main news section, despite the fact that the group's positions "would be given greater coverage" on the Women's Page.[28] While the group did not undertake any public action on women's issues in the 1960s, this effort to get the League's political opinions treated as serious news shows the evolving consciousness of local League leaders. It also reveals the feminist potential of an organization like the LWV, which taught women they had a vital role to play in government and public affairs.

Throughout the second half of the 1960s, Durham League leaders had direct, personal experience with leading men in their community who devalued women's opinions on major political issues simply because they were articulated by women. That experience sensitized them to sex discrimination several years before the women's movement identified that discrimination as part of a larger system that denied rights and freedoms to women. The intractability of the editors of the *Morning News* on this point likely heightened the women's frustration. Attention to this problem also ensured that League members remained conscious of their group's status as a women's organization throughout the second half of the 1960s, even though the national organization did little to promote that image in those years.

While the League and especially the YWCA increased their attention to gender issues as the 1960s wore on, Durham's African American women's clubs moved in the opposite direction. The Durham chapters of both Alpha Kappa Alpha sorority and the National Council of Negro Women had long been attentive to black women's needs; both groups saw themselves as serving a critical role in preparing black women for leadership both within their homes and in the world. In the first half of the 1960s, the city's Alpha Kappa Alpha chapter retained some women-centered work. In 1965 the city's AKA alumni chapter sponsored a self-esteem workshop for teenage black girls.[29] At the AKA regional conference in neighboring Raleigh the following year, the keynote speaker emphasized that women were crucial in the effort to "save the world," and noted, "The Negro man is not taking his place as the head of his family and women, therefore, must assume leadership status."[30] In the last years of the 1960s, however, African American women's groups increasingly turned their focus away from women-centered activism. Historian Deborah Gray White has argued that Dorothy Height, the president of the National Council of Negro Women beginning in 1958, believed that black women would be helped most by improving the situation of the entire race, and shifted the NCNW's focus away from women's issues and toward a more general civil rights agenda.[31] Black women's organizations in Durham followed this trajectory, and many clubs in the city developed a particular focus on increasing economic opportunity for African Americans. Many groups sponsored workshops on economic growth, especially business ownership by African Americans and black men and women's patronage of those businesses.[32] This shift in emphasis is one possible explanation for the lack of involvement in feminism on an organizational level by African American women's clubs in Durham in the 1970s.

As the 1970s dawned, most of Durham's historically white women's clubs were committed to integrating their memberships. Many of the city's women's organizations had spent the previous decades devoting at least some of their time and thought to the ways in which women's lives were shaped and, in many cases, constrained by their sex. When the women's movement emerged, Durham women turned these same organizations into effective channels for feminist change.

Integrated Feminism and the Women's Movement in Durham

In May 1973, Durham resident Gail Bradley, a longtime officer of the League of Women Voters on the local, state, and national level, addressed the annual meeting of the North Carolina LWV. In her speech she told the audience, "I make no apologies for saying that I am a women's liberationist. The heart of the women's liberation movement today is the ERA we are fighting for, but the real heart of women's liberation is the changed perception of woman's role in the society in which she lives, in which she wants to take a full and equal part in participating in what happens to her family, her city, her state, her country, her government, and everything else." Later in the same speech, Bradley stated, "I do not believe volunteerism is dead."[33] Taking these two themes together, Bradley offered a description of the feminist community that developed in Durham in the early years of the 1970s. Through the Women's Center at the YWCA, Durham women were exposed to a wide range of feminist issues, from feminist views on work and child care to sexuality and relationships with men. Other women's groups, notably the League of Women Voters, focused exclusively on bringing about structural and legal changes in women's status, and the LWV poured its energy into work for the Equal Rights Amendment. And while NOW was never a sustainable organization in Durham—three separate attempts were made to launch a chapter between 1971 and 1975, none of which lasted more than eighteen months—several women spoke at meetings of other women's groups on NOW's behalf and raised their awareness of issues such as sex stereotyping in education and children's books. As the ideas of the women's movement began to circulate in Durham, the city's middle-class women's organizations reacted in diverse ways. And the groups that pursued feminist action in Durham were racially integrated. Several years of integrated activism in the city's women's organizations created the opportunity for a biracial feminist community to develop and thrive far from the ideological tensions of feminism's intellectual home in the nation's urban centers.

Working through existing organizations rather than abandoning them for new, explicitly feminist ones was both a pragmatic and a personal choice for Durham women. They knew how to create successful community projects through those organizations. The groups already had the respect of community leaders, and many of the women did not see the necessity of creating alternative organizations in order to accomplish their goals. The YWCA in particular had a long history of successfully developing potentially controversial projects that benefited women and girls, such as the Cooperative School for Pregnant Teens. Creating independent feminist spaces or organizations was not a primary goal for most members of Durham's feminist community.

Members of Durham's mainstream women's organizations heard the new ideas being promoted by national feminist leaders and translated those ideas into a language that was relevant to a large percentage of the Durham community. Women used their existing community groups, with which Durham residents were already familiar, to mediate between national ideas and local conditions. But working through existing groups was not a method without flaws. Working within the confines of "respectable" women's organizations meant that feminist ideas were disseminated through a range of programs, and there was no way to ensure individuals' attendance at all meetings and events. Women could therefore work on the issues with which they felt most comfortable and avoid confronting the more radical aspects of feminism's agenda. Using existing organizations also created a movement that was almost completely middle class.

In spite of these shortcomings, however, the feminist community that emerged in Durham was vibrant and multifaceted. Women working through their community organizations, especially those with a strong history of women-centered activism, developed an interracial feminist community in a southern city. Looking back on their work some thirty-five years later, women who were active in the YWCA Women's Center believed that their activism helped shift public opinion in favor of feminism, a shift that may not have occurred if explicitly feminist groups had been major players in Durham's feminist community.[34] Mainstream women's organizations were the heart and soul of the women's movement in Durham.

Despite Gail Bradley's plea to her fellow League members to embrace a broad feminist agenda, the Durham League of Women Voters did not as an organization undertake a wide-ranging feminist program. But the chapter did provide significant womanpower on the feminist issue that fit most easily within its existing organizational structure and purpose: the Equal Rights Amendment. The League's long-standing focus on voting, lobbying, and legislative solutions to problems made the ERA a natural fit for the organization. League members believed that the best way to win state legislators to their side was to provide them with facts and polling data showing the impact of the amendment and its widespread support.

Members of the Durham LWV were enthusiastic supporters of the ERA. Durham League women wrote letters and lobbied legislators in their battleground ERA state throughout the 1970s. As historians Jane Sherron De Hart and Donald Mathews have argued, tension existed between the women sent by the NOW national office and many North Carolina activists. The local women felt that NOW was insensitive to the need to moderate certain parts of its rhetoric in order to appeal to North Carolina legislators.[35] The minutes from Durham League meetings on the ERA reveal these concerns. Board members talked frequently about the need for rational, polite letters that highlighted the ways in which the amendment would benefit North Carolina women. A letter from Gail Bradley, who was one of the Durham League's representatives to North Carolinians United for the ERA (NCUERA), the statewide ERA coalition, stated that a new flyer was to be used in the fund-raising materials for 1974 as "the [previously used] NOW flyer was a little too militant for other organizations."[36] Creating a new flyer was in keeping with NCUERA's overall public relations approach for the 1974 campaign. The PR Committee stated in May 1974 that its objectives for the coming push would be a "*Positive Approach*—get the real set. [sentiment] out and *Identify with N.C.*"[37] League women clearly saw their letters and lobbying efforts as countering both the outside-agitator image of NOW and what they perceived as the irrational and emotional appeals of organized anti-ERA women. An article in the March 1975 LWV newsletter, for example, urged members to write their legislators in support of the ERA, but emphasized that letters should be "extremely polite, very low-key and pleasant."[38]

League policy required members to study issues for several months and then agree on a consensus position before a chapter could take public action on the topic. Some members of the Durham League were concerned that this approach, reflected in the group's decision to work only on the ERA and not pursue other feminist action, was contributing to the organization's loss of influence in the community. The February 1970 board meeting included a fraught discussion about the direction the group should take as it moved into the new decade. Some members worried that by the time the League studied an issue, members' opinions were already set, and that the chapter would inevitably adopt a predetermined position. This faction was concerned that the League was not "ahead of its times . . . in comparison to ten or fifteen years ago." Other board members believed that stagnant membership had created this problem. In 1970 the board debated the degree to which the League should court "young activist women." One bloc argued, "Sweeping changes in regard to program activities might need to be made in order to involve persons who want to see action." The opposing group believed that "it would be unwise to embark upon active projects without sufficient background study simply to involve members who want to 'do' something."[39] Clearly the organizational culture of the League was becoming a problem. Some members felt that the League should be more active in engaging with feminism and the "young activist women" who were involved in the movement, while others were hesitant to embark on projects before reaching consensus for fear of endangering the League's image of respectability within the community. In the end, the Durham LWV stuck to traditional League procedures, limiting their feminist activism to their work on the ERA. As chapter 5 will examine, however, by the last years of the 1970s even these procedural constraints were being challenged in action if not in spirit, as ERA ratification came to be the leading, and at times the exclusive, policy pursued by the Durham League.

Members of the Durham LWV worked tirelessly for ERA ratification in North Carolina, but the embrace of feminism by the chapter as a whole was partial. Instead of turning their organization fully toward a diverse set of feminist issues and throwing themselves wholeheartedly into an effort to change their community's gender norms, LWV women, for most of the 1970s, selected from the national feminist agenda the issues that best fit with their organization's political culture. Members of the League who wanted to pursue more explicitly feminist activism were free to do so in other organizations. And many did: Gail Bradley became the treasurer of the local NOW chapter in 1973, the same year she addressed the state LWV convention. But as an organization, the Durham League of Women Voters encountered feminism through the same lens of legislative action as it did poverty, civil rights, and other issues of the day. It studied all sides, usually adopted a fairly liberal stance on the issue, and then put all the womanpower of the organization behind achieving their goal. The LWV was a vital ally in the fight for the ERA in North Carolina, but it was not a participant in the full range of feminist activism occurring in Durham in the 1970s.

The YWCA, by contrast, became the center of Durham's feminist community. When the national YWCA leadership announced its goal of "revolutioniz[ing] society's expectation of women" in 1970, the members of the Durham chapter took that directive to heart.[40] From July 1971 until the end of the decade, the YWCA building on Chapel Hill Street housed the Durham Women's Center.[41] Leaders of the Durham YWCA saw the opening of the Women's Center as a way for the group to reaffirm its commitment to addressing women's needs. A spring 1971 review of the chapter by the national YWCA staff members argued that interrogating its position as a women's group was an important step that the Durham YWCA needed to take, stating, "More fortunate perhaps than some associations, the Durham YWCA has *not* been faced with a struggle to maintain itself as an autonomous, women's Christian organization. In a sense, however, we viewed the lack of threat as somewhat regrettable because organizations that are forced to examine and redefine or reaffirm their goals find themselves in stronger position[s]. We agreed that [the Durham YWCA] could welcome creative activists who might wake [them] up."[42] After this report, the YWCA began developing the Women's Center, a project headed by Program Committee chair Muriel Smith.[43]

Smith's original vision was not for a women's center but rather for a women's library, which would gather books, bibliographies, and other items examining women's rights or women's history, as well as pamphlets and materials prepared by volunteer groups in the Durham area. In her proposal for the library, Smith wrote to Rose Butler Browne, the YWCA president at the time, that as the size of the library's collection increased, she hoped the library would become a "dynamic force in [their] community."[44] By the summer of 1971, Smith and the Program Committee had expanded their vision to include not only the library but also the Women's Center, which would provide meeting space to the city's women's groups.[45]

Over the next several years, the center continued to evolve. Rather than serving as meeting space for other women's voluntary groups, as Smith originally envisioned, the center quickly became a hub for feminist service providers, especially those in the fields of health and sexuality. By 1972 the YWCA had an office at the center that offered abortion counseling, and the chapter was working on abortion legislation as well, likely joining the national YWCA and many other liberal Protestant and Jewish groups in arguing that legalization of abortion nationwide was the only way to ensure that women of all classes had equal access to the procedure.[46] Throughout the first half of the 1970s, the Women's Center continued to work on health and sexuality issues, hiring Connie Winstead to run the Women's Health Collective in 1974 and housing a rape crisis hotline by 1975.[47] Winstead recalls the Health Collective being well received, stating that the YWCA "did good outreach" with women in the community.[48] In addition to counseling for "problem pregnancies," the Health Collective also gave surveys to every woman who visited regarding their experiences with obstetricians and gynecologists in the city and from those data created a list of doctors who were "sensitive" to a "women's rights perspective."[49] Both Winstead and Gilna Nance, another YWCA Women's Center leader, argue that the "visibility" of the women's health collective was instrumental in bringing the first "free-standing" abortion clinic to the area in the late 1970s.[50]

By 1975 the YWCA Women's Center also housed a day care center, and Triangle Area Lesbian Feminists (TALF) kept an office and held meetings there. By the end of the 1970s, the Women's Center was cosponsoring coffeehouses and other social events for lesbians with TALF at the center.[51] These activities of the Women's Center, along with ERA work undertaken by LWV members and other activists, were the most visible feminist efforts in Durham and contributed tremendously to Connie Winstead's assessment that by 1980 the women's movement was "more visible and widely accepted" in the city.[52] Fellow Women's Center veteran Gilna Nance agrees with Winstead's assessment of the changes in the city's attitude toward feminism, stating that after she left Durham in 1976 "public opinion progressed closer to the values of the group."[53]

In addition to running the Women's Center and providing numerous feminist services, the YWCA also offered women opportunities to explore the intellectual underpinnings of the women's movement and the movement's broad goals. The chapter did not create stand-alone consciousness-raising groups, which were a primary way many women around the country engaged with feminism on a personal and intellectual level.[54] Rather, the YWCA sponsored a series of public "Women's Workshops," day- or weekend-long sessions where women, in small groups, heard speakers and discussed their own feelings and opinions on a wide range of feminist topics. Workshop sessions addressed such issues as sexuality, work, the Equal Rights Amendment, "changing patterns in male-female relationships," and other topics. More than 285 women attended the first workshop, in the autumn of 1972.[55] In November 1973, the daylong "Women's Town Meeting" featured Martha McKay, a leader of the National Women's Political Caucus, as the keynote speaker. The meeting included sessions on black women, "women and their bodies," women's economic and legal problems, child care in Durham, and "restructuring personal relationships." The article about the "town meeting" that appeared in the *Carolina Times*, the city's black newspaper, also noted that there would be a lunchtime play by the Feminist Theatre Troupe of Chapel Hill and that "creative child care" would be provided.[56] In addition to the workshop series, the YWCA also continued to operate the Women's Library, which held a wide range of feminist and leftist periodicals. By 1975 women coming to the Women's Library had access to feminist, peace, and environmentalist newspapers from around the South and the country. Titles included *New Carolina Woman*; the *Women's Rights Law Reporter*, published by Rutgers University; the *Southern Feminist Connection*; and *Distaff*, a feminist paper published in New Orleans that focused on African American women and feminism.[57]

The leadership of the YWCA had clearly embraced most of the agenda of national feminist leaders. Historian Judith Ezekiel has argued that the split between liberal and radical feminism, which was so important within the movement's intellectual vanguard, did not resonate with the women whom Ezekiel studied in Dayton, Ohio.[58] This was true for the women of Durham as well. The YWCA Women's Center offered women access to a range of feminist activities from writing a letter in support of the ERA to reading radical feminist newspapers and books at the library or getting a referral to a sympathetic gynecologist. The library and the workshops introduced women in Durham to the intellectual side of the women's movement, while the Women's Center provided numerous feminist services. Failing to promote small consciousness-raising groups did not mean that the feminist community at the Women's Center lacked engagement with feminist ideas or analyses. Though the structure was different from that favored by the movement's national leaders, raising women's consciousness about the beliefs and goals of the women's movement was exactly what the Durham YWCA was doing. It was possible for women to participate in the activities at the YWCA without reading any of the literature at the library or attending any of the workshops. But the fact that a grounding in feminist theory was not the only way to join the feminist community did not mean that feminist theory did not circulate among Durham feminists. As will be discussed later in this chapter, many of the key ideas of second-wave theory were clearly moving through Durham. Women simply encountered those ideas through different means than those identified by historians of the movement.

Remaining within the YWCA also gave feminist programs legitimacy within the community. Coming to the women's workshops or stopping by the library seems to have been an acceptable thing for women to do, since those programs were housed at the YWCA. And if Winstead and Nance's assessment of the shift in public opinion is correct, feminist programs run under the auspices of the YWCA increased the acceptability of feminism more broadly. But the fact that feminist action was conducted by a "respectable" organization did not decrease the potential of the message that women received at the workshops or the library. Durham YWCA members undertook a wide range of feminist programs in the first half of the 1970s, including some, like providing abortion referrals, that were controversial.

The Durham YWCA's embrace of feminism also was not a case of a local chapter simply following the orders of the national board. Each YWCA chapter implemented the various national platform planks in its own way and was free to prioritize those issues as the chapter saw fit. This freedom meant that the Durham YWCA's feminist work was done because its members believed in the projects and not simply because they were following directives from the national leadership. In other cities—Indianapolis, for example—the local YWCA received the same national platform and did markedly less feminist work.[59] Also, unlike other women's civic groups, the YWCA had to be financially self-supporting through memberships and class fees in order to operate its facilities and offset involvement in programs and classes for low-income women and children, whose fees the group routinely waived. Had an appreciable number of people not participated in the group's feminist work, therefore, it is unlikely that the organization would have been able to sustain it. As chapter 5 will explore, this exact circumstance challenged the YWCA in the last years of the 1970s. Before 1977, however, undertaking abortion advocacy and other feminist programs did not cause a backlash in Durham sufficient to threaten the YWCA's financial footing.

The leadership of the YWCA in Durham's feminist community also led to a women's movement that was racially integrated. The Durham YWCA had integrated slowly, but in 1970 Rose Butler Browne, an African American woman and retired dean of the local black college, was elected to a two-year term as president of the organization.[60] By 1972 demographic changes in Durham, specifically white flight from the city's center, meant that the majority of community members using both of the YWCA's facilities—the Central, formerly all-white, building and the Tubman branch building—were African American.[61] Thus, when the YWCA began to undertake its feminist work, it would have been counterproductive, and all but impossible, for that work to involve only white women. African American women were vital members of the Durham YWCA, both in leadership positions and as community members participating in the various programs and workshops. The contrast between the racial makeup of two southern feminist communities—Durham's based at the YWCA and Memphis's centered around a NOW chapter—is striking. As historian Stephanie Gilmore notes, in spite of the efforts of Memphis NOW's white members to create a space that was welcoming to black women, "Memphis NOW was a white women's group in both perception and reality." Gilmore attributes the group's difficulty in attracting members of color largely to the group's image both nationally and locally, recounting that one prominent black woman activist in the city did not join NOW because she viewed NOW "as first being white and therefore suspect."[62] In Durham by 1970, no one could make a similar claim about the YWCA. The feminist community that emerged, therefore, managed to bridge the racial divide in a southern city.

Women in Durham encountered issues such as marriage, child rearing, and sex through the Women's Workshops and town meetings sponsored by the YWCA, in spaces that were already racially integrated and attuned to the distinct relationship black women had to a variety of feminist issues.[63] The Women's Workshops offered numerous sessions dealing with African American women's unique relationship to the women's movement. The YWCA's leadership in the city's feminist community helped make feminism acceptable to many of Durham's African American residents. In 1974 the *Carolina Times* ran a four-part series of articles outlining the reasons why black women should join the women's liberation movement. Author Geraldine Rickman highlighted the fact that black women "respond to issues affecting [them] as they affect all women," such as child care and equal pay.[64] Throughout the early 1970s, the *Times* also ran a sexual health advice column titled "Pregnancy Planning and Health." In the winter of 1971, a woman wrote in asking about the importance of female orgasms, and columnist Gloria Rigsbee responded with a frank discussion of the issue, assuring the questioner that "while a woman should not worry if she does not have at least one orgasm every time she has sex, she still has a right to expect a climax some of the time."[65] Clearly Rigsbee was familiar with feminist ideas about women's sexuality and sexual pleasure, even if it is impossible to know whether she had read Anne Koedt's "Myth of the Vaginal Orgasm." None of these articles—either Rigsbee's column or the series urging black women to join the women's movement—generated negative letters to the editor or other indications of community disapproval. Central feminist beliefs were moving through Durham in the early 1970s, and while certainly not everyone agreed, there were no expressions of public outrage over these ideas in local newspapers, nor did the YWCA or the LWV report attacks on their positions to the national leadership or discuss them among themselves in meetings.

Another indication of the open reception some feminist ideas found in Durham was the success of several new, explicitly feminist groups regarding the issue of sex stereotyping in schools and children's books. In 1970 a group of Chapel Hill feminists that included historian Sara Evans began Lollipop Power, a small press that printed nonsexist children's books. Evans saw the press's books as "*tools* in the service of women's liberation and human freedom."[66] Ideas about nonsexist education and child rearing became part of the broader discussion about education in Durham that took place the following year, in anticipation of the city schools' court-ordered integration at the beginning of the 1971–72 school year. The Durham Charrette, the interracial group that developed plans for school integration in Durham in the summer of 1971, had a curriculum committee that directly addressed the issue of sexism in education. The committee was made up of both students and parents and resolved that "as with black studies, the role of women as a productive part of . . . society should be included in courses at all levels. Textbooks in the elementary grades should be changed to picture the roles of both men and women away from their stereotypes."[67] The committee issued a recommendation stating that sex should play no role in a teacher's assessment of "a student's ability in a given discipline" nor in guidance counselors' work in helping students decide what career to pursue.[68] The Curriculum Committee also considered the issue of sex education. Students on the committee argued that "appropriate" sex education was needed, and parents agreed with the students' recommendations while noting that "such education should be done on a purely factual basis while leaving the corresponding moral decisions to the children themselves."[69]

After the charrette concluded in August 1971, the issue of nonsexist education remained in the public consciousness, largely due to the efforts of educator and NOW member Amanda Smith. Smith spoke tirelessly on the issue of childhood socialization and education throughout the early 1970s. In 1973 an article about sex stereotyping in children's books appeared in the *Carolina Times*.[70] That same year, NOW led a panel discussion for students and parents on issues of sex discrimination in the city's public schools.[71] The success of efforts to raise awareness about sex stereotyping in education, the sexual health columns in the *Carolina Times*, and the consistent growth of the YWCA Women's Center all demonstrate that in the middle years of the 1970s, the concerns and the language of the liberation movement had become acceptable to many in Durham.

In spite of this openness to at least parts of the women's movement, new, explicitly feminist organizations struggled to gain traction in Durham. A NOW chapter began meeting in Durham in the spring of 1973.[72] The group was never large, however, and it had difficulty maintaining momentum. In July 1973, the chapter newsletter highlighted three major projects planned for the coming months: a feminist book fair, a survey of the credit situation for women in Durham, and a committee to evaluate the need for a rape crisis center and consider alternative projects to address the issue.[73] That fall the chapter was also looking into the discriminatory practices at the Belk-Liggett tobacco factory (particularly the issue of restrictive maternity leave) and discussing the refusal of the Durham newspapers to use "Ms."[74] But NOW took no public action on any of these issues. The YWCA was already operating a feminist library and a reading room at its Women's Center when NOW held its feminist book fair. It is unclear whether NOW members were instrumental in beginning the rape crisis hotline that the YWCA operated; neither the organizations' archives nor discussions with YWCA members revealed details about the hotline's founding. But the YWCA provided the space and much of the womanpower for the project. And NOW's credit study never got off the ground. The credit task force was "reconstituted" in September 1975, after the federal Equal Credit Opportunity Act had passed, and an investigation of its implementation would have been a timely project for NOW. There is no evidence, however, that its findings were used for any projects or made public in any way, nor even that the study was carried out.[75] The NOW chapter that "reconstituted" the credit task force in 1975 was on its last legs, however. The group appears to have disbanded in the winter of 1975–76.[76]

There are several possible reasons for NOW's struggles. From interviews she conducted in the 1980s, historian of Durham Jean Anderson concluded that at least some of NOW's struggles were due to what many activist women in the city perceived as its "confrontational tactics."[77] At the time, ERA activists like Gail Bradley expressed similar reservations about the pro-ERA material that the national NOW office produced for use in North Carolina. When reflecting back on Durham NOW's struggles, Miriam Slifkin, a Chapel Hill resident who served as North Carolina NOW president in 1979, highlighted additional problems. Slifkin recalled, "[Because NOW was] issue-oriented . . . what happens is people get concerned about an issue that hits them, and they'll come onboard and then they get burned out."[78] Slifkin further argued that because of the difficulties in keeping members involved in NOW for the long haul, the amount of information with which the national NOW office "bombarded local offices" presented a challenge. In her recollection, national NOW was constantly sending local chapters information about a wide range of national issues. Acting on all the directives from the national office left little time for members to think about the local context and what issues were most pressing in the local community.[79] Slifkin also argued that groups like the AAUW or League were more stable because their members had "programs and . . . socialize[d]," creating a sense of a group that was larger than the particular crisis at hand.[80] Taken together, Slifkin's remarks suggest that Durham-area NOW achieved some successes when presented with crises but was less adept at creating a sustainable feminist community. The Women's Center run by the YWCA provided such a community, and because of its wider base of activism—not only letter writing and lobbying about a particular problem such as discrimination at area tobacco factories but also incorporating services such as abortion referrals and the feminist coffeehouse that was a hub of Durham's lesbian feminist community—the Women's Center was a more broadly based and longer-lasting endeavor.[81]

Some Durham feminists, however, were dedicated to creating an explicitly feminist group in the city. One was Gail Bradley, the longtime League activist who, along with her husband, was one of the founding members of Durham NOW. In the face of NOW's continued difficulties, Bradley began a chapter of the Women's Equity Action League (WEAL) in the city in early 1976. By 1977 Bradley had become a leader in North Carolina WEAL, but it is unclear if the local chapter continued to meet. The state group, however, remained active on the kinds of liberal feminist projects, focusing largely on legal equality, for which the group was known throughout the late 1970s.[82] The organization's most notable success was a task force designed to increase women's employment within the state government. By late 1977, WEAL was "impressed" by the efforts made by the governor's office since the summer to increase hiring of women.[83] The group continued to be active at the state level, joining the North Carolina Coalition for Choice in early 1979 and writing letters in favor of the ERA throughout the decade.[84] But WEAL does not seem to have been a major player in bringing feminist ideas to Durham specifically. Durham women—including several former presidents of the LWV—were active in the group.[85] Its focus and purpose, however, were on the state and national levels, as its members lobbied and wrote letters to elected officials.

Despite the efforts of Gail Bradley and others, the feminist community in Durham was dominated by existing organizations. Introducing feminism to a community through existing women's organizations helped reassure residents that the ideas of the women's movement were not solely the province of women in the nation's biggest cities but were important to their neighbors and friends in Durham as well. The leadership of women's groups that were already racially integrated helped to overcome many of the obstacles between African American women and feminism that existed among the movement's leading intellectuals. The YWCA's leadership in particular made feminism appear respectable to many Durham residents.

Feminism did not come to Durham through marches and mass demonstrations or primarily through new feminist organizations. The goals of the women's movement were pursued in Durham most thoroughly, and most effectively, through existing women's organizations that had authority in the community and the respect of Durham residents. The primary role of these organizations made it more difficult for women outside those circles—notably poor and working-class women, black and white—to become active in the feminist community. And it enabled some women, especially those in the League of Women Voters, to work toward feminist changes in society's laws without tackling issues of personal politics such as sexuality. Women who had cut their teeth in community activism through the League of Women Voters or the YWCA had a long history of mediating between national movements' concerns and local conditions in Durham and translating those concerns into projects that would be effective in their city. They were pragmatic, autonomous actors in shaping the second wave, and it was their work and their creativity that determined the contours and content of the feminist activism that took place in Durham.

CHAPTER THREE

Feminist Coalitions and the ERA

Indianapolis

In the spring of 1974, Lynn Schrum, head of Indiana NOW, sent a letter to all the NOW chapters in the state reminding them that the state NOW office had decided "to low-key [their] abortion fight until ERA had passed."[1] The letter was directed at least partially at the Indianapolis NOW chapter, which had gone against the policy and held a pro-choice rally on April 13, 1974.[2] Indianapolis NOW members felt that they had no choice but to break Indiana NOW's policy and organize the rally. Right-to-Life, one of the largest antiabortion groups in the country, held a demonstration in Indianapolis that April day. While the NOW members carefully avoided direct confrontation with their opponents, they felt a public showing in support of *Roe v. Wade* was essential, stating, "Our sole purpose is to defend our hard-won right to legal abortion."[3] Indianapolis NOW's decision frustrated state president Schrum, who had been trying since the previous December to improve the relationship between Indiana's NOW chapters and Hoosiers for the ERA (HERA), the umbrella organization that coordinated pro-ERA work in the state. In December 1973, Schrum wrote to a member of the HERA Policy Council, imploring her to give NOW information about any action on the amendment's behalf. Schrum stated, "Several chapters are growing concerned that nothing in the way of announcements, progress, or planning seems to have taken place with regard to the ERA."[4] The two organizations' relationship remained tense until HERA disbanded in 1976.[5]

The difficulty between HERA and Indiana NOW highlights the challenges of working for feminist change in a conservative context. Feminists in Indianapolis, both those in newly formed feminist organizations such as NOW and those in existing women's groups like the League of Women Voters, agreed early in the 1970s to make ERA ratification their primary goal. In 1977 they achieved that goal as Indiana became the last state to ratify the amendment. The protracted fight for the ERA in Indiana demonstrates that work by a multifaceted coalition of feminist groups was necessary for the amendment's success. In the early 1970s, the League of Women Voters, HERA, and the Indiana Women's Political Caucus—the state branch of a national feminist political group founded in 1971—led the fight. By 1976 HERA had declined, and NOW chapters from around the state worked together with LWV and Indiana Women's Political Caucus members—and eventually staff from the national organization ERAmerica—to finally win ratification. Throughout these years, activists often had to choose between publicly supporting a wide range of feminist causes or deferring work on issues other than ERA until ratification of the amendment had been achieved. ERA leaders feared that vocal support of a wide-ranging feminist agenda by pro-ERA organizations would harm the amendment's chances of success in the Indiana state legislature.[6]

The activism of so many groups on behalf of the ERA also demonstrates the importance of having multiple points of view among activists working on the same issue. Large women's organizations had all spent time in the 1960s doing women-centered activism and were therefore more primed to become active participants in the women's movement. In North Carolina, there was no equivalent to Indiana NOW, a statewide organization that embedded work on the amendment's behalf into a broad and explicitly feminist agenda. In Indiana NOW worked alongside members of mainstream women's groups and the fairly conservative HERA. It was only through the loosely coordinated efforts of all these groups, working toward ratification for somewhat different reasons and in different ways, that the ERA passed in Indiana in 1977.

Securing ERA ratification remained the primary goal of most Indianapolis feminist groups until that goal was achieved in 1977. But it was not the only feminist issue under discussion in the city. In their meetings, many women's groups devoted increasing amounts of time to discussing a range of feminist ideas. The League of Women Voters periodically published lists of feminist books in its newsletter under the heading "recommended reading."[7] The city's NOW chapter and the women's liberation group that preceded it used a variety of public tactics, from street theater performances to bridal fair pickets to creating sections on feminism and women's issues in local bookstores, to raise public awareness of feminism's critiques of American society.[8] The city's Mayor's Task Force on Women established a well-regarded rape prevention program in 1974.[9] While many of these projects were affected by the statewide ERA fight, the necessities of working for the ERA did not prevent women's organizations from creating diverse feminist programs. As was the case at the Durham YWCA, feminists in Indianapolis used the "respectable" spaces of the League of Women Voters or the Mayor's Task Force to launch projects and organize discussions inspired by the women's movement. But in Indianapolis, these efforts were joined by a much more robust group of explicitly feminist organizations.

Unlike the existing women's organizations, however, explicitly feminist groups were seen as radical by many Indianapolis residents and by the members themselves. In 1972 feminist activist Myra Ferris was fired from her job with the State Board of Health for her "unladylike" behavior, which she and other feminists interpreted as referring to her activism with Indianapolis Women's Liberation, a group that predated and then became part of Indianapolis NOW.[10] NOW was the most visible explicitly feminist group in the city, and Indianapolis NOW members identified themselves as "radical" activists in 1974.[11] In Indianapolis, "radical" seems to have been a label attached to, and adopted by, explicitly feminist groups that did not restrict themselves to behind-the-scenes activism and that publicly articulated and acted on a wide-ranging, explicitly feminist agenda. In considering NOW a radical group, Indianapolis residents had much in common with their peers in other cities that were not intellectual centers of the women's movement.[12] Unlike in Durham, however, such community perceptions were not an obstacle to a long-lasting NOW chapter. Many feminists in Indianapolis appear to have embraced the label, and while its identity as a radical organization created tension between NOW members and other, more conservative members of the state ERA coalition, this tension did not cause NOW to disband or the visibility of feminism in Indianapolis to decrease.

This mixture of organizations was the leading characteristic of Indianapolis's feminist community, and one that enabled that community to secure ERA ratification well after the national movement for the amendment had stalled. Feminism in Indianapolis benefited from the fact that women with many points of view and many political backgrounds became engaged in the women's movement. These multiple points of view proved essential in securing ERA ratification, a goal that required feminists to persuade lawmakers from many backgrounds to agree with the feminist position on the amendment in the face of a vocal anti-ERA movement. In North Carolina there was no radical voice as a consistent part of NCUERA, and the group stagnated by the late 1970s, failing to secure ratification in a state that many national pro-ERA leaders considered a better target than Indiana. As already documented, a feminist community involving women from many backgrounds did exist in Durham, but it remained largely behind closed doors at the YWCA, and the Durham Women's Center was never a central player in the ERA effort in North Carolina. The many viewpoints present in Indiana's ERA fight kept that movement innovative and dynamic and contributed to its ultimate success.

The majority, although not all, of Indianapolis's women's organizations joined with the several new, explicitly feminist groups in the city to mediate between feminist ideas and their neighbors and fellow residents. This vast and diverse coalition worked together—not without tension but ultimately effectively—to achieve one of the women's movement's major objectives at a time when the ERA was losing ground at every turn. Grassroots feminism in Indianapolis highlights the impact one overriding goal could have in shaping feminist action. Its story also shows how a conservative city could come to support a key piece of feminism's agenda.

Women-Centered Activism in Indianapolis in the 1960s

Unlike their peer organizations in Durham and Denver, all the major women's groups in Indianapolis in the 1960s devoted time to exploring their identity as women's organizations. Not only was the amount of women-centered discussion within the organizations higher, Indianapolis clubwomen were also more likely to hold public discussions about women's changing roles and identities than were their peers elsewhere. An examination of the kind of women-centered work and discussion occurring in these groups reveals that all of them—from the YWCA and the LWV to smaller religious groups like the National Council of Jewish Women—were primed to become channels for feminism in the following decade. But not all these organizations took that route. Because a common background did not translate into feminist activism on a consistent basis, the connection between the racial situation in each chapter and its future feminist work is even clearer in Indianapolis than in the other cities. The diversity of organizations that became sites of women-centered activism in 1960s Indianapolis is one of the distinct features of the city, and one that set the stage for the multifaceted and diverse feminist coalition that emerged around the ERA in the following decade.

The Indianapolis LWV was similar to its sister chapters elsewhere in that it devoted the majority of its program in the early 1960s to issues of foreign policy and good government. But in the second half of the decade, the Indianapolis LWV also emphasized its identity as a women's organization far more than did other League chapters. In 1965 the group's president, Jean Tyler, offered a reflection on an article that had recently appeared in *Ladies' Home Journal*, which asked if suburban housewives were "suffering from isolationism of the heart." The magazine article claimed that women were seeking to manage their homes as "safe little islands."[13] Tyler urged her fellow Leaguers to think about the obligation to the wider world they had undertaken by joining the League and encouraged them to continue to embrace "the challenge and responsibility for 'homes' throughout the world." Tyler argued that League members met that responsibility "not by learned decree or massive demonstration but quietly and effectively by studying, discussing and acting wherever their efforts [were] needed governmentally."[14] The structure of the League was clearly still an important piece of the group's identity and function to Tyler, but in this article she merged that structure with attention to the League's identity as a women's organization.

The Indianapolis League was more explicitly conscious than other chapters of its potential to prevent women's isolation in their homes and give them an outlet for discussion and debate as well as fellowship. An article in the November 1967 bulletin, for example, argued that a woman's place was not merely in the home but was "wherever she [was] needed." The article's author asserted, "We believe . . . that there are many other women like us, who want to FACE these problems for their own sakes (or as one mother of four put it, 'for their own sanity')."[15] While claiming a role for women in all aspects of government and citizenship, the Indianapolis League was very aware of its importance as a women's organization. Jean Tyler and other group leaders also saw the group as providing a middle way in "the brawl between the 'feminine mysticers' [*sic*] and the 'home and husband' advocate."[16] Coming in the late spring of 1967, this reference to "feminine mysticers" was likely a reference to NOW, which had been founded by *Feminine Mystique* author Betty Friedan and others the previous fall. In this same report, Tyler argued that the League was designed to allow women to blend their family commitments with work for the organization and other volunteer activities. She urged members to continue to make the organization flexible enough to accommodate the growing number of mothers of young children in the chapter, as well as women who worked outside the home.[17] Throughout her presidency in the mid-1960s, Tyler was a vocal advocate for the role the League played in women's lives as well as the good the group did for Indianapolis, the state, and the nation. Given the League's sustained involvement in feminism in the 1970s, she was not alone in her beliefs about the centrality of gender to the group's purpose and appeal.

In 1966 the League participated in the largest public discussion to date of women's position in society. In the fall of that year, the Indianapolis National Council of Jewish Women (NCJW) sponsored a program titled

"Women on the Move: A Forum on Employment," which was cosponsored by virtually every women's group in the city, including the LWV and the YWCA.[18] The daylong program featured panels such as "the crisis in the home," which focused on day care issues; "the service dilemma," which addressed the lack of Social Security and other protections for domestic workers; and "what can one woman do," a discussion led by local activists (including future LWV president Linda Leary) that explored ways in which women could work toward solving problems surrounding women's employment.[19] Mary Hilton, the deputy director of the federal Women's Bureau, gave the keynote address, and Dorothy Height, president of the National Council of Negro Women, former member of the YWCA national board, and one of the organizers of the 1963 March on Washington, gave a dinner speech.[20] The "Women on the Move" forum was one of the first women-centered projects undertaken by a coalition of Indianapolis women's groups during the 1960s. Coalitions of women's organizations had previously worked on issues such as crime and dropout prevention, but in the latter half of the 1960s many Indianapolis's women's groups began to focus on women-centered programming.[21] The presence of one of the highest-ranking woman in government, as well as such a nationally prominent activist as Height, speaks to the importance of the conference for the women of Indianapolis.

Mary Hilton's speech suggested one approach to women's rights work that proved appealing to many Indianapolis women in the 1970s. Hilton discussed three "great improvements" that the country had recently made: the first two were legislation related to civil rights and the War on Poverty, both issues that engaged large numbers of organized Indianapolis women. The third achievement was the "great national dialogue on the status of women." Hilton claimed there was widespread agreement on the need to remove "any barrier to full partnership, economically and socially" and also proudly claimed, "There is nothing of militant feminism, but a new, enriched concept of the feminine."[22] This contrast between feminism and femininity became a visible part of Indianapolis's feminist community and highlights the multiple points of view that women working to improve women's position in society brought to their feminist activism.

Although the turnout was good and most groups found the meeting productive, the newspaper coverage of "Women on the Move" demonstrated the press's negative opinion about the event. Women spending their day discussing issues of work were treated not as a newsworthy event but rather as an oversized coffee klatch. The tone of the article in the *Indianapolis Star* demonstrates how seriously reporter Lorraine Nelson took the event she was covering. The piece began: "Almost everyone was late. No matter. There were recipes to exchange, punch bowls to borrow, and all kinds of one-upmanship to play *vís a vís* [*sic*] weight loss on the diet circuit. Someone finally passed out ashtrays and that signaled the keynote address."[23] The article also made no mention of Height's presence, despite the fact that Height—who had been on the planning commission for the famous 1963 March on Washington—was a far more prominent figure than Hilton. This omission reinforced the notion that women's issues were only the concern of white women. The reporter never mentioned that black and white women were working together to find solutions to issues that affected all women. The omission of the presence of Height or any other African American women, as well as the patronizing tone with which the media covered the event, foreshadowed the skepticism that feminists would encounter in Indianapolis when they began their work.

The Indianapolis chapter of the National Council of Jewish Women was the primary sponsor of the "Women on the Move" forum. While the event was the organization's largest and most public action in the sphere of women's issues in the 1960s, throughout the second half of the decade the group sponsored a series of conferences and panel discussions that addressed women's concerns. It was in these discussion-based forums that women's issues found their fullest exploration within the NCJW. The organization's theme for 1965–66 was "A Woman's Place Is in the World."[24] In 1967 the chapter hosted a daylong workshop, "Family and the Changing Society," which included a session titled "The Feminine Mystique."[25] However, other than working with Women in Community Service—the national job placement and training program for low-income women—the group rarely translated these discussions into action. WICS was organized by four prominent women's organizations and had its local office at the YWCA.[26] When the project began in 1964, former NCJW president Bertha Lichtenstein was elected the head of the effort in Indianapolis.[27] NCJW members frequently discussed women's issues in their organization and through its sponsorship of "Women on the Move" encouraged women throughout Indianapolis to consider the role of gender in their lives.

Another Indianapolis women's group with a long history of liberal activism that became a feminist group in the 1970s was Churchwomen United (CWU). In the 1960s the organization undertook a public, decade-long project dealing with issues of gender. Beginning in 1960 the organization offered marriage preparation workshops to the public.[28] A pamphlet advertising the series posed questions such as "Should husbands help with housework? Are there a number of things which are clearly a wife's or a husband's responsibility?"[29] These questions did not challenge the assumption of a male breadwinner/female housewife dynamic, as feminists would in the coming years. But the discussion of husbands helping around the house shows that the members of CWU were aware of the shifting expectations for postwar marriages and families. The family ideal in the 1960s was moving away from the notion of companionate marriage, which emphasized the husband-wife relationship as the key to a happy marriage, and toward an ideal of family "togetherness" in which mother, father, and children were all critical to a happy marriage and home.[30] By incorporating these changes into its marriage preparation classes, CWU endorsed the latest ideals and trends in family life. By 1969 the organization's Speakers' Bureau was offering talks on the "Changing Role of Women in a Changing World," demonstrating that the group remained attentive to issues of gender and took its progressive understanding of women's roles into the larger community.[31]

CWU also played an important role in bringing together women from various racial and religious backgrounds who were members of other women's groups in the city. For example, Louise Batties served on the board of the League of Women Voters and was active in the city's National Council of Negro Women chapter, in addition to participating in Churchwomen United. She put her League experience to use as the head of the CWU's Legislative Committee in 1966.[32] Caroline O'Dell represented Tabernacle Presbyterian Church at the CWU and was also on the YWCA board of directors.[33] Large umbrella groups like the CWU helped build connections between women and enmeshed them not only in discussions of women's roles but more generally in a broad liberal agenda in the 1960s. In 1962 the state CWU launched a three-year project called "Assignment—Race" aimed at ending Jim Crow in Indiana, including segregation in schools and on public transportation.[34] As part of that initiative, the Indianapolis chapter of CWU developed a "pilot program in open occupancy" in 1964 as an attempt to remedy the housing segregation that prevailed in the city.[35] In 1966 the state CWU issued a statement of opposition to the bombing of North Vietnam.[36] CWU was the only mainstream women's group in Indianapolis to publicly oppose the conduct of the Vietnam War at this early date, and many groups (notably the League) never took an official position on the war. CWU, then, was at the leading edge of liberalism throughout the 1960s, introducing its members to many controversial issues. The group was devoted to staying on top of current issues, and as feminism became an increasingly hot topic members engaged in wide-ranging discussions of the movement and its implications for them as progressive Christian women. An engagement with current affairs, including trends in marriage and family life, prepared CWU members to take an active part in discussions about feminism in the 1970s.

More than other groups studied here, the Indianapolis YWCA publicly articulated its identity as a women's organization throughout the 1960s. Throughout the decade, the YWCA's board of trustees and board of directors battled the leadership of the city's United Fund to counter the fund's desire to merge the YWCA with the YMCA.[37] Because of the drop in attendance and the United Fund's belief that the YWCA was offering "a program of activities not in demand in today's society," in July 1963 the organization refused to increase the YWCA's funding until the association either agreed to consolidation with the YMCA or radically altered its programming and obtained a new and more suitable facility.[38] The United Fund and the YWCA fought over these issues for the remainder of the decade.

In the face of this debate, the women on the YWCA board of directors developed an argument for their organization's existence based on its role in providing a space devoted solely to women and girls. YWCA board members considered such space essential. At the United Fund meeting in the fall of 1963, trustee spokesman Edwin Plum was able only to defend the group's "fine job" of working with women and girls in general terms and stated simply, "No other agency is especially qualified to do this job."[39] By 1966 the women of the YWCA board of directors were speaking in their own defense as a women's organization, explaining to the United Fund, "To the extent that a girl growing into womanhood develops a clear and healthy concept of what it means to be a woman—to that extent will she be able to accept her role in the world—whatever it may be; wife, mother, unmarried professional woman, etc."[40] YWCA members claimed that their organization was one of very few in the city devoted to developing such an understanding in girls and to helping women in all aspects of their lives. Feminists would make claims about the nature of womanhood, the degree of preparation required for it, and the range of roles open to women that were very different from those in the YWCA's statement. Indianapolis YWCA members were not, as a group, early feminists. But they were devoted to providing space for women and girls to grapple with personal issues, issues that members of the YWCA believed were uniquely female.

In pursuing its goal of serving as a women's space with something to offer women and girls at all stages of life, however, the board of the YWCA focused primarily on serving women like themselves. The vast majority of the YWCA's programs were designed for stay-at-home mothers. The Indianapolis association had the largest Mother's Morning Out (MMO) program of the three YWCAs studied here. MMO consisted of small groups in suburban areas that offered socializing opportunities to both young mothers and women whose children were grown and who needed new activities to fill their time.[41] The bulk of the participants were young mothers who were described as coming from "small houses [with] many children [and] little money."[42] The organization also designed a few programs for women who worked outside the home, such as monthly luncheon get-togethers for women working downtown, and provided office space in its downtown building for the WICS project beginning in 1965.[43] Throughout the 1960s, the Indianapolis YWCA understood its mission as providing opportunities for personal growth to women at all stages of life.

Despite its professed attention to all women's needs, however, suburban white women and girls were the primary focus of the Indianapolis YWCA's programming. For example, there is no evidence that the group took an active interest in the WICS project for low-income and minority women beyond providing its office space. YWCA board members focused on serving women like themselves in the way that they themselves had been served by the YWCA, and they saw no reason to change those methods. The chapter had difficulty translating women's new options and roles into programs and action or even acknowledging that women's lives were changing. Group leaders were also unsure of their chapter's mission in relation to the goals of the national organization along these lines. In 1965 the Indianapolis board of directors answered "yes" to a national office question about whether the chapter recognized "the urgent need for women, as women, to assume responsible leadership in changing community patterns to assure a good life for all people." But the board noted, "There was a feeling that there is not as much awareness of changing community patterns as this statement assumes."[44] Such vague statements were typical of the Indianapolis YWCA's relationship with the national office. Board members knew that they should answer "yes" to headquarters' question. But they did not alter the chapter's programs in any way, nor did they press for further information from the national office to try to understand what changes national leaders were referencing.

This disinclination to engage with the changes occurring around it was even more marked in the YWCA's work with African American women and the poor. Throughout the 1960s, the Indianapolis YWCA did as little as possible in working with both of these communities, despite the fact that the group's main building was located in a low-income black neighborhood. The closing of the Phyllis Wheatley branch in 1959 and the lack of effort to integrate former Wheatley members into the Central YWCA seriously hampered the influence of African American women within the organization. Beyond starting Mother's Clubs for inner-city women, the YWCA did little to reach out to the city's low-income black community. Middle-class African American women who were members of the association were restricted to a few tasks, such as planning luncheons, and new black members were usually directed into the social circles that had been carried over from the Wheatley branch and provided no path into leadership within the organization as a whole.[45]

Late in the decade, the board of directors admitted that it had problems translating concerns into action, especially with regard to race relations. But it was not terribly worried about that fact. In reporting the outcome of a 1969 antiracism workshop to the national office, the board stated that "as a call to dialogue," the workshop had "done well." As "a call to action," however, they were unsure "what seeds [had] been planted" but argued that "it was a beginning."[46] The Indianapolis YWCA did not see directing action as its role. No further workshops on racism were planned in the following year to build on this "call to dialogue." If members were made aware of issues, then board members believed that they had done their job. This attitude was markedly different from that of YWCA members in Durham and Denver, and it affected the way women in the Indianapolis YWCA interacted with feminism in the 1970s.

By the end of the 1960s, all the major women's groups in Indianapolis were aware that women's lives were changing, and they had begun to hold workshops and hear speakers about those changes. The League of Women Voters, Churchwomen United, and the National Council of Jewish Women all provided their members with space to discuss the impact of women's changing role on their lives and emphasized the beneficial role such groups could play in members' lives. At the YWCA, more traditional forms of women-centered action occurred. The Indianapolis YWCA was a deeply conservative organization and refused to involve low-income and African American women in the chapter's leadership or create programs that considered the needs or interests of those communities from their point of view. In Indianapolis all women's groups undertook women-centered activism of some kind. Those chapters that built on this work and developed feminist commitments in the 1970s, however, were the groups that married a focus on women and gender with a generally liberal perspective. Liberal beliefs did not automatically make a group more likely to become feminist. But the depth of liberal commitment within an organization in the 1960s foreshadowed a group's likelihood to engage with feminism in the 1970s.

The diversity of groups that held such ideals led to a broad range of organizations undertaking feminist action in that decade.

Feminism in Indianapolis

In the early 1970s, Indianapolis resident Harriet Van Deusen had an epiphany. As she explained to the Indianapolis NOW newsletter, *IndiaNOWpolis Woman*, "One day I discovered I was a woman and I was oppressed." Over the next several months, that realization motivated Van Deusen to leave the League of Women Voters and the National Council of Jewish Women and relinquish her seat on the YWCA board of directors. She gave up her life as "a conventional college educated mother of one young son" and began participating in a group called Indianapolis Women's Liberation. Van Deusen also used her position as an assistant manager of a local bookstore to organize the first women's book section in the area.[47] The movement of Van Deusen and other women like her from existing women's groups to new feminist organizations—Indianapolis Women's Liberation (IWL) in the first years of the decade or the local NOW chapter that began meeting in the spring of 1972—created a feminist community and a context for feminist activism quite different from that of Durham.

National, explicitly feminist organizations such as NOW and the Women's Political Caucus were visible members of the feminist community in Indianapolis.[48] But existing women's groups like the League of Women Voters and Churchwomen United also became important channels for feminist action. Indianapolis residents saw Indianapolis Women's Liberation and the NOW chapter that succeeded it as radical organizations. The radical image of NOW may have limited its appeal to women in Indianapolis, but women both within and outside explicitly feminist organizations worked together in Indianapolis to achieve one of the most sweeping goals of the women's movement. In 1977, well after the surge of ratifications around the country had ended, Indiana became the last state to ratify the Equal Rights Amendment. NOW's perceived radicalism created space into which more moderate women's groups could step and made the work of existing women's groups on behalf of the amendment appear less threatening.[49] And the multiple points of view present in the feminist coalition pushing for the ERA helped its advocates persuade legislators of many different backgrounds to support a key feminist goal.

Women's organizations in Indianapolis appear to break down along the familiar liberal/radical split outlined by scholars of the women's movement.[50] In their public activism, existing women's organizations and the Indiana Women's Political Caucus appeared to be liberal feminist groups focused on reform and formal equality for women. These groups were also unlikely to use public tactics like marches or strikes, instead favoring lobbying, letter writing, and behind-the-scenes negotiations. Indianapolis Women's Liberation and Indianapolis NOW instead used street theater and pickets to push both for legal equality and for changes in gender norms. Within the meetings and offices of women's groups, however, these distinctions broke down. In Indianapolis "radical" groups undertook "liberal" action, and women's groups worked on a wide range of feminist issues. NOW was an important part of the statewide ERA coalition, and the League of Women Voters published lists of suggested feminist reading that included classic texts of radical feminism such as Robin Morgan's *Sisterhood Is Powerful*.[51] Groups like the League and Churchwomen United were also engaged in racially integrated feminist activism, since those organizations had integrated their memberships the previous decade. New and old women's organizations came together in Indianapolis to create a diverse feminist community that succeeded in one of the women's movement's biggest goals. Work on this goal sometimes compromised other feminist projects, but it stands as a major triumph for women in a conservative state that was considered unlikely to ratify the ERA.[52]

Harriet Van Deusen's decision to leave the League of Women Voters and the YWCA to pursue feminist activism suggests that the relationship between those organizations and feminism in Indianapolis was quite different from that in Durham or Denver. The YWCA in particular faced a dramatically different set of circumstances in 1970 than it did in the other two cities, with a few members finally becoming forceful voices for integration of the leadership and programs of the organization that year. These women faced opposition to their work from a conservative faction within the board of directors, and it took a tremendous amount of effort to move the group toward racial equality within the chapter. There was little time or energy left among these women to move the YWCA in a more feminist direction as well, even if they had been interested in doing so. The Indianapolis YWCA, therefore, did far less feminist work than other YWCAs studied here. The city's other women's groups, however, were open to the message of the women's movement and became important participants in the state's ERA fight. As the 1970s wore on, many women's organizations came to embrace an increasingly wide range of feminist ideas and projects.

YWCA members at the organization's 1970 convention, where the organization declared its intention to "revolutionize society's expectations of women." Photograph by Carolyn Litowich, courtesy of the Sophia Smith Collection, Smith College.

The Durham YWCA Building at 515 Chapel Hill Street. The building's size and prominent location speak to the YWCA's long-standing presence in Durham, a reputation that eased the group's movement into feminist activism. The building was sold in 1979, as the YWCA's finances eroded, partially because of the group's feminist commitments. Courtesy of the North Carolina Collection, Durham County Library.

Members of the Indiana League of Women Voters participating in a pro–Equal Rights Amendment demonstration during the national League's 1974 convention in San Francisco. The League was one of the many organizations that worked to ensure Indiana's ratification of the amendment in 1977. Courtesy of the Indiana Historical Society, M0612.

Members of the Colorado League of Women Voters demonstrating on the steps of the Colorado capitol, 1967. The long-standing tradition of women's participation in politics in Colorado facilitated the successful passage of many feminist laws and programs in the late 1960s and early 1970s. Courtesy of the League of Women Voters of the United States.

The Indianapolis YWCA had made only halting steps toward integrating African American women into the chapter throughout the 1960s. In 1970 the national organization adopted the One Imperative, a strongly worded call to eliminate racial discrimination in all its forms.[53] In September 1972, two members of the national YWCA staff came to Indianapolis to investigate the chapter's compliance with the One Imperative. They were not encouraged by what they found. Relations between the YWCA and the African American community were bad, with many black residents "still concerned about the loss of the Phyllis Wheatley branch, lack of black staff, and token black leadership in decision-making in the Board and Committees." The national staffers also expressed concern at the loss of black staff and the lack of effort to recruit new black members, as well as the perception of the YWCA as a "reacting organization" in Indianapolis, rather than as a group on the cutting edge of community concerns. Most troubling of all, they found that there was no "specific and conscious effort made by the leadership to fully integrate in policy and practice." While the staffers praised the efforts of Pree Jones, head of the chapter's Racial Justice Committee, they implored the organization to give more time, resources, encouragement, and attention to the efforts of that committee.[54]

In March 1973, the YWCA undertook a self-evaluation in order to examine the group's progress on the recommendations made by the national staffers the previous fall. Three members of the chapter—Natalie Boehm, Doris Fletcher, and Jean Harr—wrote a summary of the findings. Their draft summary was a sweeping indictment of the YWCA's leadership in the community and the role of the board of directors within the chapter. The document pointed out problems ranging from the organization's lack of engagement in community affairs to the significant amount of attention paid to the planning of classes and ensuring funding at the expense of work on racial issues.[55] Boehm, Fletcher, and Harr urged the board to "promote [a] contemporary image—one which deal[t] with commitment to issues" and to "go out to the community and participate in community affairs."[56] They also had much to say about racism within the group, questioning why inner-city programs were never mentioned in the organization's publicity materials and why the inner-city and suburban versions of the Mothers' Morning Out programs had different names and never met together, despite the fact that they were the same program in everything but name.[57] The evaluation also revealed the alarming frequency with which previous affiliation with the Wheatley branch continued to determine the scope of one's participation in the organization. The building had been sold and the branch deactivated in 1959, yet in 1973 it was still necessary to issue recommendations opposing the policy of directing branch members into luncheon hosting instead of committee work and encouraging efforts to "erase [the] image of Phyllis Wheatley YWCA" and that image's influence on how African American women served the Indianapolis YWCA.[58] Boehm, Fletcher, and Harr even found it necessary to state that anyone who did not support the One Imperative against racism should not be in a teaching position or on the board of directors. Their report noted that "not all board members support[ed] the imperative" and warned the board of directors not to hold its meetings at places with "restricted membership."[59] In general the three women argued that the board of directors was not serving the group well, stating, "Board meetings are physically uncomfortable and intimidating," and the policies established by the board "don't reflect our resolutions." They also charged that the board members consciously restricted who held leadership roles through "meeting time[s] and place[s which] determine who [would] serve on the Board."[60] Boehm, Fletcher, and Harr's draft statement called on the Indianapolis YWCA to completely overhaul almost everything it did, in order to become a group dedicated to racial justice and social change.

The changes that were made between these draft recommendations and the report that the board issued to members reveal how accurate Boehm, Fletcher, and Harr's critiques were and how intransigent YWCA leaders were in the face of such criticism. Where the draft had called on the group to "erase [the] image of the Phyllis Wheatley YWCA," the final report merely instructed members to "continue to ask former Phyllis Wheatley YWCA women to serve on committees as well as luncheons."[61] The final report did include the recommendations against holding meetings in segregated locations as well as the instruction that "*anyone* who [did] not support the Imperative should *not* be on the Board."[62] But the overall tone of the final report suggested that race was the YWCA's only issue, and a fairly minor one at that. Holding "rap sessions" between board members, staff members, and volunteers was one of the report's primary recommendations, suggesting that to solve the race problem board members only needed to talk more with the group's African American members.[63] The broader criticisms of the organization that Boehm, Fletcher, and Harr had articulated were nowhere to be seen. With the exception of prohibiting people who did not support the One Imperative from serving on the board, all criticisms of the board of directors were stricken from the final version. The three members who wrote the draft had crafted a plea to their peers to take racism within the organization seriously and take major steps to make the group an engaged member of Indianapolis's liberal community. The changes made between the draft and final versions show that that plea went unheeded.

The YWCA's continued racial problems and general conservatism presented serious obstacles to any member who may have wanted to turn the organization into a channel for feminist work, for several reasons. At the most basic level, the organization was consumed by the difficult process of racial reform and had little time to pursue feminism. There were occasional discussions about women's issues, but these most often took the form of raising awareness of and expressing support for the work of other groups rather than having YWCA members undertake activism under the organization's auspices. The women-centered activism that the YWCA had pursued in the 1960s through the Mothers' Morning Out program continued in the same form as previously. When these programs were changed, it was to give them a stronger focus on racial issues; two of the three programs listed under "Women" in the association's 1971–72 annual report were a workshop titled "Black—White—Uptight" and discussions led by members of the Racial Justice Committee.[64]

Even when the YWCA had contact with the women's movement, the board was resistant to adopting the new ideas and practices promoted by feminists. The group came closest to a thorough engagement with the movement in the early spring of 1972. That February board member Pat Ulen opened the board of directors meeting with a talk about the Greater Indianapolis Women's Political Caucus, urging YWCA members to become more active participants in politics at the precinct level.[65] The next month, Harriet Van Deusen encouraged the group to begin using women's first names, instead of their husbands' first names, on mailings and in newsletters. The meeting minutes noted that no agreement was reached on Van Deusen's suggestion and that the Public Affairs Committee would "discuss the question further."[66] The subject was promptly dropped. Moreover, there is no evidence that the organization took up Ulen's call for using the YWCA to encourage women's political participation. The board was not interested in pursuing even such moderate goals. The issue of women's names was not addressed again until late 1974, when a motion was made to switch to women's first names and to use "chairperson" instead of "chairman." The recommendation passed, but only with the provision that husbands' first names be included in parentheses after women's first names, and three members still voted "no" even with that caveat.[67] It seems likely that the board's reluctance to act on this issue was a factor in Van Deusen's decision to leave the organization and pursue feminist activism through explicitly feminist groups.

The YWCA board struggled to understand the place of its organization within the rapidly changing context that the women's movement was creating. In 1973 the group noted in a press release that the year's programming would "reflect the impact of several forces affecting, if not changing, the traditional view of women's role in the scheme of things."[68] Another statement from the same year noted that the YWCA was aware of the increasing "importance of the feminine role in community life."[69] The language of the second statement in particular harkened back to the earliest days of the YWCA in the late nineteenth and early twentieth centuries, when women articulated a rationale for their presence in the public sphere based on their femininity, morality, and decency, qualities that they would bring to bear on the larger community through reform and volunteer work.[70] Many of the women of the Indianapolis YWCA were still deeply attached to that worldview. The association rarely undertook feminist action. Occasionally members were encouraged to write letters in favor of the ERA, but this occurred only when a woman who was also active in the League of Women Voters was the head of the YWCA board of directors.[71] In its recommendations for the 1974–75 program year, the Public Affairs Committee announced its intention to "support and promote mainline organizations in the community in the areas of Women and our Imperative."[72] The emphasis on mainline organizations was most likely directed at NOW, the most visible explicitly feminist group in the city, and indicates a continuing discomfort with some feminist tactics. In Indianapolis the YWCA was not the force for women's advancement that the organization strove to be at the national level and was in other cities.

Throughout the 1970s, the League of Women Voters in Indianapolis was more open to feminism than was the YWCA. The League's initial reaction to the women's movement was not positive, however. An article in the September 1970 bulletin, written by president Donna Langfitt, expressed hostility toward the women's movement, and especially the Women's Strike for Equality organized by NOW to mark the fiftieth anniversary of the Nineteenth Amendment. Langfitt wrote, "Yes, Virginia, there is still a League of Women Voters. The women's lib movement ran away with our amendment. At least we thought it was ours."[73] Later in the same article, however, Langfitt noted, "Although the League is the direct inheritor of the original women's rights movement and our members have chosen to work on governmental issues which affect both men and women, there is always room for another point of view. In some areas I'm sure most of us would agree there is need for improvement."[74] It appears that the style of NOW's action and the fact that it co-opted the anniversary of the Nineteenth Amendment upset Langfitt more than the targets of NOW's activism.

As the 1970s progressed, League members slowly but steadily undertook more feminist work. In January 1971, some members suggested studying abortion laws, a topic described in the bulletin as a "completely new issue" for the group.[75] Despite members' interest, however, the board decided not to recommend a statewide study on abortion and birth control laws, believing that reaching a consensus among a majority of members statewide would be very difficult.[76] This decision highlights the ways that the League's structure sometimes limited the group's ability to take timely and decisive action on feminist issues. The requirement of reaching consensus among the members before the organization could act meant that most members would have to come to support at least some aspects of the women's movement before the LWV could become a force for feminism. But the Indianapolis League was moving in that direction. In December 1971, when discussing program ideas for the coming year, a faction within the organization urged board members and those responsible for planning the program to "quit shying away from 'women-oriented' issues."[77] A few months later, President Betty Williams reported that the results of a questionnaire mailed to the entire membership indicated that most members wanted "to see a women's rights position, 'as long as it [did] not include some of the militant feminist views.'"[78] At the beginning of 1972, the group was on its way toward presenting a new point of view on feminism in Indianapolis, one that contrasted with Indianapolis Women's Liberation but still supported core women's movement ideals.

At precisely the moment that Indianapolis LWV members expressed this desire to support women's rights, Congress passed the Equal Rights Amendment. In states like Indiana and North Carolina, where the ERA was hotly contested, ratification of the amendment became the focus of the League's feminist work. The Indianapolis LWV's work in support of the ERA will be examined in more detail later, but its members worked steadily on the amendment's behalf until the Indiana legislature ratified it in 1977. The amendment proved a valuable recruiting tool for the League.[79] ERA work was particularly effective in bringing younger women into the organization, a development that thrilled the group's leaders.[80]

Working on the ERA's behalf brought League women into contact with members of explicitly feminist organizations and exposed them to a wide range of feminist topics. In the fall of 1973, League members began volunteering with a rape prevention program sponsored by the city's Mayor's Task Force on Women.[81] The following year a bulletin article by the chapter's ERA coordinator featured a list of important books on women's history and the women's movement, including an anthology of feminist writings titled *The Feminist Papers from Adams to de Beauvoir* and *Sexist Justice* by Karen DeCrow, the newly elected president of national NOW. The list also identified two books as "down-to-earth guides [to feminism] aimed at the average man or woman."[82] The next month the League sponsored an "Issues Workshop" where Virginia Dill McCarthy of the Indiana Women's Political Caucus discussed the impact of the ERA.[83] In 1975 the chapter organized a program on pornography and obscenity laws.[84] Working for the ERA brought the Indianapolis League into the feminist community in Indianapolis, and by 1975 the group was regularly exposing members to a broad range of feminist issues.

Other women's organizations around the city also became channels for feminism. As it was in the 1960s, Churchwomen United remained on the cutting edge of liberalism in the 1970s and introduced its members to feminism early and often. In 1971 the group's national governing body added sexism to the list of problems that the organization was committed to combating and also stated that CWU should work "to develop among women a sense of their own identity, and to enable them to become full participants in today's society."[85] That same year, Indianapolis CWU sponsored a series of panel sessions addressing a wide range of issues, including "women's liberation," "the new family," and "human sexuality."[86] In 1973 CWU was among the original participants in the Women Against Rape (WAR) program developed by the Mayor's Task Force on Women. Some of the questions addressed by WAR at its initial organizing meeting, such as "Why do rape victims hesitate to report the crime? What happens to convicted rapists? What kind of person is a rapist?" show that the group was grappling with the questions and theories about sexual violence that feminists were beginning to raise.[87] CWU also held workshops titled "Men, Women, and Families" and "In the Beginning Was Eve," tackling women's issues in a theological context.[88] CWU served as an important conduit for its members to learn about the new ideas being promoted and concerns being raised by the women's movement and facilitated members' participation in large-scale feminist projects such as WAR.

African American women's organizations and groups also engaged with the dialogue of the women's movement, some of them from a very early date. The Fortnightly Club, an African American women's literary club, often read and discussed controversial or provocative books, usually focused on racial issues. They read and discussed the works of James Baldwin, for example, in 1963.[89] In 1968 they discussed a book that examined gender and race issues in tandem, exploring the impact of slavery on "achieving womanhood—acquiring manhood—marriage and love."[90] In 1969 the group decided to focus its readings on works by and about accomplished women, and by 1971 its schedule consisted almost exclusively of works by women authors.[91] In that year, the members read and discussed both Maya Angelou's frank autobiography, *I Know Why the Caged Bird Sings*, and the best-selling feminist tract *The Female Eunuch* and devoted an additional meeting to a discussion on the status of women.[92] They continued to engage with the ideas of the women's movement throughout the decade, reading books about new professional opportunities for black women and trying to secure black feminist poet Nikki Giovanni as the speaker for the annual dinner meeting.[93] The Fortnightly Club was always just a book group and never undertook action, but it was an important space for African American women to grapple with the interactions of race and gender and the impact of the women's movement on those relationships.

African American women were also well represented in the fight for the Equal Rights Amendment once it took center stage among women's rights activists in Indiana. Audra Bailey, the president of Hoosiers for the ERA, led an ERA workshop for the Alpha Kappa Alpha sorority in the fall of 1974, as women's groups organized to work for ratification during the 1975 legislative session.[94] Meg Mallory, an African American woman and head of HERA's Black Women's Caucus, gave an impassioned speech to the Indianapolis National Council of Negro Women chapter in 1974, urging greater participation by black women in the ERA fight and the women's movement more broadly. Mallory emphatically challenged the reasons given by African American women for not participating in the movement: "Some of the most disturbing remarks I have heard from Black women and Black men are 'Black women don't need it; they're already liberated,' or 'We have to get behind our men.' . . . By 1973 almost one-third of all Black families were headed by women. My question is: where are the men for these Black women to stand behind and push?"[95] Indianapolis women of many races embraced feminist ideas by the middle years of the 1970s. CWU, the League, and HERA were racially integrated organizations.

Men and women from different political backgrounds also found common ground on several feminist issues. Ideas of the women's movement gained some influence in the administration of Republican Indianapolis mayor Richard Lugar, who served from 1968 to 1975.[96] Lugar established the Mayor's Task Force on Women and named fellow Republican Mary Ann

Butters as its head. Butters was a well-known feminist in the city, having written numerous articles supporting the women's movement for the *Indianapolis Star*, the city's largest newspaper.[97] The task force's major project was the Women Against Rape program, which Butters launched in the fall of 1973. In April 1974, CBS News sent a correspondent to Indianapolis to report on the program, and the reporter hailed WAR as the most successful rape prevention program in the country. By the time CBS came to town, WAR was responsible for the presence of women police officers and women prosecutors dedicated to handling rape cases. The program was also credited with improving local hospitals' collection of physical evidence and treatment of rape victims.[98] The program's office was staffed by volunteers drawn from both the local NOW chapter and women's groups including the League of Women Voters and Churchwomen United.[99] In addition to supporting the WAR program, Mayor Lugar also endorsed the Equal Rights Amendment, agreeing in January 1975 to become the first member of a "Men for the ERA" group formed by HERA.[100]

Richard Lugar and Mary Ann Butters are examples of grassroots Republican feminists, and their involvement in feminist action in Indianapolis shows how widespread acceptance of some feminist ideas had become. Butters was a major player in the city's feminist organizations, serving as the first public relations chair for the Greater Indianapolis Women's Political Caucus.[101] Historian Catherine Rymph has documented the presence of an influential group of feminists in the upper echelons of the Republican Party in the 1970s. Women such as First Lady Betty Ford and Indianapolis native and Nixon administration official Jill Ruckelshaus worked hard on behalf of the ERA, reproductive rights, affirmative action, and other feminist issues they believed were in keeping with their party's traditional libertarian principles.[102] Indianapolis demonstrates the presence of such Republican support for feminism at the local level as well.

Indianapolis residents heard about feminism not only through publicly funded efforts like the WAR program and mainstream women's organizations but also through newly formed, explicitly feminist groups. On Mother's Day 1970, an article written by Mary Ann Butters appeared in the *Indianapolis Star*, outlining the ideas of the women's rights movement and noting the presence of a new feminist group, Indianapolis Women's Liberation, in the city. IWL received over eighty phone calls as a result of the article and established four new consciousness-raising groups for the new members.[103] In August of that year, IWL conducted its first public action. A small group of women came assembled at the Circle, a central gathering point in downtown, to pass out literature in observance of Women's Equality Day, as NOW's national leadership had named the fiftieth anniversary of the passage of the Nineteenth Amendment. At lunchtime the pamphleteers were joined by a theater troupe that performed a short play portraying the many guises of male chauvinism. The crowd was largely polite, and there was little harassment from the audience, "although more trouble had been expected."[104] The event was described as the city's "first run-in with the Women's Liberation movement."[105]

IWL was the city's first explicitly feminist group, and the first surviving newsletter of the organization, from April 1971, portrays a group of women with wide-ranging leftist interests.[106] There was an article explicating the connections that IWL saw between racism, sexism, and the Vietnam War and calling for women to join together in the search for peace.[107] Another piece, written by a member of the local welfare rights organization, analyzed the position of women on welfare and announced a "welfare banquet" to be hosted by members of the local welfare rights organization to raise awareness about the meagerness of welfare allotments.[108] There was also an ad for Lollipop Power, a small press organized by North Carolina feminists that produced nonsexist children's books.[109]

In 1972 IWL organized a statewide women's liberation conference to be held at the Indianapolis YWCA that included talks on "women's interests and arts [and] community communications," as well as politics and "lifestyles."[110] The newsletter outlining the conference schedule also featured an announcement of a "gay liberation prom" and included the phone number of a "gay women's" group. There were also phone listings for abortion, birth control, and day care providers and the Indiana Women's Political Caucus.[111] The tensions between lesbians and heterosexual women that divided several nationally prominent women's liberation groups apparently did not trouble the women of IWL, at least not publicly.[112] Lesbian issues were given equal footing with problems of low-income women and information about reproductive health. IWL embraced an expansive feminist agenda. This ecumenical approach allowed feminists to devote their energies to whatever they found most interesting or important, ranging from politics to "community communication" to the arts. But it did not shield feminists from being identified with the most radical branch of the national movement in the eyes of many citizens of Indianapolis. As a newspaper article regarding IWL's 1971 observation of Women's Equality Day noted, the women met with "both support and hostility" from the public.[113]

In March 1972, a month before the IWL's statewide conference, the Indianapolis chapter of NOW held its first meeting.[114] For several months, the two organizations existed side by side. The state NOW coordinator sent a notice of IWL's April 1972 conference to the national NOW office, and Indianapolis NOW invited IWL members to perform a play for NOW's 1972 Women's Equality Day celebration.[115] During the period when the two organizations coexisted, they appear to have followed the liberal/radical split between NOW and less formal women's liberation groups that historians have documented in other cities.[116] The NOW chapter's first action was to host a public appearance by NOW president Wilma Scott Heide. In her speech, cosponsored by the Indiana Women's Political Caucus (IWPC), Heide emphasized NOW's reform-minded goals, stating that feminists believed in "legal, economic, social, and political equality of the sexes. And equality [was] not to be equated with sameness."[117] Indianapolis NOW also cooperated with statewide NOW efforts to change the wording and content of a no-fault divorce bill that was working its way through the state legislature.[118] In 1972 the NOW members were far less radical than their sisters in IWL, who spelled America with a "k" and wished militant, leftist Northern Ireland leader Bernadette Devlin a happy Saint Patrick's Day in a March newsletter.[119]

By late 1972, however, NOW and IWL were growing closer together. Both sent representatives to a "public inquiry" held by the state civil rights commission to discuss sex-based discrimination.[120] Sometime in 1973, IWL ceased to exist as a separate organization, and many of its members joined NOW. NOW embraced new tactics and a broader feminist agenda in 1973, likely as a result of its new members and their more radical background. Indianapolis NOW's agenda for its first year had focused largely on issues of women's image in the media and advertising, and the group had six committees: "administrative, women's image, education, legal, family, and poverty."[121] In the summer of 1973, the list of priorities shifted. Education, legal, family, and poverty were dropped, and the group adopted image and health, as well as a general "legislation" item, as their major issues for action in 1973–74.[122] Under the rubric of health, NOW focused primarily on abortion rights and rape. In 1973 the chapter's Health Task Force helped establish an abortion clinic at General Hospital, the largest public hospital in the city.[123] NOW's Health Task Force also supported and raised awareness of the Women Against Rape program run by the Mayor's Task Force on Women.[124] NOW's other health-related work included monthly discussion meetings of the feminist health guide *Our Bodies, Ourselves* and sponsoring a pro-choice rally in downtown Indianapolis in April 1974.[125]

The influence of former IWL members could be seen not only in the issues NOW addressed in 1973–74 but also in the tactics it employed. In March 1974, Indianapolis NOW picketed a local bridal fair and distributed over six hundred copies of Pat Mainardi's article "The Politics of Housework," which satirized the traditional division of household labor and husbands' reaction to attempts at change from a feminist perspective.[126] Visible public actions such as the pro-choice rally and the bridal fair protest were not Indianapolis NOW's style when the chapter first began. The group's two major actions in 1972–73 had been persuading WIFE radio to cancel a program called "Feminine Forum," which members described as "extremely degrading to women," and to create a referral service of doctors, lawyers, and other professionals who were "sympathetic to women."[127] Indianapolis NOW never abandoned behind-the-scenes and legislative work. For example, in early 1974 the chapter urged women who were having difficulty getting credit cards in their own names to file a complaint with the state civil rights commission.[128] But the merger with IWL helped move NOW in a direction that even national feminist leaders would have recognized as radical, both in terms of tactics and issues, and which Indianapolis residents certainly defined as radical.

In August 1974, the chapter met to vote on its priorities for 1974–75. After discussing a wide range of issues, from working with rape victims to establishing a feminist library at the women's prison, the group settled on two areas: employment and education. The group considered focusing on ERA and abortion rights but decided that the existing statewide coalitions—HERA and the Indiana Freedom of Choice Coalition—were handling those areas and that NOW would cooperate with those groups but not duplicate their efforts.[129] Throughout the fall of 1974, the employment task force worked hard on a range of issues and met with some success, most notably convincing the state police board to remove height requirements for state troopers in order to make the job open to more women.[130] The group also ran articles in its newsletter outlining the Equal Employment Opportunity Commission definition of employment discrimination and began to work on eliminating discrimination in the life insurance industry, which had many corporate offices in Indianapolis.[131] NOW continued to work on health issues throughout the fall of 1974 as well, drumming up support for a proposed rape shield law and opposing a bill that mandated fines for anyone who distributed contraceptive information to minors.[132] In September members were preparing to go to Bloomington for a statewide pro-choice rally organized by Bloomington NOW. But the rally was canceled after "more moderate members" of the Bloomington pro-choice coalition decided, according to the Indianapolis NOW newsletter, that "a rally attended by IU students and radical activists (like [them]) would convey the wrong image of pro-choice activists."[133]

The collapse of the Bloomington pro-choice rally highlights NOW's biggest problem throughout the decade. The statewide umbrella organizations that worked on two of feminism's biggest issues in those years—abortion and the ERA—were dominated by moderates who hesitated to give NOW a leading role in their groups for fear of being tainted by NOW's image. For the most part, NOW cooperated with the statewide organizations, aware of the realities of Indiana politics and the state's deep conservative leanings. At the state level, NOW began making the ERA a priority over other issues in spring 1974. State NOW president Lynn Schrum sent a letter to the chapters reminding them that the organization had agreed to "low key [their] abortion fight until ERA [was] passed."[134] She also reminded members that the May 1974 primaries were essential for the fate of the ERA in Indiana, stating, "Now is the time to defeat any candidate not pro-ERA."[135]

Throughout 1975 Indianapolis NOW abided by the wishes of HERA and the state NOW office, and the group's public action decreased substantially. In January of that year, the chapter decided that its number one priority for the year was ERA ratification, a decision that put its public activities under the direction of HERA leadership.[136] Until HERA was dissolved in the spring of 1976, Indianapolis NOW conducted few public events in its own name. But the group continued to offer its members opportunities for consciousness-raising and behind-the-scenes feminist action. In July the chapter held a "female sexuality workshop," and that fall the group hosted a discussion of Susan Brownmiller's groundbreaking feminist analysis of rape, *Against Our Will*.[137] The organization also compiled bibliographies of feminist books, which were given to local bookstores so that the stores could establish feminist sections.[138] The chapter's one public event in 1975 was its October observance of "Alice Doesn't Day," a nationwide NOW event designed to demonstrate the centrality of women to businesses across the country by encouraging women to strike for one day.[139] Indianapolis NOW's downtown rally attracted over one hundred people, "NOW members and non-members alike," and brought new members into the chapter.[140]

Not all of NOW's members were happy with the decision to leave pursuit of some of the biggest feminist goals to moderate coalition groups. Some felt that the decision had sapped the chapter of its energy and its influence in the community. One anonymous letter to the editor in the June 1975 chapter newsletter stated: "Something has happened to our NOW organization. No longer can we be called an action group—one called on to give immediate response to sexist problems in our community. Where is our visibility in Indianapolis? Perhaps there should be serious consideration to changing our Indianapolis NOW to Indianapolis LATER (Ladies Affected by Tired Effortless Rhetoric)."[141] This member's opinion apparently remained in the minority, however. Indianapolis NOW respected the political realities of Indiana and in 1975 believed that a moderate lobbying effort was the best way to secure ERA ratification. When this tactic failed and HERA was dissolved in 1976, NOW was poised to reclaim a leading role in the fight for the amendment. But in 1975 the chapter's leaders agreed to respect the wishes of the statewide NOW leadership and continue to offer feminist programs almost exclusively behind closed doors.

Another new, explicitly feminist organization which found a home in Indianapolis was the National Women's Political Caucus (NWPC). Formed in June 1971 by such prominent national feminists as Gloria Steinem, Bella Abzug, and Shirley Chisholm, the NWPC's goal was to increase the number of women holding office and help political candidates who supported feminist positions.[142] The Greater Indianapolis Women's Political Caucus (GIWPC) was founded in November 1971 and drew members from all of the city's women's organizations.[143] The statewide WPC's original statement of purpose focused on encouraging women to run for office, but the Indianapolis chapter quickly moved beyond that limited goal.[144] In March 1972, the group sent a list of "recommended goals and program areas" to the committee that was creating the Mayor's Task Force on Women. Encouraging women to run for office was number 7 on the list, after suggestions to improve enforcement of fair employment and other antidiscrimination laws, "improved guidance and counseling for girls," and calling on women's organizations to increase the involvement of low-income people in the civic life of the city.[145] That fall the GIWPC organized a conference on women's "changing roles" that was open to the public. The conference focused primarily on educating women about career opportunities and on handling discriminatory practices.[146] The GIWPC focused its action on equality issues and eschewed pickets, marches, and other public tactics. Such tactics garnered Indianapolis NOW its radical reputation. The GIWPC, by contrast, enjoyed a substantial amount of community support. In November 1973, state representative Julia Carson wrote a letter to GIWPC leader Virginia Dill McCarthy praising the group for "drawing 'moderate' feminist elements together."[147] Once the fight for the ERA began, the GIWPC became a key organization directing the work of those "moderate feminists" on the amendment's behalf.

The ERA in Indiana

The Equal Rights Amendment, the primary focus of feminist work in Indianapolis beginning in 1973, brought feminists in the city a victory that few of their peers nationwide expected. From 1973 until 1977, the fight for the ERA was *the* feminist issue in Indiana, drawing together a huge group of women from around the state. The necessities of persuading state legislators in a conservative state to ratify a feminist amendment also created tension among the groups that made up the HERA coalition about action on other feminist issues. As a result, Indianapolis lacked some of the feminist infrastructure found in other cities—it did not have a Women's Center, for example—but the Equal Rights Amendment was ratified in the state well after its momentum had stalled nationally.[148] Indianapolis feminism and the ERA were intimately linked; by 1975 the amendment had garnered the bulk of feminists' attention and energy. As the state capital, the city was at the center of the ERA fight. And the possibility of feminist action using different public tactics or on different issues was limited by the contingencies of persuading state legislators to pass the ERA. Indianapolis feminists' work on the amendment's behalf highlights the compromises necessary to achieve legislative feminist goals in a conservative environment. It also demonstrates how, in spite of the tension within HERA, the multiple points of view held by pro-ERA activists in Indiana were critical to the amendment's success.

The Equal Rights Amendment passed the U.S. Congress in March 1972, and by the fall of that year the Indianapolis LWV was working to secure its ratification in Indiana. The League's October general meeting featured Virginia Dill McCarthy of the IWPC and Mary Ann Butters of the Mayor's Task Force on Women as its speakers; the women's talk was titled "The Equal Rights Amendment—What's in It for Us?"[149] That month's issue of the League bulletin also featured an article on the amendment that stated, "The amendment would not nullify all laws distinguishing on the basis of sex, but would require that the law treat men and women equally," and "the amendment would restrict only government action, and would not apply to purely private action."[150] The article also identified the LWV as part of a statewide coordinating committee that worked primarily to provide speakers on the amendment and to recruit state senators to sponsor the ratification bill in the 1973 legislative session.[151]

The League was active throughout the 1973 ERA ratification campaign, urging members to write letters and call their congresspersons and imploring women to keep the pressure on after the amendment passed the Indiana House of Representatives and moved on to the state senate.[152] Despite these efforts by one of the city's most respectable women's groups and others, the state senate failed to ratify the amendment.[153] But LWV leaders were proud of what their organization accomplished despite their ultimate defeat, telling members, "Everything you did last time [spring 1973] was in preparation for the next round in 1974. You made friends, clarified issues, you learned where your weaknesses were and just where to put your greatest efforts next time."[154] League leaders were not discouraged. Rather, they became even more eager to take on the state legislature over the amendment the following year.

Despite the upbeat tone of some leaders, fissures were already emerging within the LWV over the group's feminist work, and as the fight for the ERA wore on and the League consolidated its work under the umbrella of HERA, the most moderate voices came to dominate ERA efforts. In the February 1973 League bulletin, the organization's president, Betty Williams, noted, "The question has been posed concerning any restrictions imposed upon a member who opposes a League position. . . . We do not ask that they remain silent, but do ask that they not associate themselves with the League in making their views known."[155] While Williams did not state which issue some members found problematic, later in the same article she urged members to write their legislators on behalf of the ERA. As the amendment was the only new issue on the LWV's agenda in early 1973, it is likely that ERA support had generated disagreement among some members.[156] And while the League dealt with resistance from its more conservative members, it was also, in the opinion of one member, losing many feminist members to other organizations. A bulletin article reporting on a statewide LWV meeting in the fall of 1973 noted that in the opinion of the keynote speaker, who had recently attended a national NOW meeting, "many League members went elsewhere to find an organization that would give strong support to the ERA."[157] The same article announced the formation of Hoosiers for the ERA, the statewide ERA coalition that replaced the less formal Coordinating Committee for the ERA after the failure of the 1973 ratification effort and urged active participation in HERA as a way in which the League could give strong support to the amendment.

HERA was founded in the fall of 1973 and involved men and women from an array of organizations. Initially members of the League, the AAUW, and the Business and Professional Women (BPW) made up the bulk of HERA's members.[158] In 1974 members of these groups throughout the state mobilized under HERA's banner to persuade state legislators to consider the amendment again. Indiana's legislative sessions were shorter in even years than in odd, so getting the ERA on the agenda for 1974 was crucial and challenging. HERA struggled, however, in getting off the ground. The coordinating committee that had led the 1973 efforts did not pass its research along to HERA. The first task the new group undertook in October was therefore an assessment of the voting records from the previous session to determine which legislators who voted "no" on the ERA were the most likely to switch their votes.[159] HERA also faced internal debates about tactics for the fall, with one faction favoring a major petition drive while another group felt that legislators were not swayed by petitions and that such a drive was therefore a waste of time and resources.[160] The communication difficulties that plagued HERA throughout its existence were also apparent from the beginning: in a memo regarding the petition drive debate, HERA president Judy Head (a member of the Indianapolis chapters of both the LWV and NOW) noted that some people had already begun gathering signatures, even though the group had not definitely decided to go ahead with the drive.[161]

Tension between HERA and NOW first emerged in the winter of 1973, and problems between the two groups complicated feminist action in Indianapolis for the remainder of HERA's existence. That winter state NOW coordinator Lynn Schrum pleaded with HERA leader Paula Coale for more cooperation between the two organizations:

> There seems to be a problem in the state concerning the ERA and NOW and I hope we can work out a solution. Several chapters are growing concerned that nothing in the way of announcements, progress, or planning seems to have taken place with regard to the ERA. We know HERA is at work but it does seem likely that NOW should have some action working. Is there some problem I am not aware of? Can I be of any help? . . . I am really not trying to be demanding, but I must have some information about what you are doing and planning so that I can pass it on.[162]

At this time, NOW's state leaders were requesting that members toe HERA's line and tone down their rhetoric and action. Chapters were also encouraged to minimize public action, especially actions in support of reproductive rights.[163] In return Schrum needed something from HERA—a project for NOW or at least news of what was planned—so she could assure NOW members that they were not staying quiet for no reason.

In spite of Schrum's pleas, little information came to Indianapolis NOW about the ERA in 1974. That spring Indianapolis NOW chose to disregard the state NOW office's rule about downplaying other issues and hold a pro-choice rally in April in order to provide a counterpoint to an antiabortion demonstration in the city. The group did go out of its way to avoid "confrontation with [its] opponents" in planning the rally, but simply conducting it violated state NOW's rules, which had been established at HERA's request.[164]

Many of the leading women in HERA were put off by the radical image of

NOW. Virginia Dill McCarthy, a prominent local attorney, head of the IWPC, and a lobbyist for HERA, argued that being associated with NOW was "death for a politician," and she therefore believed that NOW and HERA should not be closely linked.[165] The leaders of HERA were determined to pursue their goal using what they referred to as "the soft touch." They urged their members to "play up equality for all" and "keep a sense of humor" when talking to legislators.[166] By the summer of 1974, HERA had determined that "women's lib turn[ed] people off " and urged its members to use a "sensible approach . . . to convince people of the worthiness of ERA."[167] Apparently "women's lib" and a sensible approach were two different things in the minds of HERA leaders.

The leadership of HERA believed that the amendment was a moderate piece of legislation. The slogan chosen by HERA for its letterhead cast the issue in gender-neutral language: "It's a matter of simple justice."[168] In the letter sent by HERA to newly elected legislators in the fall of 1974, the group stated that the amendment would bring "all people—men, women, boys and girls—into the mainstream of life and [give] each the endowment of freedom of choice under the law."[169] Such language reflected not only HERA leaders' beliefs about the amendment's effects but also the realities of politics in a conservative state like Indiana. The group's leaders were extraordinarily aware of the need to be polite and to play by the political rules if they wanted to achieve their goal. As the earlier discussion of Durham women's ERA work shows, an emphasis on decorum was part of women's efforts to secure ERA ratification wherever the amendment became a contentious issue and women worked on its behalf over a length of time. But in Indiana, HERA took caution and pragmatism to an extreme. The rhetoric employed by HERA distanced the ERA from the women's movement as much as possible.

In addition to a rhetorical emphasis on equality and equal rights and a downplaying of other feminist goals, HERA also was willing to cede control of efforts to secure ratification of the amendment. In 1975, the first year the amendment came up for consideration with HERA at the helm of the ratification drive, the organization had grown to include every major women's group in the state, from Churchwomen United and the National Council of Jewish Women to the African American sorority Delta Sigma Theta and a host of women's professional organizations.[170] Despite this large and diverse base, HERA leaders agreed to relinquish control of lobbying to the amendment's legislative sponsors. HERA leaders informed members that Senator Tom Teague, a Democrat and the amendment's lead sponsor in the state senate, would accept sponsorship only on the condition that the sponsoring senators be given full control over the targets, style, and content of HERA's lobbying efforts.[171] In other words, HERA would be operating under the direction of the sponsoring legislators. This decision was announced in January 1975. At precisely the moment when Indianapolis NOW decided to devote all its energies to the ERA, control of the ratification process was willingly given away by HERA's leadership. This decision likely heightened tension between the two groups and contributed to NOW's year of pessimism and minimal public action in 1975. The Indianapolis League was expressing its displeasure with HERA as well; the board noted in its 1974–75 annual report that the group's ERA work had been hampered by "frequent communication breakdown between [it] and the HERA structure."[172]

These concerns, and particularly the decision to relinquish direct control of the lobbying efforts, brought to a head questions about the leadership style of Audra Bailey, who served as HERA's president from 1974 until July 1975. Bailey, born in 1909, was two generations older than the youngest feminist activists.[173] She valued decorum and sought to keep all of HERA's constituent organizations in line at all times. She stated that because of the wide range of other issues in which HERA groups were involved—issues on which they often did not share common ground—she was "not sure it was (or would be) helpful to HERA to have lobbying efforts somewhat apart from HERA policy and strategy."[174] In other words, member organizations should hold to the HERA line or else keep quiet on the ERA.

Bailey issued this directive in April 1975; the timing made it a surprisingly assertive statement. HERA had suffered a humiliating defeat just six weeks earlier. After the ERA passed the state house of representatives in early February, antifeminist congresswoman Joan Gubbins and others killed the bill in the Senate Governmental Affairs Committee. Within the week, Virginia Dill McCarthy, who had been working with the senate sponsors to coordinate HERA's lobbying efforts, sent a tense letter to one of the senators stating, "We promised you before this session began that we would make every effort to use low-key in-Senate lobbying for your convenience and the convenience of other senators. We believe . . . that we have succeeded in that dignified effort remarkably well. . . . We do regret that we are unable to guarantee such lobbying techniques in the future."[175] League women who had worked on the ERA campaign sent equally angry notes to Senator Gubbins and to the bill's sponsors, explaining that the group was "appalled by [their] lack of leadership in the state and [felt] that the action of the Senate on the ERA item [was] unforgivable."[176]

In contrast to the immediate and frustrated letters sent by McCarthy and the League, Audra Bailey waited a number of weeks before writing to the members of the senate. When she did write, she merely stated, "Many in our ranks . . . feel we were 'put down' and treated as inferiors by action of the Governmental Affairs Committee. As a result, they have taken on a degree of militancy to make them initiate action for making changes in voting booths come next election."[177] Compared to the letters from other women involved, Bailey's note read like an exchange between friends, with her warning the senators to be alert lest they find themselves out of a senate seat come November. Bailey's extreme caution was undoubtedly a contributing factor to the election of a new HERA president in July 1975, when Laurie Scholl, a NOW member, was elected. But by then the damage had been done. Tension between the conservative faction headed by Bailey and other members of the HERA coalition had driven the organization apart, and the coalition dissolved in March 1976.[178]

After the collapse of HERA, Indiana NOW moved into a leading position on ERA work, alongside the League of Women Voters, the Indiana Women's Political Caucus, and newcomer ERAmerica.[179] ERAmerica was founded nationally in 1976 to reinvigorate the stalled ratification effort, and it enlisted the support of celebrities such as Alan Alda as well as first ladies Betty Ford and Rosalyn Carter. By November 1976, ERAmerica had opened a branch in the state. ERA Indiana received contributions and members from local chapters and national offices of NOW, the League, the AAUW, the BPW, and the AFL-CIO.[180] The organization sponsored a legislators' luncheon and ran television and newspaper ads, as well as coordinating the ERA efforts of organizations throughout the state.[181] In January 1977, ERA Indiana hosted a fund-raising reception with prominent Republican ERA supporter Maureen Reagan.[182]

While ERA Indiana courted legislators and facilitated the activism of a bipartisan group of amendment supporters, Indiana NOW staked out a more radical position of ERA support. On January 5, 1977, Indiana NOW began a daily ERA vigil outside the Indiana statehouse, which was designed to "daily remind the legislators that Indiana [was] waiting for ERA ratification." Indianapolis NOW member Marion Wagner coordinated the event. The vigil was explicitly modeled on Alice Paul's National Women's Party's pro-suffrage vigils outside the White House in the early twentieth century. Participants made sashes and banners and stood silently outside the state capitol, while other NOW members distributed literature nearby. The vigil offers a fascinating capsule of how the various kinds of pro-ERA activism worked together. The vigil was held from midnight to 1:00 p.m. daily; afternoons were left open so that participants could make appointments to speak to their legislators. The fact sheet on the vigil noted, "It is important that this in-person contact be made. This is one of the *main tactics* of the Antis."[183] The combination of direct protest action and one-to-one lobbying shows the creativity and flexibility that women in Indiana used to see the ERA to success there. In no other case that I have studied were these two kinds of activism embraced simultaneously by a single group of women in such a public way.

NOW and ERA Indiana's combined efforts paid off, and on January 19, 1977, Indiana became the thirty-fifth and final state to ratify the amendment.[184] Actions like the ERA vigil on behalf of the amendment did not occur in North Carolina, where ratification efforts failed. The lack of such sustained, public pressure by ERA activists was one of the contributing factors to the amendment's different fates in Indiana and North Carolina. Indiana NOW members saw themselves as filling the same role that Alice Paul had served and were able to help the ERA find similar success, at least in their state. The ERA vigil made the multiple points of view, the many different kinds of women who supported ERA, visible to everyone. Despite its success, however, the effort had clearly been a tense one. Just two days after the victory, ERA Indiana's campaign director sent a memo to her peers in unratified states noting, "Coalitions, by their very nature, are difficult animals."[185] In the face of these difficulties, ERA supporters in Indiana persevered and secured one of the women's movements major goals at a time when most hope of doing so seemed lost. And the multiple points of view that created such difficulties within the coalition were key to the amendment's success.

Women's groups in Indianapolis came together to achieve one of the major goals of the women's movement. Many of those groups had begun undertaking women-centered activism in the 1960s and were open to the ideas of feminism. ERA work brought many mainstream women's organizations like the League of Women Voters and Churchwomen United into contact with a range of feminist ideas, and those groups undertook increasingly diverse programs of feminist action as the 1970s progressed. Not all women's groups in the city became channels for feminism, however. Unlike in Denver and Durham, the Indianapolis YWCA was a deeply conservative organization hampered by racial tension throughout the 1970s, and the chapter was not part of the city's feminist community. Grassroots feminism was part of a larger agenda of progressive politics in Indianapolis. Women's organizations that pursued liberal political aims in the 1960s folded feminist ideas into their activism, while those without such liberal beliefs did not.

Situating Indiana's ratification of the ERA within the context of feminist activism in Indianapolis highlights the compromises necessary in achieving that goal. Especially on the issue of reproductive rights, some feminists felt that their voices were stifled. ERA work limited feminists' ability to publicly implement a broad feminist agenda, although many groups advanced such an agenda within their meetings and private events. And the push for the amendment also brought a diverse group of women from a host of organizations into feminist action. Feminists in Indianapolis were limited by the conservative milieu in which they operated and the goals they set for themselves. In spite of these limitations and difficulties, women's groups discussed a range of feminist ideas. Moreover, they created successful projects like the WAR program, and perhaps most importantly, women in the state achieved passage of the ERA—one of the major goals of the women's movement—in a deeply conservative community.

CHAPTER FOUR

"Not by Tearing Down"

Politics and Feminism in Denver

In January 1968, Blanche Cowperthwaite, head of the Colorado Commission on the Status of Women (CCSW), briefed her Fortnightly Book Club on the commission's current projects. She explained that the commission's primary focus was expanding the reach of its programming into the rural areas of the state so that women there had access to the child care centers and marriage and legal counseling the organization offered. Reflecting on Cowperthwaite's talk, the book club's secretary noted, "To one like myself who had not thought much about all this, the report given by Mrs. Cowperthwaite was very exciting indeed. The work which her commission is trying to accomplish can very easily revolutionize our society—not by tearing down and not by violence, but by making use of the abilities and intelligence and skills of women which at present are all too frequently ignored, not only by society, but by women themselves."[1]

This quote and the setting in which it was made highlight several uncommon aspects of the course of feminist action in Denver. The activity of the CCSW demonstrates the state government's commitment to women's issues, a commitment predating the emergence of feminism as a national mass movement. No city or state government in the other locations studied here was as supportive of feminism as was the state of Colorado. Indeed, a YWCA national staff member who visited Denver in 1975 noted the "general [positive] atmosphere about rights for women which [was] prevalent in the community" as one of the "aids" to the Denver YWCA chapter's overall health as an organization.[2]

The fact that Cowperthwaite was keeping her book club abreast of the latest work of the CCSW was also not unusual. Cowperthwaite and other women involved in the commission routinely spoke before women's groups in the city and encouraged group members to work with the commission as needed. While the Colorado government's involvement was unique to Denver, women's organizations in Denver worked together on major feminist projects such as securing ratification of the Equal Rights Amendment and creating rape crisis hotlines, just as their peers did in Durham and Indianapolis.

The politics of the Fortnightly Club members, who so enthusiastically perceived sweeping changes in women's roles as the commission's objective, reveals another characteristic of many Denver feminists. Many members of the Fortnightly Club identified as "old die-hard Republicans," and many of Denver's most committed feminists were also active members of the Republican Party.[3] Republican feminism flourished in Denver, and Denver feminists' numerous legislative victories came through bipartisan work in the state legislature.[4]

Largely because of the productive relationship between feminists and the state government, most feminist action in Denver focused on issues of equality that could be addressed through legislation. The vast majority of Denver feminists were committed to bringing about changes in women's legal status and educational and job opportunities by working within existing legal and governmental channels. The state government and several women's groups understood reproductive rights and reproductive health as essential pieces of this overall change in women's status as well. A focus on formal equality was dominant in the community's understanding of feminism; the nature of the "revolution" that the Fortnightly Club secretary foresaw makes this clear. She believed that American society could be made more equitable toward women without "tearing down" the entire social structure. Even the Denver NOW chapter pursued most of its activism through legal and legislative channels as late as the mid-1970s, placing the chapter at the least radical end of a spectrum of tactical choices and activist targets that created many debates within NOW nationally in those years.[5]

This fruitful partnership between state and city officials and feminist activists created a situation that, in hindsight, had problems as well as benefits. Because the CCSW ran the Denver Women's Center, women's organizations like the YWCA that operated centers in other cities chose not to do so in Denver. Therefore, there was no visible, physical feminist space independent of the state government and its funding. Also, there was no group analogous to Indianapolis Women's Liberation, no group that publicly identified as a radical feminist group for any length of time and presented its analyses of patriarchy and women's oppression to the public. There almost certainly were consciousness-raising groups unaffiliated with any organization that met to discuss women's lives and the obstacles presented by patriarchy and sexism. But Denver did not have the kind of sustained, public radical feminist presence as Indianapolis had nor the behind-closed-doors radicalism of the Durham YWCA. The feminism that found the most welcome reception in Denver was focused on legal and legislative remedies to women's problems rather than large-scale challenges to the structure of American society. This brand of feminism was the most acceptable in all three cities studied here, but alternative voices were present in Indianapolis and, to a lesser extent, in Durham. In Denver no alternatives were heard.

This chapter begins by discussing the context in which feminists in Denver operated by outlining the state's unique history with regard to women and electoral politics. It then examines the engagement of Denver women's groups with debates about women's discontent that appeared in the national media in the early 1960s, and the level of women-centered activism the groups undertook in those years. Finally, it documents the women's movement in Denver. Feminist action in the city was pursued both by existing women's organizations and by a large and active NOW chapter founded in November 1970. Coalitions of women from various organizations successfully achieved a range of feminist goals, often by working through the Colorado government. But because of the close relationship between feminists and the state, Denver's feminist community was fragmented and publicly addressed a relatively narrow slice of the women's movement's critiques of society.

Women and Politics in Colorado

Colorado's long history of women in politics is a primary reason for the state's openness to feminism in the 1960s and 1970s. Colorado women won full suffrage in 1893 and immediately became active participants in all the major political parties.[6] When the Populist-controlled state legislature granted Colorado women full suffrage in 1893, the Populists expected to be repaid by receiving a substantial majority of women's votes in the 1894 election. To counter this feared bloc vote, Colorado Republicans increased opportunities for women's participation in the GOP. As historian Rebecca Edwards has noted, women's participation in the two parties was roughly equal within a year of women gaining suffrage.[7] In 1895 three women, all Republicans, won seats in the Colorado House of Representatives.[8]

Women's participation in state politics continued throughout the twentieth century, and in the years after World War II, Colorado consistently had one of the highest numbers of women legislators of any state in the nation.[9] In 1955 seven women served in the state house of representatives—

three Democrats and four Republicans. Allegra Saunders, a Denver Democrat, became the first woman elected to the state senate four years later. There has been at least one woman in the Colorado house every year since 1937.[10] While these numbers represent a higher percentage of women legislators than in many other states, women in the Colorado legislature still constituted only a tiny percentage of the one hundred–person legislature by 1960. But the tradition of women's participation in politics and the consistent presence of women officeholders had important ramifications for women's political action in the state.

The presence of women in the halls of the Colorado legislature was well established before the emergence of the women's movement in the late 1960s. Working alongside women legislators did not necessarily make the men serving in Colorado's legislature more open to the demands of feminists than their counterparts elsewhere in the country, nor were women legislators automatic feminists. But an acceptance of women holding office gave Colorado feminists an advantage over many of their peers in other states. Activists in other places who wanted to use legislation to bring about feminist change had first to establish relationships within the state legislature and undergo other forms of "political socialization" before they could pursue their agenda. In the context of the ERA fight, historians have defined political socialization as learning both the processes of lobbying and coalition building and how to work effectively in the face of a passionate and influential opposition.[11] This socialization process was long and often painful for women in other states. One ERA activist in North Carolina noted simply, "We just didn't realize it [political socialization] was going to be that difficult."[12] In Colorado many women—and many women's organizations—were already familiar with the workings of state government, and officials in state government were accustomed to their presence in the statehouse. Feminists could therefore proceed straight to lobbying for specific bills and programs, without having to first learn the basics of political action or persuade others of the legitimacy of their presence.

Throughout the 1960s, the government of Colorado paid attention to issues that became part of the women's movement at the end of the decade, giving a unique slant to a broader trend in the politics of many booming western cities of the era. Since World War II, large numbers of highly educated people had immigrated to Denver to work in the city's defense and technology industries.[13] These new citizens supported probusiness governments that were moderate to progressive on social issues and also, according to historian of Denver Carl Abbott, embraced a "reform ideology" reminiscent of the Progressive Era.[14] Abbott has described Republican governor John Love, who served as the state's chief executive from 1963 to 1973, as the perfect match for the political climate of Colorado in the 1960s because he was a "pragmatic moderate" who wanted to cut state spending but embraced progressive measures such as environmental protections.[15] The emphasis on reform in both city and state government, together with a long-standing western emphasis on individual freedoms and rights, suggest possible reasons for Colorado's embrace of women's rights issues in the 1960s.[16]

The clearest example of this embrace came in 1967, when Colorado became the first state in the country to liberalize its abortion laws.[17] Colorado's previous law had allowed abortions only to save the woman's life. The 1967 law allowed doctors to perform abortions in cases of rape, incest, or severe fetal defect, even if the woman's life was not in danger. It did not, however, provide abortion on demand.[18] The bill's sponsoring legislators argued that changing the law would "eliminate much of the social and physical anguish which comes from having an unwanted or deformed child."[19] Other bill supporters also noted the disparity in abortion access that occurred when the procedure was illegal. Floyd Marks, district attorney of a suburban Denver-area county, testified to the House Committee on Health, Welfare, and Institutions that "well-to-do parents" could afford safe illegal abortions while the poor could not.[20] The bill's proponents also reminded legislators that the bill did not "force anyone to get an abortion . . . but allow[ed] a distraught mother a chance to make a moral choice."[21] After many hearings and much debate, the bill passed on April 8, 1967, by a 40–20 vote in the state house of representatives.[22]

Support for the abortion reform legislation was bipartisan, and bipartisan support of women's issues was not unique to Colorado. Historian Catherine Rymph has argued that many women within the upper echelons of the Republican Party "responded positively" to the ideas and programs of feminism, especially the ERA.[23] The GOP had a long history of supporting the ERA, but the Republican women who worked for its ratification in the 1970s understood the amendment not merely as a libertarian measure ensuring each person the right to determine her or his own course in life but rather as part of a larger feminist agenda.[24] Rymph and others have highlighted leading Republican women's hope for using their party's traditional support of women's rights—support based on an ideal of individual liberty and minimal government intervention in individuals' lives—to advance a feminist agenda in the 1970s.[25]

A study of Colorado shows that there were Republican feminists at the grassroots as well, and that in Colorado they were pursuing key parts of the emerging women's movement's agenda, in cooperation with Democratic politicians, several years before the movement gained national prominence. Women's issues found a particularly welcoming reception in the decade-long administration of Republican governor John Love. In addition to overseeing the abortion law reform in 1967, Governor Love convened the Colorado Commission on the Status of Women in 1964.[26] The original charge of the Colorado commission was to focus not only on discrimination against women in Colorado's laws but also on women in government more generally. The commission continued to meet and expand the scope of its activism for over fifteen years. Blanche Cowperthwaite became CCSW chair in 1967 and helped ensure the commission's perpetuation by persuading the state to make the commission a statutory agency in 1972.[27] That same year, the CCSW opened the first of seven Virginia Neal Blue Women's Resource Centers. The purpose of the centers was to "advance the welfare, status, progress and best interests of women throughout Colorado."[28] Throughout the 1970s, the CCSW worked hard on legislation affecting women and also facilitated women's involvement in government, operating a drop-in day care facility at the capitol building where women who wished to speak to their representatives or otherwise participate in the legislature could leave their children.[29] The CCSW served as an internal advocate for women's concerns in government and a central location for advocating changes in legislation and government services well into the 1970s.

Women legislators' standing in both political parties also contributed to the welcoming legislative environment that feminist activists encountered in the 1970s. Until the 1974 election, women legislators were members of both parties equally, with Republicans often holding a slight edge.[30] Issues that became closely linked with the women's movement, such as abortion, were debated in Colorado before feminism became a national movement and often found support among men and women in both parties. This bipartisan support of legislation and programs benefiting women, combined with the presence of women legislators in both parties, made it more difficult for feminism's detractors to tar all Colorado feminists with the brush of radicalism once the national women's movement emerged. By contrast portrayals of feminists as radical women out of touch with the mainstream opinions of their communities created hurdles for feminists in states like North Carolina when they needed legislation to achieve feminist goals.[31]

In Colorado the state government was attentive to women's issues before there was a national movement urging it to be so. The state government's predisposition to work on issues that affected women, even in the absence of grassroots agitation for such work, established a markedly different context for Denver feminists than their peers encountered in other cities in the 1970s. Even before the rise of the women's movement, this unique context also influenced the types and amounts of women-centered activism that women's groups undertook in the 1960s.

Women's Issues and Women's Organizations in 1960s Denver

The greater openness to women's participation in electoral politics and greater attention to women's issues by the state government put Denver's women's organizations in a very different milieu than that of their sister chapters elsewhere. In the 1960s, many of the women's groups in the city embarked on paths that differed greatly from those of their peer organizations in Durham or Indianapolis. The YWCA did not have to defend its right to exist, as the Indianapolis chapter did. Nor was it in the midst of working through integration of the organization in the context of the civil rights movement, as the Durham chapter was. Denver YWCA members did not engage with those issues but instead used the group's space to hold discussions about members' sex lives and lobby for reproductive rights, issues that the Durham YWCA did not take up until the 1970s and with which the Indianapolis YWCA was never comfortable. At the Denver League of Women Voters, the differences ran in the opposite direction. Unlike the Durham and Indianapolis chapters, the Denver LWV paid no attention to gender issues in the 1960s. Its members did not discuss the role of their group in getting women's voices into public discourse or breaking down women's isolation—they may have felt there was no need for such conversations or actions in the welcoming environment that Denver provided. For both of these groups, the level of engagement with women's issues in the 1960s serves as an accurate predictor of the level of more explicitly feminist work that the chapters would undertake in the 1970s.

As the 1960s began, leaders of the Denver YWCA urged association members to use the women-only space the organization provided to talk about their lives. A member's report from a regional conference on women in society stated that women's role then was "more confused and complex than ever before," and that there was a correspondingly high need for women's organizations to help women come to grips with the changes in their lives.[32] The YWCA board of directors frequently called members' attention to media discussions of women's new roles. The entire board watched a television series about women sponsored by *McCall's* magazine and reported on it to the membership.[33] The members of the YWCA's Young

Adult committee, who organized programs and classes for women under forty, were particularly attentive to these issues. In April 1960, they had a lengthy discussion about an article in *Time* magazine that outlined the "disenchantment" young women felt about marrying early and the potential of wasted years after their children were grown.[34] In 1964 the committee opened its meeting by reading extensively from an article on women's rights that appeared in *Reader's Digest*. The article stated that the idea that women had to choose between marriage and a career was a "false choice" and concluded by urging "women, married or unmarried, to arise as individuals committed to perfecting themselves as human beings."[35] The members of the Denver YWCA believed that their organization helped members do precisely that.

Beyond providing space for discussing members' lives as women, the Denver YWCA was also active throughout the 1960s in lobbying for improved reproductive health and reproductive rights in their city and state. The chapter's consistent attention to this issue set it apart from the Durham and Indianapolis chapters. In 1960 the Denver YWCA sent a letter to the Board of Health and Hospitals supporting Planned Parenthood's proposal to establish family planning clinics in Denver's public hospitals.[36] In 1963 YWCA members sent letters to the state senate expressing support for a bill to allow women on welfare access to birth control and family planning information upon their request.[37] The following year, the national YWCA adopted the topic of "sex morality" as a programming focus for the coming three years. The organization's national leaders envisioned this topic as primarily addressing the changing mores of young people and helping adult women understand those changes.[38] The Denver chapter did not maintain that narrow focus. Instead, YWCA members took the opportunity to discuss the changes that the sexual revolution was creating in their own lives. In their 1964 report to the national headquarters, the board of directors noted that in young adult programs such as the YWCA Wives clubs, "there is little 'study' as such [of sex morality], but a great deal of less formal discussion goes on in all clubs and many classes, although the stated subject may be completely unrelated."[39] In other words, younger members of the Denver YWCA were using meetings to talk about their sex lives. The Durham YWCA used the "sex morality" goal more in the way that the national organization had intended and opened the Cooperative School for Pregnant Teens as part of fulfilling that goal. The Denver YWCA took the issue in a very different direction.

As the 1960s progressed, the YWCA continued its work on reproductive health. In the fall of 1966, Polly Bullard, the Denver YWCA's executive director, represented the national YWCA at a family planning conference.[40] In 1967, as the abortion reform legislation awaited the signature of Governor Love, the YWCA urged its members to call the governor's office and express their views on the bill.[41] It is unclear what position the YWCA took on the abortion reform in 1967, but based on the group's previous work on reproductive rights and its enthusiastic support for repealing all abortion laws in 1971, the organization almost certainly supported the bill.[42] Issues of sexuality and reproductive health were seen as within the proper sphere of activism for the Denver YWCA and were the focus of most of the women-centered activism occurring within the chapter in the 1960s. YWCA members felt comfortable discussing issues of sexuality not only at meetings but also in public.

No other organization in Denver undertook as much women-centered activism as did the YWCA. But the local American Association of University Women chapter kept members abreast of legal changes that had an impact on women, and encouraged women's participation in the legislative process. Many of these discussions occurred in the second half of the 1950s, well before other women's groups were discussing similar issues in other cities. Again the context established by Colorado's long history of women in electoral politics shaped the actions and discussions of the city's women's organizations. The Denver AAUW had a committee that investigated the status of women in employment, politics, and education throughout the 1950s.[43] In February 1956, it restated a standing policy of encouraging "qualified" members to run for public office. That spring the group circulated a questionnaire to sitting legislators that solicited their views on the status of women, along with other topics such as international relations and individual rights.[44] Later that year, three of the chapter's members ran for the state legislature, including future CCSW head Blanche Cowperthwaite.[45] In 1957 the Public Affairs committee researched anticipated changes to the state's divorce laws. The committee recommended that the AAUW oppose the bill, which would have mandated counseling, a six-month waiting period, and one year of residency in Colorado before one could seek a divorce in the state.[46] The AAUW actively participated in the public discussion about changes for women that were beginning to seem possible in the 1960s.

The situation at the Denver LWV was quite different. In contrast to the Durham and especially the Indianapolis chapters of the organization, the Denver League of Women Voters undertook virtually no women-centered activism in the 1960s. While other Leagues around the country argued passionately for their role in interpreting women's changing options and alleviating suburban women's physical and intellectual isolation, the Denver League was quiet on the issue.[47] There is no evidence of discussion about the media portrayals of housewives unsatisfied with their lot in life, as there was in other Leagues around the country and in other Denver women's groups like the YWCA. League members volunteered with the local Women in Community Service program, which helped low-income women find work, but the organization was not an official sponsor of the program. The group undertook no other women-centered projects.[48] The chapter also did not engage with the state's changing divorce laws in the late 1950s nor the abortion law reform in the 1960s. These omissions are particularly striking, as studying and lobbying for legislative changes were a focus of LWV work.

The Denver League was a vibrant organization in these years. It faced intense criticism from community members in the early 1960s for its support of the United Nations and was actively involved in creating desegregation plans for Denver schools. The desegregation effort took an entire decade, from the mid-1960s to the mid-1970s.[49] The group's leaders occasionally expressed concern about how the changing patterns of women's lives were adversely affecting League membership. In the mid-1960s, leaders were worried about the loss of women who "dropped out" of the League to go back to work.[50] In response the chapter began a unit (the small discussion groups that League members attended) downtown. The downtown unit met during a weekday lunch hour and was created for "working gals who [could not] get out evenings."[51] The creation of this unit is the only evidence that the League was aware of the changes in women's opportunities in the 1960s. While the organization made this structural accommodation to the changing pattern of many women's lives, it did not engage in women-centered activism, nor did League members see a role for the organization in interpreting or facilitating those changes.

While the very different context provided by Colorado explains much of the Denver YWCA and LWV's difference from their sister chapters in other cities, the demographics of each organization's leadership likely also played a role in the divergent paths that the two groups took not only from that of their national peers but from each other's. Throughout the 1960s, the Denver YWCA's largest program was the YWCA Wives, a group designed for young suburban mothers with small children at home. YWCA Wives meetings provided nursery facilities for preschool-aged children as their mothers gathered to discuss political, social, and personal issues. In 1964–65 approximately 750 women participated in YWCA Wives clubs throughout the city.[52] The next year, the organization created several new

YWCA Wives clubs, as the existing groups were "at capacity," and the YWCA leadership believed there was a "great need" for the services that the clubs provided.[53] The organization continued to focus many of its classes and program offerings on young adult women and stay-at-home mothers into the 1970s.[54] In addition to providing opportunities for socialization, YWCA Wives clubs also gave women leadership opportunities. Each group had its own officers, and a YWCA Wives representative always sat on the YWCA board of directors.[55]

Not only the active involvement of younger women but also the high level of turnover in the YWCA's board of directors contributed to the flow of new ideas through the organization, particularly in the latter half of the 1960s. Only one person who served on the 1967–68 board held a formal leadership role in the chapter in 1970–71.[56] Many of the women who served on the board were also quite young. In 1970 six of the approximately twenty-five board members were under age thirty-five.[57] The YWCA made working with young suburban women and giving those women leadership opportunities a priority. That, coupled with the high turnover in the board of directors, kept new ideas circulating in the organization's leadership, which may explain its more progressive stand on women's issues.

There was far less turnover in the League of Women Voters. Women in leadership roles in that group also tended to be somewhat older than YWCA leaders. For example, Kay Schomp was president of the LWV from 1969 to 1971.[58] In 1969 Schomp was in her early fifties, and the youngest of her six daughters was in school.[59] The League, unlike the YWCA, had no programs specifically for young mothers of small children. While other Leagues around the country discussed the important role the organization could play in the lives of such women, the Denver League was quiet on that issue. This may have been because League members believed that the YWCA Wives programming was meeting the needs of younger women. But Denver's YWCA Wives program was not exceptionally large compared to the other two cities studied here, and the program's presence in Durham and Indianapolis did not prevent the Leagues in those cities from engaging with these issues and trying, especially in the late 1960s, to recruit new and younger members. Recruiting younger women and integrating them into the leadership of the organization were not priorities for the League in the same way as for the Denver YWCA. A more stagnant membership meant fewer points of view were present among the organization's leaders, especially in the last years of the 1960s and the early 1970s, when the ideas of the women's movement were becoming widely known.

Women's groups in Denver engaged with women's issues in very different ways than did their peer chapters in other cities. YWCA members used meeting time to talk about their sex lives, and the group lobbied on behalf of what was, at the time, a major reform of the state's abortion laws. The League of Women Voters, by contrast, saw itself as a lobbying organization without any special mandate or need to focus on gender issues. These choices established patterns that persisted into the 1970s with the rise of the women's movement. Coupled with the context created by the state government, the decisions made by women's organizations shaped a unique feminist community in Denver in the 1970s, one that found much legislative success but was in many ways fragmented and partial.

Feminism in Denver

For the first half of the 1970s, women in explicitly feminist and preexisting women's organizations in Denver worked together with legislators to secure many of feminism's goals. The Colorado Commission on the Status of Women provided a central location within the state government for coordinating feminist projects, and the CCSW was instrumental in many of feminism's successes at the state level. The group funded women's centers and lobbied on women's behalf at the state legislature. In addition to the CCSW, women's groups that predated the women's movement occasionally created ad hoc coalitions to work together on a specific issue. Rather than establishing long-term, sustained coalitions, women's organizations pooled their resources for work on one particular issue. When the goals related to that issue were achieved, the coalition dissolved. Such a structure was not unlike the ERA coalitions that emerged in Durham and Indianapolis. But because the ERA fight in those cities was prolonged, the ERA coalitions—both HERA and NCUERA—became permanent features of each city's feminist landscape. Both of those groups, and especially HERA, became central places where women interested in feminism could go to find other feminist activists and served as vibrant and vital representations of the women's movement in each city. In Denver no such permanent group emerged among the city's women's groups. This lack was due to the perceived absence of a long-term problem, such as the ERA, but also caused by the strength of the CCSW.

In addition to the CCSW and the ad hoc coalitions formed by mainstream women's groups, Denver was also home to a large and active NOW chapter, whose members often joined the coalitions or worked alongside CCSW members. Denver Metro NOW was dominated in its early years by women who believed that legislative channels were the best paths for achieving their agenda, and the chapter rarely worked on issues that could not be addressed through legal or legislative remedies. Denver's overall feminist community, therefore, was oriented toward legislative change but was a fragmented community. The CCSW served as the primary center for women's activism in the 1970s. The fact that feminism flowed through a state-funded government agency, coupled with a NOW chapter that leaned in that direction as well, yielded a feminist community in Denver that addressed only some aspects of the women's movement's critiques of American society—those that could be most easily or effectively addressed through legislation. Denver feminists did not create the kind of multiperspective feminist movement that grew out of the ERA fight in Indianapolis or the YWCA Women's Center in Durham.

One of the CCSW's most sweeping projects in the first half of the 1970s was the creation of women's centers, one in each of the state's major cities. Local women in each city ran the center and decided on the types of programming they believed would be most beneficial to women in their town. Denver's center opened in the fall of 1973 and focused primarily on employment, providing a talent bank to employers and a "resource library" to women seeking jobs.[60] The steady income from the state government, coupled with the flexibility the CCSW gave each facility, enabled the centers to tailor their work to the needs of the women in each city. In a large city like Denver, with widespread and diverse job options, identifying employment for women and fitting the right woman into the right job was a time-consuming endeavor. A state-funded body like the Women's Resource Center was more capable of handling such a task than a grassroots women's group would have been. The center's existence alleviated the need for women's groups to take on such laborious and costly tasks.

The CCSW also served as the clearinghouse for lobbying efforts for the ratification of the federal Equal Rights Amendment and the passage of a state ERA. The commission coordinated the efforts of all the women's groups in the state that supported the ERA, leaving groups like the League of Women Voters, which led pro-ERA efforts in other states, to merely urge their members to write or phone their representatives if they favored the bill.[61] In the fall of 1972, the YWCA made plans to create a coalition of women's groups to work for the amendment, but that group never materialized. The CCSW was already serving that purpose; there was little need for a large-scale campaign by women's groups.[62] Women's groups were not wrong in believing the CCSW could handle what lobbying was necessary to pass the ERA in Colorado: not only did the state quickly ratify the federal amendment, but a state ERA was also ratified in April 1972, just one month after the federal amendment passed Congress. The state ERA was not as strong as feminists hoped, for it banned only discrimination by the state government and not by private companies.[63] But both measures passed, and the city's women's organizations quickly moved on to other projects. Because of this success, the ERA did not have the potential to serve as a means of bringing women into the feminist community and breaking down misperceptions about feminism, as was the case in Durham and Indianapolis.

Many mainstream women's organizations in Denver designed programming to address only one specific feminist issue, or they hosted discussions about feminism but did not undertake action. For example, the Denver chapter of the National Council of Jewish Women adopted day care as its focus and became the center of activity on that issue in the city. In early 1971, the NCJW invited representatives from other women's groups to meet and discuss their concerns about child care.[64] The Women's Ad Hoc Coalition on Day Care emerged from that meeting, bringing most of the city's women's groups together to work to improve access to day care facilities and their quality.[65] The NCJW was the leading force in the coalition, and the Ad Hoc Coalition became the single voice on women's concerns about day care in Denver. Denver NOW was beginning a study of child care in the spring of 1971, but after the formation of the Women's Ad Hoc Coalition, no other women's group in the city took up the issue on its own, and NOW's task force merged with the Ad Hoc Coalition.[66] The following year, the NCJW articulated the relationship it saw between day care and the women's movement. Better day care options, the group argued, would improve women's opportunity to go out into the world and provide the "new woman power for a new era" that members believed women wanted and the country needed.[67] The NCJW did not pursue a broad feminist agenda. But its focus on a single issue enabled many of the city's women's organizations to pool their resources and place day care activism at the direction of the council, freeing the other groups to work on different feminist goals.

Other women's groups, including many that joined the NCJW's day care coalition, did not undertake any action on their own. But they did provide members the time and space to consider the impact of the women's movement on their lives. The Denver AAUW, as an organization of women college graduates, had been attentive to issues of discrimination against women in employment and education since well before the emergence of the women's movement. In the 1970s the chapter continued to work on women's issues and to pay particular attention to problems of discrimination in work and education. In 1970 the group sent representatives to a meeting at the YWCA to discuss changes in women's labor laws.[68] The following spring, leaders also attended the meeting on abortion held by the YWCA and informed members of the findings.[69]

Over the next several years, the AAUW aligned itself more closely with other women's groups pursuing feminist goals. In the fall of 1973, the organization polled its members on issues of interest and the direction they wanted the organization to go. There was "high interest" in undertaking projects to decrease discrimination against women.[70] The head of the Women Searching for Self Committee also urged the organization to "have closer relations with other women's groups in the city such as NOW who have common goals."[71] The AAUW board members believed their organization was pursuing feminist action, even if they seldom used those exact words. By 1976 the group had affiliated itself directly with the women's movement and held a meeting that May titled "Lively Libbers and Colorado."[72] The AAUW was not a program-oriented organization like the YWCA and NOW. But it continually offered members opportunities to keep informed about the newest ideas being circulated and programs being undertaken by those more active organizations, and its members considered themselves part of the feminist community of Denver.

As an organization that ran numerous programs, and one with a long history of discussing women's issues, the Denver YWCA also began to undertake a broad range of feminist projects in the 1970s. As it had done with the debate about housewives' malaise a decade earlier, the organization provided members space to consider and debate all aspects of feminism and its impact on their lives. In the first years of the 1970s, the group regularly offered a class called "The Role of Women in Today's World," which examined the impact of feminism not only on women but also on men, the family, and society.[73] Feminism also brought changes to the YWCA itself. In the spring of 1971, the YWCA staff asked the board of directors to adopt both "Ms." and women's first names (as opposed to their husbands') in all the organization's paperwork. Those urging the change argued that the use of "Ms." would "expand women's self-perception, particularly in an age when women [were] demanding to be treated as full human beings with their own identities." The board quickly agreed and made the change in the minutes of that meeting.[74] These discussions provided the foundation for a wide range of feminist programs that the YWCA undertook in the first half of the 1970s.

As the ideas of the women's movement spread, abortion continued to be the feminist issue that garnered the most interest and support among YWCA members. The group had been working on issues of sexuality and reproductive health since the mid-1960s, and in January 1971 the YWCA Public Affairs committee organized a public meeting to discuss the national organization's position on abortion, which was shared by the members of the Denver association.[75] Committee members pointed out that even where laws had been liberalized (as was the case in Colorado), abortions were not available "on an equitable basis for the poor and affluent." YWCA women also asserted that their organization did not believe the government should be involved in questions of personal morality; the question of whether abortion was "taking a life" was therefore immaterial to the group's position on abortion laws. This argument marked the national YWCA and its Denver chapter as among the many liberal, religiously affiliated groups that supported abortion reform in the years immediately before *Roe v. Wade*.[76] Not only did the Denver YWCA keep its members updated on the latest developments in abortion legislation; by 1974 the organization was renting space in its downtown building to an abortion clinic.[77]

Denver YWCA leaders saw their organization as an important site of feminist work in Denver. Beginning in 1975, its building housed the state-funded Denver Women's Resource Center, and the organization undertook a number of feminist projects throughout the decade.[78] The most ambitious of those projects was the Better Jobs for Women program. In 1971, with a grant from the federal Women's Bureau, the Denver YWCA established a program that placed low-income women in apprenticeships for traditionally male skilled trades such as plumbing and carpentry.[79] From 1972 to 1974, the program found jobs for a racially diverse group of women and had a retention rate of 79 percent. Women who were heads of household accounted for 88 percent of the program's participants.[80] The YWCA envisioned the project as a way to combine its interest in empowering women with the organization's commitment to helping low-income women. The most important aspect of the program was its insistence on placing women in skilled trades with advancement opportunities, rather than in the low-paying, dead-end jobs that dominated in other job placement programs. As a bilingual brochure about the program stated, Better Jobs for Women would "provide training for jobs with an income *above* the Colorado average . . . open up jobs to women traditionally held by men . . . [and] temporary financial assistance [was] available for child care."[81] In 1975 national YWCA staffers who visited Denver to audit the chapter identified Better Jobs for Women as one of the chapter's major strengths.[82]

Even as they were publicly supporting reproductive rights and designing innovative programs for low-income women, some YWCA members felt that the women's movement did not appreciate their efforts. In 1974

YWCA member Alex Habenicht wrote a memo on the value of voluntarism, noting that volunteering was continually denigrated because women were "accosted on all fronts by a society that measure[d] a man's worth by his income." This message came not only from mainstream culture, she argued, but also from leaders of the women's movement. Habenicht asserted, "Women's Lib groups claim we waste ourselves; demean ourselves by volunteering when we could be paid."[83] Opinions such as these had the potential to create tension between the women of the YWCA and members of explicitly feminist groups such as NOW. While they often worked together, some YWCA women believed that NOW women did not see them as true feminists. Whether NOW members actually felt this way was immaterial. Some YWCA members thought that feminist leaders and women affiliated with explicitly feminist groups did not value the contributions that women in voluntary groups made to the women's movement. Even at the movement's height, therefore, at least some women perceived tension in Denver between women who approached feminism and undertook feminist action in different ways.

In contrast to the YWCA, the Denver League of Women Voters never embraced feminism. The chapter first discussed the movement at a relatively early date. In November 1969, League member Judy Schuenmeyer wrote an article in the chapter newsletter discussing a national youth conference she had attended. She reported that a group at the conference added sessions on women's liberation at the last minute. She went on to explain: "Although I did not attend any of these workshops, I understand that the people in this movement feel that women are mistreated by society as a whole, particularly in the institution of marriage which they don't believe in. They do want to have children, however, but they would put them in day care centers so they could continue with their careers."[84] These were the first feminist ideas circulated by the League to its members, and as an organization, it was not interested in the misunderstood version of feminism that Schuenmeyer presented. There was no further discussion of feminism in subsequent newsletters; no member stepped forward to correct the misperceptions detailed in Schuenmeyer's article.

The following spring, Kay Schomp, the group's president, noted in her monthly newsletter column that the League was the way for young mothers to "give [themselves] a feeling of mattering in [their] community" and for older women to "feel [they] still ha[d] a purpose in life."[85] The idea that a voluntary organization such as the League was the most appropriate way for women to feel of use in the world—after raising a family—was unchanged since the late 1950s, when Leagues throughout the country were promoting their organization as a way to fight the malaise of housewives. While it certainly remained an option for such fulfillment and purpose in life, the tone of the president's letter suggests that as late as May 1970 the leadership of the Denver League was either unaware of the vast new opportunities feminism was creating for women or unwilling to engage with them.

Not until 1971 did League leaders in Denver begin to consider the impact that the women's movement had on the organization. That spring the board decided that the organization needed to consider changing the group's structure and practices in order to adapt to "changing times and the changing role of women."[86] The newsletter article, which asked for member feedback on this question, did not explicate what the changes in women's roles were or how they specifically affected the League. Articles in the June 1971 newsletter made the tensions that feminism was causing within the Denver League clear. In her monthly letter, the League president discussed various graduations she had attended that month and how "excited" she was to hear commencement speeches about women's growing role in the world.[87] The report of the state League convention, written by another member of the group and appearing in the same newsletter, exhibited far less enthusiasm for the changes brought about by the women's movement. This article described the "very heated debate" that "raged" when members of the "women's lib wing of the LWV" called on the organization to list women by their first names, as opposed to their husbands' names.[88] The fact that such a proposal caused a "raging" debate shows how far from embracing feminism the Denver League was in 1971. The next year the issue of names was raised again, and the Denver League still refused to change its practice, pleading the expense and time of revising the mailing lists.[89]

At precisely the moment when League members became aware that the women's movement was having an impact on their organization, the group was also struggling with internal tensions over how much action was appropriate for the League to undertake on any issue. In May 1971, the programming chairwoman noted, "The LWV reacts to problems, it does not initiate action," and for the next several months a debate occurred within the group about whether the lack of action was a problem.[90] By September League leaders had decided to offer more opportunities for action but also noted that the numerous members who felt they did not have time for greater involvement were free not to participate.[91] That same month, a notice ran in the chapter newsletter noting that a League task force had been established to examine "the continuing infringements on . . . individual liberties by some industry, business, various parts of the government, and—who knows who else?" and urging that the task force's work be incorporated more fully into the League's program.[92] Together with the reactions that League leaders had to feminism in the first years of the 1970s, this comment shows that the Denver League had a stronger contingent of conservative members than did other Leagues studied here. Their presence may have checked the interests of other members who wanted to move the group in a more feminist direction. Or, given the effective work that the CCSW and other women's groups were doing, Denver League members may have believed that their group did not need to engage in feminist activism.

As the 1970s progressed, the League occasionally worked with feminist organizations like the Women's Political Caucus on political topics that were of interest to both groups, such as the process of becoming a delegate to party conventions.[93] The LWV also supported the ERA, but because the federal amendment and a state version passed quickly in Colorado, that support demanded far less action on the part of the Denver League than it did for the Leagues in Durham or Indianapolis.[94] The language of the League's ERA support illustrates its understanding of the amendment's goals and the somewhat more conservative leanings of many group members. An article in the March 1972 newsletter stated that the League supported the ERA because it allowed "every person in Colorado an opportunity to develop his or her highest economic potential."[95] While this would be one outcome of the ERA, League members did not talk about the amendment in the context of a larger feminist agenda. The League continued throughout the 1970s to announce programs being conducted by other organizations, including feminist groups and projects. But the chapter never embraced feminism, continuing instead to work on issues concerning the environment, foreign policy, and other topics it had been examining for decades.

Denver's openness to women's rights not only created a different relationship between mainstream women's groups and feminist activism; it also enabled broader discussions about the relationship between women of color and the women's movement than occurred in the other two cities studied here. One of the major contributions of the Colorado Association of Colored Women's Clubs to the women's movement in Denver was facilitating such discussions by organizing an essay contest on the topic "Today's Black Woman and What She Desires."[96] In 1971 club members solicited entries and chose the winning essay to be published in the *Denver Post*. Although the *Carolina Times* in Durham published articles about black women's relationship to feminism, that paper was writing for and read by a black audience. In Denver the city's largest daily paper, facilitated by a black women's organization, provided a public examination of what feminism meant to African American women. The prominence of the essay contest again highlights the very different context that a city with a long history of women's political involvement created for discussions about feminism.

Not only does the essay contest illuminate the contrast between Denver and elsewhere; the essays submitted also provide insights into the attitudes of Denver's black women residents toward the women's movement. One woman, who identified herself as a "senior citizen," used the longtime slogan of the Association of Colored Women's Clubs, urging black women to work together "lifting as [they] climb" to improve their community. She also pointed out the double burden that black women faced as African Americans and women and urged them to no longer "accept the role of second class citizens."[97] Another entry advised black women to work together with other racial minorities, arguing that cooperation between minority groups was the best way for all of them to achieve their goals.[98]

Several of the entries in the essay contest specifically addressed the relationship between African American women and the women's movement. While one author believed that women's liberation would "add impetus to the fire that was already burning within the black woman to make a greater way for herself," other contributors were not so positive.[99] One woman, Renee Cousins, claimed that "eradication of chauvinism, traditional male-female roles and so on as advocated by the (white) Women's Liberation movement [were] not of primary concern to black women." She believed black women were instead "striving for productive co-existence with their male counterparts."[100] It is striking that Cousins did not see a connection between this goal of cooperative relationships between black women and men and the "eradication of chauvinism" that the women's movement sought. Cousins understood the "women's liberation" movement as wanting to eliminate, rather than reform, "traditional" male-female relations, and she did not believe that black women wanted to eliminate those relationships. Another entrant in the essay contest had far harsher words for the women's movement, writing, "Black women are enslaved by Women's Lib (started by white women who are tired of sitting at home, doing nothing). Yet these Black women don't realize that once the women are liberated, she still will not be—because she is Black. (It is also interesting to note the progress that Women's Lib has made compared to the early civil rights movement, and the time involved)."[101] This author urged more black women to become involved in civil rights work, arguing that only when the status of all African Americans improved could the position of black women be addressed.

These essays offer a window into the attitudes of African American women in Denver toward the women's movement at the height of that movement's national profile. They show that while some black women believed that the needs of African American women could be served by the women's movement, others disagreed. The essays also indicate the specific feminist ideas that were known to Denver women. The author who believed that the women's movement was begun by white women who were tired of "sitting at home doing nothing" knew that many feminists advocated paid employment as a solution to women's problems. The author who commented on the women's movement's desire to "eradicate . . . traditional male-female relations" had heard the challenges some radical feminists posed to the nuclear family. The essays show that African American women in Denver were aware of the ideas of feminists, had a variety of opinions about how those ideas affected black women, and in some cases were comfortable articulating their opinions in a manner that may have become public.

Women of color within the YWCA also grappled with the impact of feminism on their lives and the role that the YWCA, as a feminist organization, should play in addressing issues of both sex and race. The Denver YWCA had discussed its internal racial situation extensively in the late 1950s and early 1960s. In the second half of the 1950s, the chapter had undertaken extensive discussions and made difficult decisions about how to integrate its historically African American Welton branch into the organization. The group began by integrating its programs: by 1955 YWCA Y-Teen programs run in local junior and senior high schools were integrated, and each committee at the historically white Central YWCA had at least one African American member.[102]

The major challenge that confronted the organization was deciding how to use the Welton branch building. Changing residence patterns complicated that task. Leaders of the branch were African American women, but after World War II the population of the neighborhood surrounding the branch shifted, with many African Americans leaving the area for middle-class neighborhoods and low-income Hispanic, Asian, and Anglo families moving in.[103] The branch leadership was uncertain whether its goal should be to cater to branch members, still overwhelmingly black women and children, or begin to offer services that appealed to the branch's new neighbors.[104] By the early 1960s, the organization had decided on the latter option. The Denver YWCA consolidated all administrative functions at the downtown Central building and renamed the Welton branch the Northeast Community Center. The center offered programs that YWCA leaders believed would benefit the low-income residents of the neighborhood regardless of race.[105] White leaders of the YWCA believed that the situation was then settled; discussion of the Northeast Community Center vanished from the board of directors meetings between 1963 and 1968. Some African American members likely disagreed with this assessment, however, and began pushing the chapter to take a harder look at its racial situation in the early 1970s.

In 1970 the national YWCA adopted the elimination of racism as the organization's first priority.[106] At that moment, the relationship between African American members of the Denver YWCA and the group's leaders was somewhat tense. Several black members of the Denver chapter attended a racial justice conference in 1969 and returned to inform the board of directors that the organization needed to begin working for "equity, not equality" and designing programs "*with* regard to race, color, and creed."[107] Many African American members of the Denver chapter were sympathetic to the decision of black women within the organization to hold a separate meeting at the YWCA's 1970 national convention. The conclusions of that meeting were relayed to the Denver YWCA members: "[African American women] want us [the YWCA] to close the gap between our ideal and our practices and to move our collective power behind one issue: the elimination of racism."[108] African American women wanted to use the YWCA as a central force for reshaping race relations in the city, a position that YWCA leaders seemed reluctant to embrace. The group was less involved in the school integration discussion of the early 1970s than was the LWV, for example, even though the YWCA's minority membership was larger.

There is a striking contrast between the relationship of black women and that of Hispanic women within the YWCA to the overall organization. Hispanic members were particularly active in using the YWCA as a channel through which to explore their relationship to the women's movement. In 1971 the Denver YWCA was one of the sponsors of the first national Mexican-American Women's Conference, held in Houston.[109] The conference was designed to allow Mexican American women to address feminist issues that affected them differently than they did women of other ethnic and racial backgrounds. The weekend-long event included sessions on marriage, religion, education, and work and also grappled with class and ethnic differences within the Mexican American community. Several sessions debated whether there was a place for Mexican American women in the feminist movement and the relationship between the Chicano and feminist movements.[110] Not only did the Denver YWCA cosponsor this conference; it also paid the travel and lodging expenses of the two representatives sent by the chapter.[111]

Several Hispanic women who were active in the YWCA took the leadership skills they had gained through their YWCA work and put them to use not only in that organization but also in a group that did not have a long history of women leaders. Many YWCA members also held offices in the Denver branch of La Raza, a national Hispanic rights organization. Betty Salazar was the president of her YWCA Wives Club and the executive secretary of La Raza.[112] Elizabeth Olivarez represented the Denver YWCA at the Mexican American women's conference and worked for La Raza's Head Start program.[113] Helen Lucero was active in the YWCA and headed the Community Service Committee of La Raza.[114] These women were instrumental in increasing the representation of women in La Raza's leadership circle. In 1971 only three of La Raza's thirteen board members were women.[115] With YWCA members taking the lead, by the mid-1970s women had an equal voice on the various boards and committees of Denver La Raza.[116]

Hispanic members of the YWCA separated their work and discussions of their status as women and as Hispanics into two separate organizations—the YWCA and La Raza—while African American women sought to use the YWCA as a channel to address both sets of problems. There are several possible reasons for Hispanic and black women's differing approaches. Nationally, the YWCA made the "elimination of racism" its primary goal in 1971. While the language was race neutral, national YWCA programs designed to accomplish this goal dealt overwhelmingly with racism against African Americans.[117] Black women in Denver may therefore have felt it was the duty of the organization to become more proactive in addressing the problems and concerns of African Americans. While the Denver YWCA was committed since the early 1960s to eliminating the structure of racial segregation within the group—most notably through its decisions regarding the Welton branch—by the end of that decade the group seems to have rested on its laurels. Discussion of racism dropped off as the group focused on other issues. In the context of the new focus on eliminating racism at the organization's national level, the chapter's African American members began to push the Denver group to move beyond mere structural changes into a thorough investigation of the perhaps less obvious but equally problematic ways in which race shaped both the YWCA's decisions and the programs it created to serve the wider Denver community. Some African American members believed that many women in leadership positions within the YWCA thought that they had solved the group's racial issues. In the same month that leaders were urged to design programs "with regard to race," the northeast area coordinator urged the YWCA leadership to "accept responsibility to the community" in northeast Denver, a community that was low income and minority. Clearly, the YWCA was not as engaged with issues of race as some African American members felt it should be.

Demographic changes in Denver may have also made it more difficult for African Americans' rights groups to gain traction in the city, increasing the urgency black women within the YWCA felt in turning their organization toward the problems of the black community. Historian Carl Abbott has argued that by the second half of the 1960s, Hispanics had become the "central" minority group in Denver, occupying the economic and geographic space that was held by African Americans in many other cities.[118] In 1967 37 percent of Denver's African Americans lived within the city's "urban poverty area," while 72 percent of the city's Hispanics lived in the same area. By 1970 Hispanics also made up a much larger percentage of Denver's population, 16.8 percent, than African Americans, who accounted for 9.1 percent of Denver's population.[119] It is possible that African American women wished to use the YWCA to improve the situation of their race because, due to their relative affluence compared to Hispanics together with their smaller numbers, African American rights groups were having difficulty getting the attention and action of local politicians and government agencies. What is certain is that black women in the YWCA wanted to pursue activism centered on African Americans from within that organization, a tactic not embraced by Hispanic YWCA members.

While existing women's organizations in Denver pursued feminist projects and provided space for members to consider the impact of feminism on their lives, as well as the interactions of feminism and race, few women's groups engaged in a wide range of feminist actions, contributing to the fragmentary nature of Denver's feminist community. The creation of explicitly feminist organizations did not immediately remedy that problem. A NOW chapter was founded in Denver in the fall of 1970. In August of that year, on the fiftieth anniversary of women's suffrage, Denver NOW's soon-to-be founder, Charlotte Wolf, held a press conference announcing NOW's goals. Wolf was a sociology professor at Colorado Women's College (CWC), and she outlined NOW's positions on reproductive rights, job opportunity, day care, the ERA, and welfare reform.[120] That November a group of women who attended a conference titled "Women as Minorities" organized by Wolf gathered and founded Denver Metro NOW.[121]

The following year, Wolf articulated her reasons for being a feminist activist in an interview with the *Western Graphic*, the student newspaper at CWC. She argued that the women's movement was a continuation of the civil rights struggle, stating that the two were "pretty much the same kind of effort when one compare[d] the similarities of the situations and responses to discrimination." Wolf believed that only if the entire population was aware of the discrimination faced by women and the role "sexual prejudice" played in creating that discrimination could women become full members of society. Wolf believed that in order to raise awareness "analysis and planning" were the most important tasks of the women's movement.[122] This focus on analysis, along with the analogy to the civil rights movement and all that implied about tactics and targets of action, had lasting effects on the NOW chapter that Charlotte Wolf was largely responsible for founding.

Several characteristics of Denver NOW set it apart from the dozens of other NOW chapters that formed throughout the country in the early 1970s. Sociologist Jo Freeman has argued that as large numbers of women not previously part of the women's movement joined NOW in those years, the membership of the organization became more diverse, moving somewhat away from its original makeup of highly educated career women.[123] For the leadership of Denver NOW, this was not the case. Virtually all the officers who served in the organization's first two years had at least a bachelor's degree; many held advanced degrees. Several of the women who led Denver NOW in its first years were attorneys or were involved in politics or government.[124] The background in politics of NOW's most active members, combined with the Colorado legislature's tradition of work on women's issues, gave Denver NOW a decidedly legislative slant. Wolf and other early chapter leaders believed in the ability of government to improve the circumstances of women's lives through legislation or government-supported programs. Most of Denver NOW's action throughout the 1970s was focused on achieving feminist goals by working through the state legislature. As the chapter matured, it began to use a wider range of tactics and to undertake consciousness-raising work among its members. But the group always used lobbying and other legislative methods extensively, a fact that made it somewhat unusual among NOW chapters nationwide by the mid-1970s.[125]

In the first half of the 1970s, NOW focused on using government channels to achieve its goals, using tactics more in common with the LWV than with many local NOW chapters. Denver Metro NOW's newsletters were full of announcements of projects that pursued feminist action through traditional mechanisms like lobbying state legislators. One early newsletter featured a list of bills under consideration that NOW members "should know about and be writing about." The article urged NOW members to write their congresspersons about legislation with feminist implications such as the ERA.[126] Within a year of its founding, the chapter held a workshop on grassroots political action, and members lobbied the state legislature as it considered repealing Colorado's abortion laws.[127] The ERA and abortion legislation were key feminist concerns; Denver NOW's attention to lobbying lawmakers on those issues is not surprising. But the chapter continued to focus much of its energy on electoral politics even after the feminist position on major legislative issues like the ERA had won in Colorado. At the beginning of the 1973 legislative session, NOW sponsored a buffet dinner for Denver legislators. Constituents of each congressperson were assigned to chat with him or her before dinner, and the event included presentations on NOW's position on various feminist issues after the meal.[128] In the fall of 1975, the chapter gave awards to women who had improved the lives of Denver women that year. Except for two NOW members who had worked on gaining visitation rights for inmates of the state's women's prison, every award winner held a political post.[129] Throughout the first half of the 1970s, Denver NOW used governmental means whenever possible to achieve feminist goals and applauded women who made political institutions work for feminists.

Examining the political activism of NOW members reveals another key difference between Denver NOW and the national organization. Many of NOW's most active members, and particularly those who were active participants in state politics on feminism's behalf, were Republicans. As discussed earlier, Colorado was a hotbed of Republican feminism well into the 1970s. Denver NOW was one of the primary local organizations in which Republican feminists were active. Two NOW members, Bonnie Andrikopoulos and Liz Abramson, illustrate the role of Republican women within Denver NOW. Andrikopoulos joined the group in 1971 and became the chair of NOW's abortion task force during the push to repeal Colorado abortion laws in early 1972. She served as the organization's lobbyist on abortion issues and other feminist causes for several years, was Denver NOW's representative to the National Women's Political Caucus convention in Houston, and was also involved in recruiting Republican NOW members to the Colorado Republican Women's Political Caucus (CRWPC).[130] In 1973 Liz Abramson was a NOW member and used the chapter newsletter to announce the formation of the CRWPC. Her article highlighted the difference between the CRWPC and the traditional Republican women's clubs, noting that the CRWPC would only endorse candidates who supported feminist positions on issues.[131] The following year, Abramson became an officer of NOW and was also the secretary-treasurer of the CRWPC.[132] Numerous other women who headed task forces and held offices in Denver Metro NOW were active in Republican politics in the state or identified themselves as Republicans.

NOW's efforts in the state legislature were often closely coordinated with women members of both political parties who served in that body. The newsletter article discussing efforts to repeal Colorado's abortion laws in early 1972 identified "NOW's own dear Jean Bain," a Republican representative from Denver, as the bill's sponsor. The presence and activism of women like Bain, Andrikopoulos, and Abramson highlight the existence of Republican feminists at the grassroots level. It also shows the crucial role that feminist groups such as NOW played in bringing these women together and offering them space to work with feminists from across the political spectrum. The presence of Republican feminists coupled with the tradition of a state government amenable to women's issues also contributed to the decidedly liberal (as opposed to radical) slant of feminism in Denver. Leading Republican feminists nationally argued that supporting causes such as the ERA, affirmative action, reproductive rights, and federally funded child care was in keeping with the party's traditional support of individualism and equal opportunity.[133] Denver's Republican feminists worked on behalf of these causes, and their focus on reproductive rights and the ERA suggests that they may have had similar reasons for supporting feminism. The active role of women such as Andrikopoulos and Abramson within Denver NOW meant that the chapter was unlikely to adopt a radical feminist agenda that prioritized altering gender roles over efforts to bring about equality.

Despite the influence of Republican women, Denver NOW did not completely eschew nonlegislative tactics. Beginning in 1972, the chapter offered members frequent opportunities for consciousness-raising (C-R).[134] The article that announced the creation of the chapter's first C-R groups included a very basic definition of C-R and why it was important, arguing that the experience helped women form friendships with other women. The piece defined C-R as a process through which women discovered that "what they thought was their problem is society's instead, and is shared by many others."[135] Beginning in the spring of 1974, offering consciousness-raising opportunities to members became a major focus of Denver NOW, and announcements of C-R groups with a variety of specific foci came to occupy increasing amounts of space in the chapter's monthly newsletter.[136]

In addition to a steadily increasing focus on consciousness-raising, in the middle years of the 1970s Denver NOW also pursued action on issues that could not be addressed completely within a legislative framework. One such issue was rape, a topic that also engaged not only NOW but also, briefly, a wide cross section of Denver women. NOW began discussing the issue earlier than other women's groups in the city. In May 1972, the organization held a workshop for its members that examined "law enforcement, the victim, and the attacker." The group was motivated to take up the issue partially because "Denver ha[d] one of the highest rape incidences in the nation."[137] The group continued to discuss the issue, holding a pair of panel discussions on the topic the following year.[138] By the summer of 1973, NOW had persuaded Denver General Hospital to establish a rape crisis hotline.[139] Beyond a notice of its creation, however, there is no further mention of the hotline in the NOW newsletters. Denver NOW encouraged the hospital to open the hotline but appears not to have been actively involved in its operation. While these decisions were in keeping with Denver NOW's usual choices about activism, they were much closer to the League of Women Voters' style than many local NOW chapters at this point in the 1970s.

In early 1974, other women's groups began to address rape. That March there was a daylong conference attended by all the organizations that were working on issues related to rape, including NOW and the YWCA.[140] The conference led to the creation of the Coalition on Sexual Assault, which NOW and the YWCA both joined. NOW folded its existing Rape Task Force into the coalition to avoid duplication of work.[141] The League of Women Voters informed its members of the coalition's formation, but the organization did not officially participate.[142] The coalition had subcommittees addressing health, law enforcement and legislation, counseling, and education.[143] In spite of this strong start, the effort was short-lived. By August NOW had left the coalition and reactivated its own Rape Task Force. Most of the NOW members working with the coalition had "become dissatisfied with the policies of the Coalition."[144] No further explanation was given, and the coalition was never mentioned again by NOW or any other women's group. The loss of NOW members caused it to fall apart.

Despite the false start of the Coalition on Sexual Assault, Denver NOW's consistent attention to rape and especially to laws regarding sexual assault eventually paid off. In July 1975, the Colorado legislature overhauled the state's rape laws. The new code allowed women separated from their husbands to charge them with rape, made a victim's sexual history inadmissible in court, and prohibited judges from instructing juries that rape was a difficult charge to defend against.[145] Denver NOW's preference for working on the legal aspects of rape again highlights the difference between feminists in Denver and other feminist movements that scholars have examined. Operating rape crisis centers and hotlines was often a major project of feminist groups.[146] In Denver NOW did not choose to open its own hotline but instead attacked the problem by first urging the creation of a hotline at a public hospital and then by seeking changes to rape laws. It is not that feminists elsewhere did not also work for legal changes. Feminists in Durham and Indianapolis, however, organized their own programs of outreach and support to rape victims as well as trying to change the laws.[147] Denver NOW's handling of rape again shows how Denver's oldest explicitly feminist organization believed in the efficacy of existing channels and chose time and again to use public facilities like hospitals and various levels of government to bring about the changes it sought.

But government intervention was not applicable to every situation, and NOW undertook some projects that did not focus on changing laws or government practices. Several of these episodes revolved around sex discrimination in the workplace. One of Denver NOW's first large-scale actions was to join other NOW chapters around the country in picketing their local Ma Bell subsidiary, as a discrimination case against the company worked its way through the courts.[148] Denver NOW kept a close eye on the progress made after Mountain Bell settled its portion of the lawsuit, noting in January 1973 that while the company had established guidelines for hiring and promotion, it had taken no affirmative action to meet those guidelines. The group also expressed concern about Mountain Bell's maternity leave policy.[149] NOW members also participated in pickets in cases of workplace discrimination. In November 1974, they joined a stewardesses' union that was picketing Western Airlines after the airline fired a woman who had gained four pounds over the airline's maximum weight requirement for flight attendants.[150] Picketing and public demonstrations were not Denver NOW's preferred method of effecting change. But when its members believed a problem could best be solved in that way, they were willing to use such tactics.

However, as Denver NOW broadened its tactical repertoire and gave increasing emphasis to consciousness-raising, the relationship between white and minority members of the chapter became tenser. NOW's March 1973 meeting focused on the question "Is the Women's Movement Meeting the Needs of Minority Women?"[151] At that meeting, the group adopted the national organization's resolutions on minority women, and it declared that the problems of minority women had "officially become the concern" of Denver NOW.[152] The following month, a minority women's task force was formed that included both African American and Mexican American women. According to task force head Corina Aragon, the group hoped to come to collective decisions about the most pressing problems of minority women and to make those concerns "a concern of all women."[153]

In the spring of 1974, as consciousness-raising became a major focus of Denver NOW, the minority women's task force decided to withdraw from NOW and become its own autonomous organization.[154] While neither the minority women who left nor those who stayed in the organization noted the increased attention to C-R as a reason for the departure, many historians of minority women's relationship to the women's movement have argued that issues of family relationship and the notion of sisterhood, both of which frequently emerged out of C-R, were often problematic for women of color.[155] The withdrawal of the minority women from NOW created a stir in the city, and the *Denver Post* ran an article about the split. In that article, task force leader Aragon explained that the primary reason for the separation was the need for minority women of different backgrounds to learn how to work together. Only after achieving that goal, she argued, would they focus on teaching nonminority women how to work with minority women.[156] Charlotte Hebeler, Denver NOW's president at the time, told the *Post* that while she knew the women were still feminists, NOW was losing "some very active members." But she also pointed out that not all of the chapter's minority members were leaving.[157] The task force voted six to three in favor of splitting from NOW; it is unclear whether the three women who opposed the separation stayed in NOW or went with the task force.[158] NOW tried to address the concerns of its remaining minority members by focusing on the questions "How do minority women set their priorities? Do they consider racism or sexism their first concern?" at its June 1974 meeting.[159] After that meeting, however, the topic was never raised again. The Minority Women's Task Force continued meeting for several years as its own organization, and NOW announced its programs and sent representatives to its meetings.[160] But the specific concerns of minority women were not a major part of Denver Metro NOW's agenda after 1974. Rather, NOW was one of many groups that throughout the first half of the 1970s used the amenable climate of the Colorado state government to pursue its goals, goals that were more focused on gaining legal equality for women than grappling with the complex personal relationships between women of different races. The tensions that emerged when more-personal issues were considered likely increased this tendency among the chapter's leaders.

Feminists in Denver were more successful than their counterparts in Indianapolis or Durham in encoding feminist principles of equality into local laws and governments. The state government's attention to women's issues before the emergence of the women's movement meant that feminists in Denver had allies among political leaders, and they used those alliances effectively. Whenever possible, feminists used legislative channels to pursue their goals. Such efforts often had bipartisan support in the statehouse, and grassroots Republican feminism flourished in Denver. Many leading women in Denver NOW were Republicans as well. Government support and Republican women's activism meant that liberal feminism was quite successful in Denver. That very success made it difficult for more-radical feminist programs, focused on issues of personal politics, to develop.

The political system worked for feminists in Denver, and they did not believe it was necessary to fundamentally alter that system in order to bring about the revolution they sought. Those coming to feminism from Republican backgrounds were also more comfortable with feminist ideals of equality and individualism rather than with altering gender roles. Feminists in Durham and Indianapolis found success in other ways, by doing more consciousness-raising or by establishing a more comprehensive women's center. In Denver, government action and legislation were feminists' chosen tactics, and they used them effectively throughout the first half of the 1970s. In the second half of the decade, however, Colorado's history regarding women and politics began to lose its influence, as it did in the local contexts in Durham and Indianapolis. As the next chapter examines, the rise of organized antifeminism dramatically altered the political calculations of liberal women's groups and feminist organizations in all three cities.

CHAPTER FIVE

Responses to Conservatism and the Evolution of Political Tactics

In the fall of 1977, a Denver television station aired an editorial segment discussing the pros and cons of a proposed new water treatment plant. The Denver League of Women Voters had publicly and repeatedly opposed the new plant because, the organization believed, it would enable more development than the sensitive environment around Denver could "responsibly" handle.[1] The television commentator accused the group of being "left-wing" and "partisan," and urged citizens to give the League's positions "the minute attention they deserve."[2] The language and tone of the segment suggested that giving the League "minute attention" would reveal that the group was not the fact-based, nonpartisan organization it claimed to be but was instead a mouthpiece for the Democratic Party. While this was not the first time the Denver League had found its positions opposed in the media, it was the first time that such opposition was used to tar the entire organization and question everything it stood for. Such an attack was a marked change from a decade earlier, when the Denver League was also advocating a controversial position: strong support for the United Nations. In the mid-1960s, the chapter reported that a local radio personality had "editorialized in an adverse way" about the United Nations but said nothing to discredit the League itself simply because the organization supported the UN.[3] Nor did its support of the UN undermine, in the 1960s, the community's perception of the League as a nonpartisan group. In 1977 neither of those statements was true any longer.

The different reactions that local media personalities had to the Denver League's positions demonstrate how the political climate was shifting at the end of the 1970s. Nonpartisanship was no longer an option for politically active organizations. The preferred method of political action in the "consensus era" after World War II, which had been crafted in part to "diminish partisanship [and] limit the influence of interest groups," was crumbling.[4] Consensus-era political culture emphasized facts, figures, and specialized knowledge. Civic organizations and concerned citizens at the local level drew on this culture to guide their activism and made their case to politicians using polling data and other forms of what they believed to be objective facts. The League of Women Voters had been particularly enthusiastic in embracing this culture, as it fit neatly with the group's founding purpose of helping women become engaged and informed citizens in a nonpartisan way.[5] Local Leagues, therefore, had a particularly difficult time dealing with the political world that emerged with the increasing visibility of conservative activists in the 1970s. As League women and other local-level liberal activists saw it, emotional, irrational appeals began carrying more weight with politicians than facts and dispassionate advocacy. For liberal women's groups, especially those involved in feminist work, this new political world threatened their effectiveness as local political actors.

These tactical shifts occurred in the late 1970s because of the increasing influence of grassroots conservative activists. The rise of conservatism affected politics in myriad ways. Conservative activists were explicitly partisan; no liberal women's group had an explicit partisan identity in the 1970s. They worked on issues and positions that were increasingly associated with the Democratic Party in those years, but groups like the LWV or the YWCA did not make allying themselves with that party a priority. Nor did all of them seek to make the Democratic Party more responsive to their needs and beliefs, as conservative activists did with the Republican Party. Additionally, the tactics that socially conservative women used were diametrically opposed to those successfully used by liberal women for several decades. Conservative women appealed to legislators' and citizens' morality and made personal appeals; many liberal women, at least at the local level, saw themselves as urging politicians to do what was in the best interest of the majority of their constituents based on facts and polling data.[6]

Phyllis Schlafly's STOP ERA campaign was the first national conservative effort to successfully utilize these new tactics, doing so several years before antiabortion and antigay groups gained national prominence. Examining pro-ERA women's reactions to their opponents is therefore particularly useful in highlighting liberal women's efforts to recalibrate their political actions and make sense of the new political world in which they found themselves by the late 1970s.[7] Liberal women's organizations were not passive in the face of these changes. Some groups changed their political tactics; others sought to return to their previous position in the community as providers of objective political facts. For those groups that chose the latter path, doing so meant abandoning feminist work. By 1980 it was impossible to undertake activism on women's issues and not have other activists consider your group part of one camp of the burgeoning culture wars between liberals on the one side and social conservatives on the other.

Members of women's organizations and their allies in the wider women's movement were at a loss, however, about how to rebut or even describe the political style favored by STOP ERA. Over and over again, feminists throughout the country used the word "emotion" to describe their conservative opponents' political style and tactics. While there was certainly emotion behind feminist activism, "emotional" was not how ERA proponents and other feminist activists described their political work. Feminists in Denver, Durham, and Indianapolis, as well as many of their colleagues in the national office of ERAmerica, described conservative women's tactics as "emotional" in order to denigrate them. To the minds of these activists, emotion and politics should not coexist. In order to be politically effective, they believed, one had to leave one's emotions behind. The political success of women who were using "emotional" appeals—STOP ERA activists sending loaves of bread to North Carolina legislators with notes that read "From the bread bakers to the bread winners," for example—and seeking what liberal activists saw as personal, rather than political, responses from legislators disturbed and startled feminist activists.[8]

ERA support was never the only feminist work being done at the local level, however, and non-ERA feminist activism was also affected by the changing political climate. If one examines all the feminist work of women's organizations in the second half of the 1970s, it becomes clear that liberal women's organizations—especially those that predated the women's movement—had lost much of their influence in local politics by 1980. Tracing how liberal women's organizations in Denver, Durham, and Indianapolis understood their political opponents and navigated the shifting political terrain of the second half of the 1970s illuminates the ways in which the rise of conservatism not only led to new issues being discussed and a new perspective becoming prominent in American politics but fundamentally altered the way politics worked at the local level.

Denver: New Challenges

As chapter 4 has outlined, feminists in Colorado—a state with a long history of official openness to women's involvement in politics—did not need to engage in the kind of labor-intensive coalition building that their peers in Indianapolis or Durham did. Instead, Denver women's groups worked together under the auspices of the Colorado Commission on the Status of Women. The CCSW provided a network for feminist action in Denver and throughout the state. But the group was dependent on bipartisan political support in order to survive. The lack of connections among women's groups independent of the state government became increasingly problematic as the 1970s progressed. Whereas a large bipartisan group of men and women supported feminist causes in the first half of the decade, by the late 1970s feminism had become strongly identified with the Democratic Party. The transformation of feminism into a single-party issue was in many ways a result of the burgeoning conservative attacks on many feminist gains in Colorado and the state GOP's shift to the right. Feminists in Denver—long a bipartisan, government-centered community—had difficulty coming together to create a sustained response to their conservative opponents, and at the end of the 1970s feminists found themselves on the losing side of several key battles.[9]

Feminism first came under organized fire in Colorado in 1975. An anti-ERA organization called Wake Up Colorado was founded that year. Denver's women's groups all responded to this threat. The local League of Women Voters, which had never been active on feminist issues, mobilized its members promptly. The chapter's February 1975 newsletter printed a "call to action" by the League's national leadership that encouraged members to speak publicly in favor of the amendment, both to civic groups and to state legislators. Denver League members hoped that their vocal support of the ERA would defeat Wake Up Colorado's first attempt to overturn the amendment through rescission legislation—essentially a bill taking back the state's ratification of the ERA—in the state legislature.[10] The League focused its work on "public education," giving speeches to other women's and civic groups and issuing press releases to local media that outlined the impact that the amendment would—and would not—have on Colorado women.[11] The YWCA also began focusing on the ERA after Wake Up Colorado's creation. In February 1975, the YWCA board of directors urged members to take "active notice" to prevent the amendment from being repealed.[12] The YWCA also established a new committee to work on the ERA and other equal rights issues that summer.[13] After Wake Up Colorado's effort to achieve rescission through the legislature failed, the group began circulating anti-ERA petitions in the spring of 1976 and succeeded in securing enough signatures to place rescission of the ERA in the hands of voters through a ballot initiative that November.[14] In the summer of 1976, after the petition campaign had successfully placed rescission on the ballot, ERAmerica established a branch in Colorado; its office was in the YWCA's downtown building.[15] The hard work of women's organizations paid off. The 1976 ballot initiative to repeal ratification failed by the same 2–1 margin that the amendment had passed by in 1973, and the state amendment remains in effect today.[16]

While the fight against ERA rescission pulled new women into feminist action, especially members of the League of Women Voters, the effort did not lead to the kind of large-scale, statewide feminist organizing in Colorado that occurred in states where ratification of the ERA was a protracted battle. During the mid-1970s, the CCSW continued to serve ably as a central organization for feminist action throughout the state. The commission coordinated the efforts of all the women's groups in the state that supported the ERA. Commission members had written the state-level version of the amendment, which passed in 1973, and lobbied actively for both the state bill's passage and ratification of the federal amendment.[17] As chapter 4 has documented, the CCSW's efficacy and reach made it difficult for other women's groups to create long-lasting statewide organizations.[18] Such groups simply were not necessary in order for feminism to thrive in Denver.

The ERA rescission effort was not the only obstacle that Denver feminists were facing in 1976, however. In that year, Denver Metro NOW saw a steep drop in its donations. Leaders pleaded with members to contribute money beyond their dues so that the group's office in the First Unitarian Church could remain open. Articles in the group's newsletter argued that the office provided "absolutely essential services" both for the group and in an outreach capacity to the city.[19] That February the chapter wrote a public service announcement designed to introduce women in Denver to feminism and to NOW. The message emphasized "the many different meanings of feminism, and how many different types of women [could] fit into NOW."[20] The PSA marked the first time that NOW had needed to actively recruit members from the general population, and the first time the organization had felt the need to communicate with the broader Denver community about what feminism was and how NOW served feminist goals. The PSA apparently did not have the impact the group had hoped; in April 1976 the chapter created a public relations task force charged with creating a media campaign "aimed at informing the general public about NOW and its meaning to Denver women."[21] These outreach efforts, as well as NOW's emerging financial difficulties, were indicators of the changing political terrain in Denver in 1976.

With hindsight it is clear that 1976 was a pivotal year in Denver and marked the beginning of a rapid shift in Denver politics. Discussions among leaders of ERA work in Denver provide a window into feminists' struggles with the new political climate they were encountering. In their correspondence with one another, and with citizens writing for information, leaders of ERA Colorado and ERAmerica made it clear that they understood STOP ERA and its allies in Wake Up Colorado as very different from earlier political opponents. One letter from ERAmerica leader David Abrams, responding to a Denver woman who wrote looking for information on the ERA for a panel discussion, urged the woman not to "become overly frustrated by the opposition." Abrams went on to state, "Their emotional scare tactics are just that—scare tactics and emotionalism pitched at the highest point possible."[22] The tone of the letter made it clear that such "emotional scare tactics" were not the stuff of serious politics and implied that they therefore need not be taken too seriously. But while the ERAmerica leadership did not recognize it yet, such "emotional" politics were quickly becoming the order of the day. The fact-based style that had been the most effective method of political action for a generation was fading fast.

A year later, ERA Colorado leaders more fully realized the significance of this new political style, but they feared the leadership of ERAmerica still did not. In the late summer of 1977, two leading Denver members of ERA Colorado—one of whom, Sue Bollman, had a history of activism in Denver's women's organizations—exchanged heated letters with ERAmerica's executive director.[23] Bollman and her fellow Denver activist Barbara Dean accused ERAmerica's leadership of "failing to see a role in moving [them] ahead, or worse, failing to have even a basic strategy." They further complained that ERAmerica had not "dealt with [the issue] as a political one," had not "given ERA the touch of class it rightfully deserve[d]," and had instead allowed the issue to "be dragged into the gutter and swept away by the 'new right.'"[24] Shelia Greenwald, ERAmerica's executive director, replied that she shared Bollman and Dean's frustration with the lack of progress but closed by noting that anti-ERA action "and its proponents [were] unlike any other." Greenwald also stated that since Florida's failure to ratify in the spring of 1975, ERAmerica had "tried . . . to approach this like a political issue."[25]

The language used in these letters to discuss anti-ERA activists and the political fight between the two camps highlights both the shifts in politics in the late 1970s and also the confusion about and ambivalence toward those shifts felt by women who had been successful using the political methods that were being replaced. Such women were dismayed by the "emotional" tactics used by the opponents, describing them as putting an issue as important as women's equality "into the gutter." And the discussion of handling the issue as "a political one" shows how uncomfortable these women were with that shift. It is unclear what exactly treating the

ERA as a "political issue" meant. Did it mean using the kinds of fact-driven arguments that women's groups had long used and applying those tactics to the ERA? Or did it mean making more-partisan arguments to lawmakers, urging them to think about the decision as it related to their reelection prospects? Shelia Greenwald noted that she would not call a national meeting of grassroots activists until she had "the political information to allow [them] to make some decisions and plan strategy."[26] Greenwald was likely waiting for information about previous votes, political influence, and other matters in order to shape a strategy based on seeing the ERA like other political issues. At no point did she indicate that ERAmerica would move away from a focus on lobbying using polling data and other factual material. Treating ERA as a "political" issue meant avoiding making the kinds of "emotional" appeals that anti-ERA activists made. Although Bollman and Dean understood that those tactics were bearing fruit, they clearly did not want ERA proponents to adopt such tactics.

While feminists in Denver remained tuned in to the ERA fight, other challenges to feminism in Colorado were also emerging. Throughout the second half of the 1970s, the Commission on the Status of Women struggled to retain its support from the government. The state legislature imposed a severe budget cut on the group in 1976; the Denver Women's Resource Center, for example, had its funding cut by more than half from 1975 to 1976 and was forced to close.[27] The commission struggled along for a few more years, but in 1979 a majority-Republican committee of the state house of representatives voted to disband the commission.[28] Commission leaders and their allies saw the threats to the CCSW as part of the increasing partisanship and growing influence of single-issue groups in Colorado. Leaders of the commission blamed "the intense lobbying efforts of a few women organized into special interest groups." Those "special interest groups" were conservative groups opposed to abortion rights and rights for lesbian women, rights for which the CCSW had lobbied. The commission's leaders noted, "Neither the Commission nor the persons on that Commission are responsible for the controversy surrounding the issues of abortion and sexual preference and eliminating the Commission will not eliminate what certain legislators referred to as the 'divisiveness' caused by those issues."[29]

A number of women's groups, including the Denver chapters of the League of Women Voters and the American Association of University Women, called a joint press conference to condemn the Colorado house's deactivation of the commission.[30] The AAUW in particular had been watching the situation closely, alerting its members in November 1978 that the commission was likely under threat from the new legislature.[31] Once the house of representatives had acted, AAUW members voted to make reactivation of the commission one of the chapter's legislative goals for 1979.[32] It is unclear what designating an issue a priority led to in terms of action; regardless, the chapter's efforts to reestablish the commission were not successful.

One reason that the AAUW and other feminist groups were so worried about the fate of the CCSW in 1978 was the outcome of that year's elections for the Colorado legislature. While the legislature elected in 1976 had slight Republican majorities in both chambers, the one elected in 1978 had a much clearer Republican advantage: twenty-two Republicans to thirteen Democrats in the senate, and forty Republicans to twenty-five Democrats in the house.[33] More concerning to feminists than the numbers, however—after all, feminism had long enjoyed support from the state's sizable moderate Republican population—was the nature of these newly elected Republicans. The *Denver Post* reported that Democratic governor Richard Lamm defeated a "conservative Republican challenger" by a substantial margin in 1978, but noted that the new speaker of the state house and majority leader in the state senate both "represent[ed] a trend toward a more conservative style" in comparison with their predecessors, who had also been Republicans.[34] In other words, Colorado, that bastion of "modern Republicanism," was turning toward the conservative camp, with all the implications for women's issues and their political culture that such a turn held. The end of the 1970s was a newly partisan era in Colorado, one in which Republicans did not have to compromise with Democrats in order to pass their agenda and in which conservatives made up an appreciable number of the Republicans' ranks. Women's organizations saw their voice in government become one of the first casualties of that shift.

Because of the state's long history of bipartisan government support for feminist programs and issues, the sequence of events in Colorado was different from that in the other two states examined here. In Colorado conservative women did not enter politics until several years after many major feminist goals, such as ERA ratification, had been achieved. And they did not find their beliefs embraced until the very end of the 1970s, when the electoral success of conservatism was rising nationally. Conservative women became active in Colorado not only because they were connected to a national conservative movement but also, unlike in Indiana or North Carolina, because feminists were succeeding in Colorado. In North Carolina and especially Indiana, conservative women were influential in state politics quite early on, before any major legislative feminist goals had been achieved. Feminists in those states therefore had to directly respond to the increasing presence and influence of conservative women in order to secure any legislative victories.

Durham: Expansion and Opposition

Both North Carolina and Indiana were amendment battlegrounds throughout the 1970s (until 1977 in Indiana, when it became the last state to ratify), and the fight over the amendment established the context for all other debates and discussions about feminism. The ERA was the dominant feminist issue; tactical decisions made in that arena had implications for other projects. And the fate of the ERA was also tied, both directly and indirectly, to the fate of other feminist projects. In North Carolina, amendment activists from Durham and elsewhere continued to emphasize what they described as fact-based arguments free of emotion, and they shied away from partisan attacks. In Indiana pro-ERA forces were more willing to make partisan arguments, directly threatening the reelection prospects of state legislators who voted against them or, especially, those who switched their votes at the last minute to doom the amendment.

In North Carolina, as in Indiana, 1977 was a pivotal year for the Equal Rights Amendment. Historians Donald Mathews and Jane Sherron de Hart have argued that until 1977 the ERA had a chance in North Carolina.[35] Indeed, the amendment passed the state house of representatives in that year. But the state senate failed to ratify, and the amendment never passed in either chamber again. Mathews and de Hart have attributed this failure to the fact that after 1977 the ERA became a political issue like any other—not a bill about women or equality but "part of a pattern of defining political allegiance."[36] What is of interest here is how women who had fought for the ERA reacted to this defeat.

In the face of coming so close to securing ratification of the amendment, only to fall short at the last minute, pro-ERA forces in North Carolina were amazingly calm. In her postmortem report of the 1977 failure, North Carolinians United for the ERA legislative director Karolyn Kaye-Hervey singled out two members of the state senate who had pledged to support the ERA during their campaign, only to vote against it when the time came.[37] Since the ratification vote was lost twenty-six to twenty-four, these two men made the difference. She also noted the mailing of fifty thousand anti-ERA packets to state residents by members of a conservative organization in Virginia.[38] Kaye-Hervey's report, however, simply mentioned these facts. There is no evidence of letters decrying their action being sent to this organization or the two senators. Nor does it appear that NCUERA took any steps to publicly chastise either the senators or the out-of-state organization for their actions. The summary of Kaye-Hervey's report concluded by noting simply that "special appreciation was expressed to legislative observers."[39]

North Carolina ERA activists believed that their state's southern identity created different circumstances for ratification than existed at the national level. Specifically, NCUERA officials felt that the strong honor code of southern men made it unnecessary for activists to continually check with legislators regarding their position on the amendment. Once a legislator had given his word, NCUERA officials believed he would stick to it.[40] This belief caused NCUERA to refrain from asking legislators to put their commitments to vote for the ERA in writing until 1976. And the decision to make legislators put their position in writing came only after twenty-three legislators switched sides in the 1975 campaign.[41] Their reliance on ideals of southern honor likely indicates the racial makeup of NCUERA. In traditional constructions, honor was something that white southern men had and which they deployed in their interactions with one another and with white women.[42] If African American women had been prominent members of the NCUERA coalition, it is unlikely that the group would have given so much weight to traditions of honor in shaping their tactics.[43] In North Carolina (and indeed, in most of the country), white men and women were the people publicly debating and deciding the fate of the ERA.

While beliefs about southern honor shaped NCUERA activists' interactions with state legislators, there was no such framework into which the actions of anti-amendment women could be placed. Although pro-amendment women were dismayed by the various legislative manipulations used in the 1975 session to defeat the amendment, the group's most heated comments were reserved for anti-ERA activists. NCUERA members reported, "The loss of their votes [the twenty-three legislators who switched positions] was also due to the overwhelming strength of the opposition placing enormous pressure on legislators. One woman who courageously voted 'yes' had her life threatened, another was threatened with a recall petition. The tactics used by the opposition were highly emotional, bordering on unethical, and will not be forgotten."[44] NCUERA members were aware of the impact of the legislative manipulations but clearly held grassroots opponents of the amendment mostly to blame for its defeat. That understanding shaped their tactical decisions moving forward. Because they believed their primary obstacle was the "unethical" tactics—indeed criminal tactics, in the case of the death threat—of their grassroots opponents, they continued to believe that creating a contrast between those tactics and their own was the path to success.

This belief was clearly illustrated through the decisions NCUERA made in the eighteen months following the 1975 defeat. When the group announced in 1976 that it would seek written statements of support for the amendment from legislators, group leaders restated the southern ideals of honor, which they believed would make this a winning strategy: "In North Carolina, once a firm, written commitment is given, it is kept."[45] Early in 1976, NCUERA leader (and longtime League of Women Voters member) Gail Bradley reported that NCUERA would take a "positive approach" to the 1977 campaign.[46] Perhaps the clearest example of NCUERA's insistence on continuing to use nonconfrontational tactics came in June 1976, when the state Republican Party hosted STOP ERA head and nationally known conservative activist Phyllis Schlafly as the keynote speaker at its convention. NCUERA's male "political advisors" had counseled it not to make "an 'all-out' action" in reaction to that decision, so the organization kept quiet, even though it had a regularly scheduled board meeting on the same day as Schlafly's speech, seemingly a ready-made opportunity to respond.[47] The only public response in opposition to Schlafly's appearance seems to have been from leading North Carolina Republican women such as the state secretary of cultural resources, Grace Rohrer, who called inviting Schlafly to speak "a putdown" of women by the state Republican Party.[48] The presence of feminist Republicans such as Rohrer in the state government demonstrates that pro-amendment forces still had powerful allies in the state in both parties. Had they altered their tactics in the wake of the 1975 defeat, they may have been able—as their peers in Indiana were—to secure ratification of the amendment in 1977.

But NCUERA did not alter its tactics, and the amendment was once again defeated in 1977. After that year's failure, national ERA leaders expressed their unhappiness with NCUERA's insistence on continuing down the same path it had trod since 1973. While NCUERA leadership kept operating within a local context, focusing on the ERA's impact on North Carolina women, ERAmerica officials urged them to rethink their positions. In a letter to ERA supporter and state government employee Jane Patterson, ERAmerica executive director Shelia Greenwald noted that ERAmerica "disagreed with a great deal of [NCUERA's] strategy but [was] unable to direct them in any way" since Greenwald had just assumed the directorship and reorganized ERAmerica in the late fall of 1976.[49] The tension between NCUERA and ERA-NC (ERAmerica's operations in the state) remained throughout the rest of the ERA fight. In 1978 NCUERA's Karolyn Kaye-Hervey wrote a detailed assessment of where the push for the amendment stood in the state and how the two groups were working to advance their goal. She reported that not enough had been done to emphasize to grassroots supporters "the importance of the cooperative effort between NCUERA and ERA-NC." She further, and more damningly, noted, "Repeatedly, we have been asked why the opposition forces remain intact and identifiable and why we seem to undergo a major restructuring (especially in personnel) at the beginning of each campaign. I believe this question needs to be addressed honestly by everyone concerned."[50] Kaye-Hervey was not the only person who was concerned. Ruth Mary Meyer, a longtime Durham LWV member who was North Carolina League president in 1978, wrote a letter to other ERA supporters in July 1978 noting that the "complacency" with which many activists had previously pursued ratification "must be shaken."[51]

At first blush, perhaps all this reluctance to be more confrontational is not surprising. Women had been focusing their legislative efforts on fact-based, polite requests for decades, and these tactics had served them well. Perhaps North Carolina's ERA proponents did not fully appreciate how quickly or dramatically things were changing. As chapter 2 has explored, many feminists in Durham also worked hard to keep their activism focused on issues other than the ERA within bounds of traditional community gender norms that valued "ladylike" behavior by white women and "respectability" for African American women. The failure to secure ratification of the ERA in North Carolina highlights the shortcomings of that tactic. Unlike their sisters in Indianapolis, Durham women attempted to secure ERA ratification through the same political channels that they had always used. There were no thinly veiled threats to legislators about their reelection prospects, no silent vigils outside the statehouse in Raleigh. Although it is not the only reason why Indiana ratified in 1977 and North Carolina failed to do so, the more aggressive tactics used by ERA proponents in the Hoosier state certainly contributed to Indiana's ratification, especially since that ratification came two years after the amendment's previous success. By the later years of the 1970s, Durham women were hamstrung by their continued reliance on ladylike behavior and letter-writing campaigns and were unable to push the ERA across the finish line in North Carolina.

The evolving local status of the YWCA Women's Center also highlights the degree to which working within a respectable, ladylike organization no longer guaranteed feminists respectability by the end of the 1970s. Beginning in 1976, the Women's Center faced a community backlash. As chapter 2 has outlined, the Women's Center opened at the YWCA in the second half of 1971. In 1976 the Durham Women's Center was partially spun off by the Durham YWCA. The center's decision making and program planning became autonomous from the YWCA's board of directors, but the center was still "sponsored by" the YWCA, and the center's director was a paid member of the YWCA staff.[52] After gaining this level of independence, the Women's Center adopted a collective decision-making process; as center director Gilna Nance put it, "Whoever attends [monthly meetings] has an equal voice in the planning process." The two largest groups that were part of the center, the Women's Health Cooperative and the Triangle Area Lesbian Feminists group, were "large subgroups of the center, and work[ed] collectively."[53] After this transition, the Women's Center proved more controversial than it had been earlier in the decade, and that controversy had a serious impact on the Y's broader role in the community.

The controversial nature of the Women's Center's programs are reflected in both attendance at YWCA and Women's Center events and the financial status of the YWCA. Unlike the Indianapolis YWCA, the Durham chapter had enjoyed high levels of participation and stable, adequate funding throughout the 1960s and into the 1970s. In the second half of the 1970s, the Durham YWCA began to face serious financial problems. As Gilna Nance, Women's Center director from 1974 to 1976, noted, the organization was forced to sell its downtown building in 1976 because of financial difficulties.[54] In 1977 women associated with the Women's Center blamed themselves for the YWCA's financial woes: "The local community is often critical of Women's Movement activities. This sometimes results in financial problems for the YWCA as a whole; potential members won't join because of our 'radical' projects; potential contributors decide to have their names and money associated with less controversial groups."[55] The "radical" projects that troubled community members likely included the women-only coffeehouse that the Women's Center hosted, the center's efforts to persuade state legislators to extend public funding for abortion, and the work of the Women's Health Cooperative in "provid[ing] counseling and referral for women with problem pregnancies."[56]

The fact that community disapproval of the women's movement, writ large, was beginning to affect the Durham YWCA was also a substantial shift from four or five years earlier. As chapter 2 has documented, in the early years of the 1970s there were no public expressions of disapproval for the development and activities of the Women's Center, nor did the center's presence create financial trouble for the group. Channeling feminist activism through the respectable space of the YWCA made it at least palatable to Durham residents. By the end of the 1970s, the YWCA's history and long standing in the community no longer insulated the center. Running a women's center made one a partisan in the culture wars, no matter whose name was on the door.

The YWCA's money problems persisted for the remainder of the decade. In November 1979, the YWCA's president reported to chapter members that the chapter had "been trying to deal with its serious financial situation" for several years. She laid out possible ways that the group could move forward and focus on becoming "self-supporting, if not revenue-making, in all of [its] activities." This did not, however, mean abandoning work focused on the needs of women. She argued that there was "genuine interest on the part of some Y leadership that [they] use this time to shake loose and find new directions for the Y (like becoming a women's headquarters for different women's groups)," but later in the same letter noted "great respect" for the Women's Center and its Health Cooperative, even though there had been a drop in attendance at Women's Center events.[57] The YWCA was not going to abandon its commitment to feminism, even as late as November 1979, simply because it caused the group some financial problems. A commitment to meeting the needs of women and girls had been central to the YWCA since its founding in the late nineteenth century. And by the end of the 1970s, YWCA members firmly believed that a commitment to women and girls meant a commitment to feminism, both as a national organization and within the programs and practices of the Durham YWCA.[58]

While the Durham YWCA was focused on keeping its building and programs afloat, that city's League of Women Voters and Leagues around the country were also grappling with how the changing political climate affected their organizations. Of all the groups studied here, the Durham League was the most explicit in its discussions of how political culture was changing and what those changes meant for the organization. The Durham LWV's leadership first discussed the situation in the fall of 1976. That November over half of the board meeting was devoted to discussing the problem of falling attendance at unit meetings.[59] Units were the central building block of the League's elaborate structure; members met in these small groups to study and discuss an issue, and each unit took a vote on what the League's position should be. Only when all units were in agreement—when the group had reached "consensus"—could the League speak publicly on an issue. If attendance was falling at unit meetings, then the entire structure of the League would crumble. And that structure had always been vital to the League's long-standing influence in politics both locally and nationally.

In the minds of League leaders, the unit structure kept them well informed and therefore nonpartisan on a host of issues. By the end of the 1970s, Durham League members felt that their influence was slipping away, largely because of the rise of single-issue, clearly partisan groups. In early 1978, League president Jean Bruno reported in her newsletter article that it was "fascinating (maddening) the tactics that [were] being used" by anti-ERA groups.[60] Her column went on to detail the connections that amendment opponents had drawn the previous fall between a state bill allowing the governor to succeed himself and the ERA. Anti-ERA activists had urged their allies to vote against the succession bill so that the pro-ERA governor could not serve another term. In her column, President Bruno commented, "What kind of logic is that?"[61] To a reader today, it is fairly standard political logic, something akin to "the enemy of my enemy is my friend." But to the League of Women Voters in 1978, this was simply not how politics was done. One studied an issue and decided a position on that issue on its merits, without regard for how it might affect other areas of political concern. By the late 1970s, however, the League was one of a rapidly shrinking number of organizations that continued to use such tactics. The most effective methods of political action were changing fast.

But Durham League members were not willing to let that older political culture die without speaking up for it, at least among themselves. In the fall of 1979, member Phyllis Noell penned an article for the chapter newsletter in which she related a conversation with "non-Leaguer" friends. She wrote:

> As at a b—session, *everything* was wrong: Congress has no power, Congress exerts no leadership, the Presidency exerts no leadership, but can't anyway because Congress won't let it. Of course, the complaints weren't entirely true. We wonder whether the partial truths are related to a growth of single-interest groups and their one-issue lobbying power. Are we saying government is too complex for the citizenry to evaluate it all? Are we asking our representatives to be responsible leaders and govern in our best interest? Or are we saying we will refuse to support any legislator who does not save the whales or lower personal income taxes or vote "yes" on SALT II or vote "no" on SALT II. . . . The LWV with our grass-roots consensus principle and our multi-issue program offers a holistic approach for citizen involvement in government.[62]

This eloquent argument against the rise of single-issue groups embodied the whole idea behind the League. But it was an idea whose time had passed. In the same month that the League newsletter carried Noell's article, the board of directors in their meeting vented their frustration with the local newspapers' coverage of the League's voter education work. Stories using material generated by League candidate questionnaires did not attribute the material to the League, nor did a series of articles on influential Durham organizations in the *Durham Morning Herald* mention the League.[63] The League's voter education work, and especially its candidate questionnaire, had long been the most successful of its projects and certainly the most visible. In the early 1960s, the organization's candidate meetings had been essential stops not only for candidates seeking local office but also for those wishing to represent Durham at the state and national level.[64] So far did the Durham League fall that by the summer of 1980 the group adopted "increased LWV involvement in government" and "increased visibility as an objective organization" as goals for the 1980–81 program year.[65]

One reason for its declining visibility was that, for all the members' protestations, the Durham League was becoming a single-issue group, at least in its public activism. By 1980 the group was fully committed to gender politics and at least some of the tactical changes that commitment entailed. The group held only one public meeting on foreign policy issues between 1976 and 1980, while the topic had been a frequent subject of public forums a decade earlier.[66] Even though the group continued to discuss issues such as environmentalism and poverty in its meetings, the Durham League's public face in the last years of the 1970s became synonymous with the ERA. In April 1978, the group set up a booth on Duke University's campus to raise money for the ratification effort.[67] That same spring, the League created a new women's rights committee dedicated solely to the Equal Rights Amendment: learning about the ERA, the history of League involvement, and the impact the amendment would have in North Carolina; and identifying "anti-ERA strategy and prepar[ing] rebuttals."[68] Throughout 1978 League members spoke to community organizations about the amendment more than any other topic, giving speeches in favor of the ERA to the Junior Women's Club of Durham, the Durham-Chapel Hill Newcomers Club, and the Women's Office of Duke Divinity School, among other groups.[69] Group members also began volunteering for regular shifts at the ERA Action Center that ERAmerica had established in downtown Durham earlier in the year and acknowledged that they were volunteering as representatives of the League.[70]

In a time of shrinking membership and increasing demands on members' time, it is clear that those women who remained in the Durham League of Women Voters wanted the organization to work on women's issues. This sentiment was echoed some fifteen years later in a history of the North Carolina League. Marion Nichol, a member of the Durham League who served as state League president from 1979 to 1981, recalled, "The [ratification] campaign had focused attention on women's rights and concerns as never before. That focus continues to inform our thinking and modify our institutions to this day."[71] Such a focus, however, was incompatible with the League's long-standing traditions of nonpartisanship and objectivity. Durham League members sensed that at the time and, in 1980, were still unsure about whether they were willing to abandon their institutional culture in the name of gender politics.

The Durham League's concerns in 1980 that it was no longer "visible [as] an objective organization" were tied to the tremendous visibility of its ERA work, especially the visibility of that work relative to the group's activism on other issues.[72] To the general public, the Durham League could not help but look like an organization devoted solely to women's rights. That image placed it front and center in the political battles of the late 1970s, as opposition to the ERA transformed into a more general opposition to the advances made by the women's movement.[73] By the end of the decade, it was no longer possible for a group so visibly on one side of the burgeoning "culture wars" to be seen as an "objective organization." Indeed, objectivity was no longer the goal. To be successful in politics, one needed to take a side and pursue that side's agenda in a passionate, full-throated way. The League, however, was indecisive about fully embracing these tactics; the debates among the group's board in 1980 demonstrate board members' reluctance. This unwillingness to completely engage with the new political style of the day led to a waning of the Durham League's influence.

Indianapolis: In the Wake of Victory

In 1977, on the heels of its ERA triumph, the Indianapolis League of Women Voters remained an influential group in the city. In the second half of that year, the chapter "initiated a study" of a proposed expansion of the city's water treatment plant, a project that had been mandated by the EPA. Unlike the Denver chapter, which at the same moment faced mounting public criticism for its opposition to a very similar project, the Indianapolis League did not take sides on the proposal. It became involved because Indianapolis mayor Richard Lugar requested its help. In their annual report to the national office, LWV leaders noted that Mayor Lugar asked for their assistance because the project was "highly controversial."[74] The group was clearly still viewed by those with power in Indianapolis as a nonpartisan group that could marshal the facts of an issue without too much emotional investment and without choosing a side.

Like their peers in Durham, members of the Indianapolis LWV were worried about the changing political culture and how those shifts affected their organization. Indianapolis League leaders, however, prioritized maintaining their nonpartisan reputation over taking action on feminist issues once the ERA was ratified in Indiana. They were also very worried about the increasing role of, as they phrased it, "emotion" in politics. In July 1978, the national League decided to put its weight behind opposition to the Hyde Amendment, the legislative rider that prohibited Medicaid funds from paying for abortions.[75] In announcing its decision to work against the rider, the national League office told chapters that at both the state and the local level, they had "the option of supporting this position or staying quiet, but not opposing it."[76] By the time the national office made this announcement, the Indianapolis League had already decided to keep its mouth shut on the issue of abortion. The possibility of adopting health care as an item for study at the national level was first raised at the April 1978 board of directors meeting. During the ensuing discussion, president Mary Lou Rothe stated that "she would hate to see the League become involved in emotional issues such as abortion."[77] The next month, board members decided that the chapter had not done enough study at the local level on women's rights issues such as day care and employment to engage in action on those issues, even though the national organizations had endorsed action on the topics.[78] League leaders in the city clearly understood that keeping "emotion" out of their actions and continuing to undertake the kind of time-intensive, detailed study of issues were the way to move forward and retain their community influence. And steering clear of "emotion" by 1978 meant steering clear of gender politics.

Reflecting back on their work with the League during this time, many group leaders expressed continuing faith in the older political culture. Mary Lou Rothe noted, "I think the group worked best by providing study opportunities for members, developing reliable factual background material for the community, and working with coalitions of like-minded organizations."[79] Another former League president, Betty Williams, felt that "educating [themselves] was the most important aspect [of League work] since [they] could then proceed with confidence in educating the public and lobbying for [their] positions."[80] Indianapolis League members also firmly believed, as their peers in Durham did, that the group's attention to many issues simultaneously was the key to their success and influence.

Looking back at her time in the League, Nancy Smith, a third 1970s chapter president, argued that the rise of single-issue groups was one of the biggest challenges the League faced in the latter years of the 1970s, as "women's rights groups, environmental groups, etc. . . . drew many members away."[81] Smith in particular was sensitive to the shift toward single-issue groups. In 1976, when she was League president, she wrote and distributed to group members an eloquent explanation of how all of the League's positions, from ERA ratification to environmental quality to improved treatment of the poor, were connected:

> Social justice is the unifying objective of our two major human resources thrusts—equal access to housing, employment, and education and equal rights for all.... Furthermore, action to combat poverty and discrimination and to provide equal rights for all will require decisions about the use of natural as well as human resources. The League is determined to avoid the trap of both the either/or and the trade-off approaches, which imply that one set of resources can be protected only at the expense of the other.[82]

In spite of their efforts to remain nonpartisan and objective, however, the issues in which the League was interested were increasingly the sole province of the Democratic Party. And when reflecting on the League's loss of influence in Indianapolis, former leaders clearly saw this as part of the problem. Smith recalled that although the League was "fairly well-regarded" in Indianapolis in the mid-1970s, some saw the group as "too liberal."[83] Mary Lou Rothe went even further, arguing that most people in the town in the 1970s saw the League as "a bunch of liberal do-gooders who meant well, but were out of touch with reality." She further noted that over the course of the 1970s, the group was "increasingly seen as 'out of the main stream' of Hoosier values."[84] Taken together, these comments imply that "liberal" and "Hoosier values" were not the same thing. Rothe was likely highlighting the conservative nature of the town; later in her oral history she described Indianapolis as "a community very resistant to change."[85] Securing ratification of the ERA in such an environment required a years-long, total commitment from every feminist and liberal group in the state, as chapter 3 has detailed. The women in the Indianapolis LWV were unwilling to risk their community position by traveling further down the feminist road.

Not all feminist groups in Indianapolis made the same decision, however; Indianapolis NOW remained an active group throughout the last years of the 1970s by taking sides in the culture wars. As an explicitly feminist group, the organization had no choice but to do so, and its members enthusiastically supported taking on the conservative movement and bringing about feminist change in Indianapolis using whatever tactics were most effective. Newsletters from these years reveal a group actively involved in many of the key feminist issues of the late 1970s, such as domestic violence. Indianapolis NOW took a multifaceted approach to its work on that issue. Some members held leadership roles in a newly created nonprofit that opened the first battered women's shelter in the city, and the chapter's Legislative Committee drafted bills for the state legislature to increase abused women's legal rights.[86]

The difference in approach between Indianapolis NOW, an explicitly feminist organization, and the Indianapolis LWV in the years after ERA ratification reveals some of the limitations of pursuing feminist work through multi-issue women's organizations. Indianapolis NOW was free to use a variety of tactics and, importantly, to attack politicians and media outlets in a partisan way. When the city's largest newspaper endorsed Republican Dan Quayle in his contest against incumbent Democrat (and ERA supporter) Birch Bayh almost a year before the 1980 election, Indianapolis NOW leader Jill Chambers wrote a scathing article in the group's newsletter. Chambers denounced the paper's reasoning for supporting Quayle, stating, "Bayh is supposedly nixed as a favorable candidate for voting for billions of dollars of 'unnecessary' spending. 'Unnecessary' may be defined as anything to do with making the U.S. government more responsive to women, blacks, minorities, the elderly, and other marginal citizens. . . . *IndiaNOWpolis Woman* may not have as much influence on our Indiana community as the *Indianapolis Star*, but our endorsement without reservation goes to Senator Birch Bayh! And never fear, we may be small, but we *are* determined!"[87]

Being so explicitly partisan in no way contradicted the activist history of Indianapolis NOW. But leaders of the city's LWV could never have issued such a strong endorsement, no matter how badly they may have wanted to. Indianapolis LWV leaders valued their group's standing in the community as a nonpartisan, objective group; coming out publicly in support of a certain candidate would have destroyed that reputation. But by 1980, while Indianapolis NOW was small but stable, the League was continuing to lose members. LWV leaders noted with dismay that the few new members they were attracting "prefer[red] to monitor League activities via [their] publications" rather than coming to meetings and being actively involved in League work.[88] The efficacy of a multi-issue, nonpartisan group was declining throughout the country, even in Indianapolis, where the LWV had retained its influence longer than other, similar groups.

CONCLUSION

By the end of 1980, much of the forward momentum of the women's movement had stalled in Denver, Durham, and Indianapolis, as it had throughout the country. The Colorado Commission on the Status of Women had been eliminated. The Durham YWCA faced a serious budget crisis; some of the group's leaders believed that the problems were caused by the visibility of the organization's feminist work. And in Indianapolis, women's groups, explicitly feminist or not, had struggled since 1977 to regain the prominence and influence they had had in the mid-1970s while pushing for and securing ERA ratification. The revolution regarding "society's expectations of women," which the national YWCA had sought since 1970, appeared to be waning.

Such a narrative of a faltering movement, one facing an increasingly potent backlash as Ronald Reagan moved into the White House, is a common one in many historical accounts of the women's movement. Many studies also emphasize the fragmentation that occurred among many high-profile radical feminist groups in the second half of the 1970s.[1] Both the fragmentation and the backlash were forces keenly felt by many of the movement's intellectual leaders at the time. For example, a 1976 *Ms.* magazine article that documented the infighting (or "trashing") among feminist intellectuals "generated more letters than any article [the magazine] had previously published."[2] The prominence of this narrative of decline is one of the many results of the fact that, as historian Stephanie Gilmore has recently argued, the experiences and perspectives of radical feminists have dominated the scholarship on the women's movement.[3] By ending books with discussions of the fracturing of coalitions, the failure of the ERA, or the rapidly increasing challenges to abortion rights in the early 1980s, scholars of the women's movement have been one of many forces that have narrowed the public understanding of the movement.

It is not at all surprising that the reverses of the last years of the 1970s—

the failure of the ERA, the passage of the Hyde Amendment restricting federal funding for abortion, and the rise of the "pro-family" movement—left feminist intellectuals discouraged. Feminism's progress, if measured by laws and policy changes, was halted in the last years of the 1970s with much work left undone. It would be impossible for people who had devoted, at that point, roughly a decade of their lives to eliminating patriarchy not to be disheartened by the rise of the social conservative movement. But when the experiences and perspectives of women who were at the forefront of the movement are removed from the center of the narrative, a somewhat different picture emerges. As this book demonstrates, examining the accomplishments of feminist activists in cities throughout the country reveals just how pervasive changing notions about women's role in society were in the 1970s and the tremendous amount of feminist change women in organizations and cities all over the United States were able to bring about in light of those new ideas.

Focusing on the experiences of women who were not the movement's intellectual leaders shows that society's expectations for women were, in fact, revolutionized throughout the country between 1965 and 1980 to an astonishing degree. This change can be measured in several ways. The widely cited Virginia Slims polls examining attitudes toward the women's movement, which were conducted throughout the 1970s, provide one measure. In 1971, 40 percent of women approved of "efforts to strengthen or change" women's roles in society. Just one year later, that percentage was 48 percent. The same question was asked of women and men, at regular intervals, for many years. In 1974 almost 57 percent of women approved of efforts to "strengthen or change" their position in society. In 1979 the number was 64.5 percent. Just as striking was the increase of support among men—from 44 percent in 1971 to 63.6 percent in 1974 and 64.4 percent in 1979.[4] By 1979, then, nearly two-thirds of Americans were in favor of changing or "strengthening" women's roles—that at the end of a decade in which major changes had occurred. This rapidly increasing and substantial support for improving women's lives over the course of the 1970s demonstrates the impact of the women's movement. The data also show that the movement was continuing to change attitudes in the second half of the 1970s, even as the legislative goals of many feminist groups began to be effectively challenged and feminist progress was, in many cases, halted.

Women's lived experiences in the decades since the women's movement provide another measure of just how much feminists accomplished in the 1970s. Women's enrollment in college surpassed men's in the early 1980s, and the rate at which women outnumber men in college classrooms has continued to grow ever since.[5] In 2007 women were sole or equal co-owners of nearly 46 percent of all American businesses.[6] In 2012 women represented nearly one-third of all lawyers and physicians practicing in the United States.[7]

Scholars who have begun to study the 1980s have also argued that in that decade the reaction against feminism was not as pervasive as one might expect. Historian Marisa Chappell has argued that within the Reagan White House, "Americans' widespread commitment to equal rights and equal opportunities for women played a role in constraining the policy influence of traditionalist conservatives," particularly as the Reagan administration sought to battle the emerging "gender gap" in advance of the 1984 election.[8] Similarly, historian and movement participant Sara Evans has argued that "backlash was not the dominant reality of the 1980s. Indeed, the new hostility to change reflected the fact that . . . women had become omnipresent in public life."[9] Now, in the second decade of the new century, when social conservatism remains a potent force in national politics—and has more influence within the Republican Party than it did in Reagan's day—a mere 20 percent of Americans want to return to a "traditional 1950s middle class housewife" model of life for American women.[10]

For the organizations that make up the heart of this book, the world was also very different after 1980. All three Leagues of Women Voters are still active groups in 2013 and display patterns remarkably similar to those in 1980. The Indianapolis League has the most explicitly feminist identity today, with domestic violence and welfare still areas of work for the organization. Its work on domestic violence, for example, emphasizes the need for "appropriate" training for medical and law-enforcement personnel as well as adequate funding for prosecution of offenders and shelters and hotlines for victims.[11] The Durham League has merged with League chapters in neighboring Orange and Chatham Counties but appears to be a thriving organization with frequent events. While the chapter is not currently engaged in directly feminist work, it has a clear liberal bent. The chapter's central project in 2013 was rallying support for the Affordable Care Act, and the chapter's website also prominently features national LWV positions on climate change and immigration that broadly match the positions held by the Democratic Party on those issues.[12] The contrast and continuities between the Indianapolis and Durham chapters are quite similar to the work of those two chapters in the 1970s; Indianapolis was more explicitly feminist, but both were clearly progressive groups involved in a variety of important issues. The Denver League's issue profile is also similar to its 1980 profile. The group continues to be active on issues of zoning and land use and to sponsor candidate debates for local elections and school-board positions. However, no discussion of women's issues appears on its web page, and the group in general appears less closely linked with Democratic Party priorities than are the Indianapolis and Durham chapters.[13]

For the YWCAs studied here, the picture is far less positive. All three of the chapters are closed, and the Indianapolis chapter—the least active and stable in the 1970s—was the last to go, closing due to lack of funds in May 2012. Before closing its doors, the group's most successful projects were those that brought public attention to domestic violence as well as programs focused on empowering young women through education.[14] It is unclear when the Denver and Durham YWCAs closed. Nationally, however, the YWCA still has nearly 250 chapters throughout the United States and has remained dedicated to "empowering women" since its adoption of the 1970 goal of revolutionizing society's expectations of women.[15]

The women's movement of the 1960s and 1970s obviously did not accomplish every goal it set for itself. Patriarchy is still a strong force in American culture and society, rapes still occur with disturbing frequency, and women's ability to balance career and family depends precariously on very expensive day care and very meager maternity- and family-leave policies. Many other changes still need to be made in a huge array of other areas. But focusing solely on what was not accomplished obscures the tremendous victories of a generation of feminist activists who worked in all kinds of organizations in cities throughout the country to bring about one of the most rapid periods of change in women's lives in American history.

NOTES

Introduction

1. "Excerpts from Work Book," p. 1, folder 9, box 2, Indianapolis Young Women's Christian Association papers, William Henry Smith Memorial Library, Indiana Historical Society, hereafter cited as Indianapolis YWCA papers.

2. Several recent works have argued that the wave metaphor and therefore the descriptive term "second-wave" should be discarded, as they imply periods of inactivity and erode the sense of continuity in women's activism. I also feel that this metaphor has outlived its usefulness, at least as far as the second wave is concerned, and I therefore avoid using the term "second-wave," replacing it with the somewhat more cumbersome but far more accurate "women's movement." On the scholarship that advances this position see, for example, Hewitt, *No Permanent Waves*.

3. Gilmore, *Groundswell*, 19.

4. Rosen, *World Split Open*, chaps. 2 and 3.

5. On media, see Douglas, *Where the Girls Are*; Farrell, *Yours in Sisterhood*; Gerhard, *Dinner Party*. On women of color and feminism, see Roth, *Separate Roads to Feminism*; Springer, *Living for the Revolution*. On coalition work, see Gilmore, *Feminist Coalitions*; Thompson, "Multiracial Feminism"; Valk, *Radical Sisters*.

6. Enke, *Finding the Movement*; Ezekiel, *Feminism in the Heartland*; Gilmore, *Groundswell*.

7. The one exception to this is Gilmore's *Groundswell*, which examines local NOW chapters. NOW is traditionally associated with liberal, rather than radical, feminism, although Gilmore argues that we should see it as a radical group, noting quite correctly that NOW was radical in communities that were not New York, and also that the organization never described itself as a "liberal feminist" group.

8. Valk, *Radical Sisters*, 8.

9. See Echols, *Daring to Be Bad*.

10. See, for example, the discussion of socialist feminism in Evans, *Tidal Wave*, 158–68.

11. Feminist leaders at the time realized the obstacles their media image presented to recruiting a broader cross-section of women into the movement. See Freeman, *Politics of Women's Liberation*, 216–17.

12. Enke, *Finding the Movement*, 5.

13. Susan Hartmann has challenged this notion in her study of women pursuing feminist change within the institutions of the liberal establishment. However, her work is somewhat different from all the others because she examines the professional work of women who were, essentially, professional activists. Hartmann, *Other Feminists*.

14. For example, Cobble, *Other Women's Movement*.

15. Mary Lou Rothe, oral history, June 3, 2011. On the structure of the League, its history, and the centrality of nonpartisanship and objectivity to its goals, see Young, *In the Public Interest*.

16. Anderson, *Durham County*, 461.

17. For example, scholar Winifred Brienes has argued that white feminists wanted to work with black women but had difficulty doing so because they did not have a prior history of interracial cooperation. Brienes, *Trouble between Us*, 114

18. HERA Policy Council meeting minutes, December 14, 1974, p. 2, folder 2, box 1, Hoosiers for the ERA (HERA) papers, William Henry Smith Memorial Library, Indiana Historical Society, hereafter cited as HERA papers.

Chapter One. Women's Grassroots Political Activism in the 1960s

1. Quoted in Orleck, "War on Poverty from the Grassroots Up," 3.

2. War on Poverty legislation required the "maximum feasible participation" of low-income people in the planning and execution of new programs. Cazenave, *Impossible Democracy*, 138–40.

3. "League Log," June 1966, p. 1, folder 10, box 2, Indianapolis League of Women Voters papers, William Henry Smith Memorial Library, Indiana Historical Society, hereafter cited as Indianapolis LWV papers.

4. "League Log," October 1966, p. 1, folder 10, box 2; "League Log," January 1967, p. 1, folder 11, box 2, both in Indianapolis LWV papers.

5. On the League's tradition of encouraging political participation, see Young, *In the Public Interest*, 49–50.

6. Virtually all women's groups saw welfare reform as a civil rights, rather than a feminist, issue until the 1970s, when that view began to shift somewhat. On the interactions between feminist and civil rights groups pursuing welfare reform, see Chappell, *War on Welfare*, chaps. 1–3.

7. See, for example, the work of the Denver section of the National Council of Jewish Women in placing Hungarian refugee families. Board of directors meeting minutes, December 3, 1956, folder 6, box 2, National Council of Jewish Women—Denver Section papers, Peryl H. and Ira M. Beck Memorial Archives, Penrose Library, University of Denver, hereafter cited as Denver NCJW papers. On environmentalism, see *Voter* newsletter, April 1973, p. 6, folder 8, box 2, Denver League of Women Voters papers, Western History and Genealogy Division, Denver Public Library, hereafter cited as Denver LWV papers. Women's environmental work

had a long and particular history in the West, which is examined in Glenda Riley, *Women and Nature: Saving the "Wild" West* (Lincoln: University Press of Nebraska, 1999).

8. Scholars Rosalyn Baxandall and Elizabeth Ewen have argued that suburban women were drawn to NOW chapters in the 1970s because, in addition to career counseling and other services, those chapters provided "companionship, as well as strength and sustenance." For many women, mainstream women's groups had been serving that role for some time before the emergence of NOW. Baxandall and Ewen, *Picture Windows*, 215.

9. Gere, *Intimate Practices*, 13.

10. Mary Wooley, "The Woman's Club Woman," 1910, quoted in Gere, *Intimate Practices*, 1.

11. Schuyler, *Weight of Their Votes*, 57.

12. Young, *In the Public Interest*, 83–84, 137.

13. The Denver League was the largest (as the city was the largest of the three examined here), and the Durham League the smallest, in the smallest town of the three studied. For numbers on the Denver League, see Denver LWV Annual Report 1968–69, p. 1, folder 3, box 2, Denver LWV papers. On the Durham LWV, see board of directors meeting minutes, February 17 1976, p. 1, folder 4, box 2, Durham League of Women Voters papers, David M. Rubenstein Rare Book and Manuscript Library, Duke University, hereafter cited as Durham LWV papers.

14. Robertson, *Christian Sisterhood*, 3.

15. "William Preston Few," Duke University History, http://www.lib.duke.edu/archives/history/few_wp.html, accessed October 23, 2006.

16. Durham County's population went from 101,639 in 1950 to 132,681 in 1970, an appreciable jump in a county that encompasses only three hundred square miles. *County and City Data Book Historical Edition*, http://fisher.lib.virginia.edu/collections/stats/ccdb/php/historic5.php, accessed October 11, 2006. On the Research Triangle, see Bartley, *New South*, 215.

17. Brown, *Upbuilding Black Durham*, 16.

18. Anderson, *Durham County*, 221–22, 307–8. NCC's name was later changed to North Carolina Central University, but the acronym remained the same.

19. On the sit-ins and other events that pushed Durham's restaurants and hotels to integrate in the first half of the 1960s, see Greene, *Our Separate Ways*, chap. 3.

20. Hubert Humphrey carried Durham County, with 38.7 percent of the vote. George Wallace finished second, with 31.6 percent, followed by Richard Nixon with 29.7 percent. *Dave Leip's Atlas of U.S. Presidential Elections*, http://www.uselectionatlas.org/RESULTS, accessed November 6, 2006.

21. Greene, *Our Separate Ways*, 49–52.

22. Board of directors minutes, November 18, 1969, p. 1, folder 27, box 1, Durham LWV papers. In 1967 the group had enough black members to consider starting a unit that would meet in an African American neighborhood. Board of directors minutes, July 13, 1967, p. 2, folder 26, box 1, Durham LWV papers.

23. For the 1963 proposal, see board of directors meeting minutes, October 3, 1963, p. 2, folder 24, box 1, Durham LWV papers.

24. Busby, "Price of Integration," 211.

25. For more details on the Durham YWCA's integration process, see Melissa Estes Blair, "Women's Organizations and Grassroots Feminism: Denver, Durham, and Indianapolis 1960–1975," PhD diss., University of Virginia, 2008, 44–45.

26. "Teenage Program Director: Branch," September 1, 1962, p. 1, folder 4, box 34, Durham Young Women's Christian Association papers, David M. Rubenstein Rare Book & Manuscript Library, Duke University, hereafter cited as Durham YWCA papers.

27. "Basic Standards Report, Durham N.C. Young Women's Christian Association," February 1966, folder 5, box 21, Durham YWCA papers; Muriel Smith to Dr. Rose Browne, July 1, 1971, p. 2, folder 18, box 11, Durham YWCA papers.

28. The Components of the YWCA," March 1969, p. 1, folder 4, box 22, Durham YWCA papers.

29. Outline for Report of Association Review Committee of Durham, N.C., YWCA, n.d. (ca. winter 1971), pp. 3–4, folder 3, box 22, Durham YWCA papers.

30. Ibid. See also Tubman Branch board of directors meeting minutes, January 28, 1971, folder 8, box 21, Durham YWCA papers.

31. Greene, *Our Separate Ways*, 109.

32. June 1965 Bulletin, p. 5, folder 4, box 1; board of directors meeting minutes, September 23, 1965, p. 1, folder 24, box 2, both Durham LWV papers.

33. January 1967 bulletin, p. 2, folder 4, box 1, Durham LWV papers.

34. March 1967 bulletin, p. 5, folder 4, box 1, Durham LWV papers.

35. "Opportunity for All? A Durham Question," January 1968 bulletin, p. 3, folder 5, box 1, Durham LWV papers.

36. Ibid., emphasis in original.

37. Lists of OBT programs needing volunteers were published regularly, with no accompanying text. See, for example, February 1969 bulletin, pp. 5–6, and July 1969 bulletin, pp. 6–7, both in folder 5, box 1, Durham LWV papers.

38. On the national League's commitment to antipoverty efforts and especially welfare reform, see Chappell, "Rethinking Women's Politics."

39. October 1971 bulletin, folder 6, box 1; July–August 1972 bulletin, p. 6, folder 7, box 1, both Durham LWV papers.

40. On Fuller, see Greene, *Our Separate Ways*, 119, 168.

41. Fergus, *Liberalism, Black Power*, 59.

42. Ibid., 40–41, 55–56, quote on 56.

43. "From the President's Mailbox," January 1968 bulletin, p. 5, folder 5, box 1, Durham LWV papers.

44. For more examples of OBT's controversial position by the late 1960s, see Greene, *Our Separate Ways*, 171–84; and Fergus, *Liberalism, Black Power*, 58–66.

45. On the YWCA's work with working-class women in the earlier decades of the twentieth century, see Browder, "'Christian Solution.'"

46. Program, Forty-Fifth Annual Meeting, January 28, 1965, p. 2, folder 16, box 11, Durham YWCA papers.

47. Basic Standards Report, February 1966, p. 2, folder 5, box 21, Durham YWCA papers.

48. Ibid.

49. Greene, *Our Separate Ways*, 105, 110–13.

50. Board of directors meeting minutes, March 2, 1967, p. 2, folder 26, box 1, Durham LWV papers.

51. Unfortunately there is no archival material available for the city's black sorority alumnae chapters, its National Association of Colored Women's Clubs–affiliated groups, or its National Council of Negro Women chapter. The only archival source on the work of these groups is the reporting in the city's African American newspaper, the *Carolina Times*.

52. "Describes Role of Women in Bias Struggle," *Carolina Times*, April 4, 1964, p. 3A.

53. "Alpha Kappa Alpha to Observe Founders' Day," *Carolina Times*, January 22, 1965, p. 3A.

54. Ibid.

55. Ruth Johnson, "Social Notes," October 2, 1965, p. 3A, notes that AKA had been hosting an annual debutante ball in Durham since 1937.

56. Greene, *Our Separate Ways*, 211–12.

57. On the lack of reaction from the white community in the early 1960s, see Greene, *Our Separate Ways*, 73.

58. Board of directors meeting minutes, March 27, 1958, p. 2, folder 21, box 1, Durham LWV papers.

59. Taube Pine, draft of announcement, March 12, 1959, p. 1, folder 22, box 1, Durham LWV papers.

60. *Durham Civil Rights Heritage Project*, timeline, http://www.durhamcountylibrary.org/dcrhp/timeline.htm. On the impact of the *Green* decision nationally, see Clotfelter, *After Brown*, 13, 26–27.

61. November 1970 Bulletin, p. 6; April 1971 Bulletin, p. 2, both in folder 6, box 1, Durham LWV papers.

62. Greene, *Our Separate Ways*, 160–62.

63. "SOS: What's It's Purpose? What Are Sponsors After?," *Durham Morning Herald*, July 18, 1971, folder 8, box 2330, series III, North Carolina AFL-CIO papers, Pullen Library, Georgia State University, hereafter cited as North Carolina AFL-CIO papers.

64. See, for example, "Curriculum Committee: Thursday night session" meeting minutes, n.d., folder 3, box 2231, series III, North Carolina AFL-CIO papers. On sex education, see untitled clipping from the *Summer Chronicle* (Duke University student newspaper), July 23, 1971, p. 1, in folder 8, box 2330, series III, North Carolina AFL-CIO papers.

65. Charrette Steering Committee to "Dear Friends," n.d., folder 5, box 4, Durham LWV papers.

66. Outline for Report of Association Review Committee of Durham, N.C., YWCA.

67. Ibid.

68. Leary, *Indianapolis*, 221.

69. Ibid., 220.

70. Pierce, *Polite Protest*, 52, 54–55.

71. Ibid., 74.

72. "Association Review," September 20–12, 1971, p. 2, folder 1, box 3, Indianapolis YWCA papers.

73. "Tentative Draft [of United Fund presentation], Indianapolis YWCA." October 8, 1963, p. 1, folder 5, box 2; Kathryn Coy to the board of directors, March 11, 1962, p. 2, folder 4, box 3, both in Indianapolis YWCA papers.

74. In her oral history, Indianapolis League member Mary Lou Rothe recalls that the League was one of the best ways to "meet congenial people" when she moved to Indianapolis in 1958. In answering the same question, she states that she first joined the League while living in Savannah, Georgia, because it was one of the few places where "an avowedly liberal Midwesterner could feel at home." It is likely that the Indianapolis League shared these political leanings, given Rothe's long affiliation with the Indianapolis chapter. Mary Lou Rothe oral history, June 3, 2011, p. 1.

75. "President's Address," Annual Report 1964, p. 6; "President's Address," Annual Report 1965, p. 4; both in folder 11, box 3, Indianapolis LWV papers; "Longtime Civic Leader Nellie M. Gustafson Dies," *Indianapolis Star*, November 7, 1987, p. B2.

76. Board of directors meeting minutes, October 2, 1963, p. 3, folder 8, box 2, Indianapolis LWV papers.

77. Board of directors meeting minutes, September 4, 1963, pp. 1–2, folder 8, box 2, Indianapolis LWV papers.

78. Board of directors meeting minutes, April 3, 1968, p. 2, folder 12, box 2, Indianapolis LWV papers.

79. Carol Kirk oral history, May 20, 2011, p. 1.

80. Pierce, *Polite Protest*, 54.

81. Board of directors meeting minutes November 1, 1961, p. 2, folder 6, box 2, Indianapolis LWV papers.

82. Board of directors meeting minutes, March 1, 1961, p. 2, folder 6, box 2, Indianapolis LWV papers.

83. Pierce, *Polite Protest*, 49–50

84. Board of directors meeting minutes, March 31, 1965, p. 2, folder 9, box 2, Indianapolis LWV papers. The 1961 consensus had been reached on a school reorganization, not an integration, plank.

85. Annual meeting minutes, April 26, 1961, p. 2, folder 6, box 2, Indianapolis LWV papers.

86. On the 1967 study, see "Statement of League Positions," spring 1967, pp. 1–2, folder 11, box 2, Indianapolis LWV papers.

87. Pierce, *Polite Protest*, 52.

88. May 1969 bulletin, p. 6, folder 8, box 7, Indianapolis LWV papers. Other spon-

soring groups included the YWCA, the National Council of Jewish Women (NCJW), and the National Council of Negro Women (NCNW).

89. Ibid., p. 1.

90. Board of directors meeting minutes, February 6, 1974, p. 1, folder 3, box 3, Indianapolis LWV papers.

91. Board of directors meeting minutes, August 6, 1975, p. 3, folder 4, box 3, Indianapolis LWV papers. On *Miliken*, see Clotfelter, *After Brown*, 31.

92. Memorandum: To the members of the Indianapolis Board of School Commissioners, May 25, 1971, p. 1, folder 10, box 2, Indianapolis YWCA papers.

93. Board of directors meeting minutes, March 28, 1972, p. 4, folder 1, box 3, Indianapolis YWCA papers.

94. Board of directors meeting minutes, November 28, 1972, p. 5, folder 1, box 3, Indianapolis YWCA papers.

95. Doris White, YWCA executive director, to Albert G. Blakely III, May 17, 1965, p. 1, folder 2, box 4, Indianapolis YWCA papers.

96. "Progress Report of Lockfield Gardens YWCA Programs," May 27, 1957, p. 2; and "Program Analysis, Y-Teen Clubs, 1957–1961," p. 1, both in folder 1, box 6, Indianapolis YWCA papers.

97. "Indianapolis YWCA Progress Report for the Last 3 Months," March 27, 1963, p. 1; "Current Program at a Glance," January 1965, p. 1, both in folder 5, box 2, Indianapolis YWCA papers.

98. Board of directors meeting minutes, January 26, 1965, p. 3, folder 7, box 2, Indianapolis YWCA papers.

99. Agenda for board of directors meeting, February 22, 1966, p. 1, folder 3, box 4, Indianapolis YWCA papers.

100. Board of directors meeting minutes, May 23, 1967, p. 4, folder 5, box 4, Indianapolis YWCA papers.

101. Report on downtown mothers' group, May 15, 1968, p. 2, folder 3, box 6, Indianapolis YWCA papers.

102. Board of directors meeting minutes, January 25, 1966, p. 2; board of directors meeting minutes, February 22, 1966, p. 1, both in folder 3, box 4, Indianapolis YWCA papers.

103. Chappell, "Rethinking Women's Politics," 156.

104. Board of directors meeting minutes, November 4, 1964, p. 2, folder 8, box 2, Indianapolis LWV papers.

105. "League Log," June 1966; March 1972 bulletin, p. 1, folder 11, box 7, both in Indianapolis LWV papers. On the importance of CAAP office holding to poor activists, see Naples, *Grassroots Warriors*, 183–84.

106. "League Log," October 1966; Annual Report 1969–1970, p. 10, folder 2, box 4, both in Indianapolis LWV papers.

107. Board of directors meeting minutes, December 2, 1964, p. 3, folder 8, box 2; board of directors meeting minutes, March 2, 1966, p. 4, folder 10, box 2; February 1967 bulletin, p. 8, folder 7, box 7, all in Indianapolis LWV papers.

108. Board of directors meeting minutes, March 2, 1966, pp. 3–4, Indianapolis LWV papers.

109. One possibility for this openness to birth control in Indianapolis may be the state of Indiana's early adoption of a eugenic program; the state was the first to adopt such a program, doing so in 1904. See Willrich, *Pox*, 320. However, the program had apparently lost its popularity in Indianapolis in the post–World War II period. In 1957, while debating whether to begin offering its services to unmarried women, Planned Parenthood of Indianapolis leaders noted, "Public opinion in general is as much against the use of this law [the state eugenic law] as it would be against our handing out contraceptives to single women. It was agreed that even considering such a question would be bad at this time." Planned Parenthood of Indianapolis board of directors meeting minutes, February 27, 1957, p. 2, folder 4, box 1, Planned Parenthood of Indianapolis Board of Directors meeting minutes, William Henry Smith Memorial Library, Indiana Historical Society.

110. Abbott, Leonard, and McComb, *Colorado*, 301–4.

111. Dorsett, *Queen City*, 251. These figures are for the city proper; the Denver metropolitan area grew from just over 445,000 to 1.23 million in the same years. Dorsett, *Queen City*, 253.

112. Abbott, Leonard, and McComb, *Colorado*, 330. People of Asian, Native American, and Pacific Islander heritage are grouped into one category in this source.

113. Carl Abbott, "The Metropolitan Region: Western Cities in the New Urban Era," in Nash and Etulian, *Twentieth Century West*, 87.

114. Abbott, "Metropolitan Region," 87.

115. Beta Phi Chapter Social Action Seminar, February 26, 1966, pp. 3–4, Delta Sigma Theta scrapbook, Western History and Genealogy Division, Denver Public Library; "Proposal for an Effective Schools Program," March 17, 1966, p. 1, folder 69, box 2, La Raza papers, Library of the Colorado Historical Society, Denver, hereafter cited as La Raza papers.

116. "National Council of La Raza: History," http://www.nclr.org/index.php/about_us/history/, accessed September 24, 2012.

117. "Proposal for an Effective Schools Program" March 17, 1966, p. 1, folder 69, box 2, La Raza papers.

118. Clotfelter, *After Brown*, 27.

119. Unfortunately, very few archival materials survive for the council chapter after 1962, and it is impossible to fully assess its engagement with the school issue. Board of directors meeting minutes, September 12, 1962, p. 1, folder 7, box 2, Denver NCJW papers.

120. Public relations questionnaire, Annual Report 1967–68, p. 1, folder 2, box 2, Denver LWV papers.

121. "Statement Presented to the Denver School Board by the Denver LWV," November 12, 1968, pp. 1–2, folder 3, box 1, Denver LWV papers.

122. "League of Women Voters' statement to School Board, presented by Mrs. J. L. Williams," Annual Report 1968–69, p. 27, folder 3, box 2, Denver LWV papers.

123. Flyers attached to Annual Report 1968–69, folder 3, box 2, Denver LWV papers.

124. *Voter* newsletter, February 1975, p. 9, folder 8, box 2, Denver LWV papers.

125. Annual Report 1975, p. 7, folder 4, box 2, Denver LWV papers.

126. The Denver YWCA began to integrate its white, Central association with the city's African American branch in 1955. See board of directors meeting minutes, November 22, 1955, p. 1, folder 12, box 2, Denver Young Women's Christian Association papers, Library of the Colorado Historical Society, hereafter cited as Denver YWCA papers.

127. Board of directors meeting minutes, March 28, 1961, p. 3, folder 16, box 2, Denver YWCA papers. The Northeast YWCA opened in 1964. See Northeast Area Evaluation, July 31, 1964, folder 16, box 27, Denver YWCA papers.

128. Board of directors meeting minutes, September 26, 1961, p. 1, folder 16, box 2, Denver YWCA papers.

129. Adult Committee meeting minutes, January 15, 1965, p. 3, folder 1, box 21, Denver YWCA papers.

130. Board of directors meeting minutes, April 24, 1962, p. 4; board of directors meeting minutes, February 26, 1963, p. 3, both in folder 16, box 2, Denver YWCA papers.

131. See Interracial Integration Committee meeting minutes, March 15, 1955, p. 1, folder 6, box 22/23; Northeast Area Evaluation, July 31, 1964, pp. 2–3, folder 16, box 27, both in Denver YWCA papers.

132. Board of directors meeting minutes, November 26, 1968, p. 6, folder 28, box 3, Denver YWCA papers.

133. Board of directors meeting minutes, December 1, 1964, p. 1, folder 29, box 8, series VIII; board of directors meeting minutes, September 5, 1967, p. 2, folder 30, box 8, series VIII, both in AAUW of Denver papers, Special Collections Division, Auraria Library, University of Colorado–Denver, hereafter cited as AAUW of Denver papers.

134. AAUW newsletter, December 1973, p. 7, folder 1, box 6, series VIII, AAUW of Denver papers.

135. Special board of directors meeting minutes, July 2, 1968, p. 1, folder 12, box 8, series VIII, AAUW of Denver papers.

136. Board of directors meeting minutes, April 25, 1961, p. 2, folder 16, box 2, Denver YWCA papers.

137. Board of directors meeting minutes, April 23, 1963, pp. 2–3, folder 16, box 2, Denver YWCA papers.

138. Board of directors meeting minutes, May 28, 1963, p. 3, folder 16, box 2, Denver YWCA papers.

139. Board of directors meeting minutes, May 25, 1965, p. 4, folder 22, box 2, Denver YWCA papers.

140. Board of directors meeting minutes, March 29, 1966, p. 5, folder 22, box 2, Denver YWCA papers.

141. Board of directors meeting minutes, February 22, 1966, p. 1, folder 22, box 2, Denver YWCA papers. On the founding and purpose of WICS, see "27 Million Women Volunteer for War on Poverty," *Carolina Times*, January 23, 1965, p. 3B.

142. Adult Committee meeting minutes, March 12, 1965, p. 2, folder 1, box 21, Denver YWCA papers.

143. On the YWCA's assessment of what the women took away from these programs, see board of directors meeting minutes, May 25, 1965, p. 5, folder 2, box 2, Denver YWCA papers.

144. Board of directors meeting minutes, April 23, 1963, p. 1.

145. Barbara Stephenson, YWCA president, to Mrs. Paul Thompson, chair of legislative committee of Colorado Coordinating Council of Women's Organizations, January 8, 1965, p. 1, folder 3, box 26, Denver YWCA papers.

146. Board of directors meeting minutes, April 23, 1968, p. 3.

147. Board of directors meeting minutes, October 22, 1968, p. 5; board of directors meeting minutes, September 30, 1969, p. 2, both in folder 28, box 3, Denver YWCA papers.

148. The history of the NWRO is well documented in Nadasen, *Welfare Warriors.*

149. Annual Report 1965–66, p. 10, folder 2, box 2, Denver LWV papers.

150. Voters Services Annual Report 1967–68, pp. 1, 3, folder 2, box 2, Denver LWV papers.

151. Action Briefing, September 13, 1971, p. 4, folder 5, box 2, Denver LWV papers.

152. Ibid.

153. Briefing, November 15, 1969, p. 1, folder 4, box 1; program, LWV of Denver 1971–72, p. 1, folder 6, box 1, both in Denver LWV papers.

154. National Program Planning meeting minutes, December 6, 1971, p. 3, folder 6, box 1, Denver LWV papers.

155. Annual Report 1971, p. 12, folder 5, box 2, Denver LWV papers.

156. Action Briefing, September 13, 1971.

157. *Voter* newsletter, October 1971, p. 5, folder 8, box 2, Denver LWV papers.

158. Nadasen, *Welfare Warriors*, 126.

159. Chappell, "Rethinking Women's Politics," 159.

160. Despite encouragement to counter negative opinions, the League's welfare work at the national level in the early 1970s focused primarily on securing a guaranteed minimum income from the federal government, a goal most easily achieved by lobbying legislators. See Chappell, "Rethinking Women's Politics," 157, 163.

Chapter Two. Race and Feminism in a Southern City

1. Connie Winstead, e-mail correspondence with author, August 31, 2011.

2. Connie Winstead, oral history questionnaire, May 28, 2011, pp. 1–2.

3. Judith Ezekiel, a leading scholar of grassroots feminism, has argued that women undertaking feminist work in Dayton, Ohio, explicitly broke with liberal

groups such as the League of Women Voters in which they had previously been active. Ezekiel, *Feminism in the Heartland*, 37. See also Gilmore, "Dynamics of Second-Wave Feminist Activism." Gilmore's book *Groundswell* and Anne Enke's *Finding the Movement*, the other monographs besides Ezekiel's that explore nonradical grassroots feminism, consider local NOW chapters and feminist services and facilities such as bookstores and softball teams, respectively. All three books look exclusively at groups and services that identified explicitly as feminist. Enke, *Finding the Movement*; Gilmore, *Groundswell*.

4. Winstead, oral history, p. 2.

5. Gilna Nance, oral history, p. 1, June 1, 2011.

6. On the impact of the region's gender norms on southern suffragists, see Wheeler, *New Women of the New South*, 6–7; 72–73.

7. Cahn, *Sexual Reckonings*, 5, 10.

8. Gilmore, *Groundswell*, 46.

9. Higginbotham, *Righteous Discontent*, 186–87.

10. Ibid.; see also Cahn, *Sexual Reckonings*, 10; and White, *Too Heavy a Load*, 52–54.

11. Brown, *Upbuilding Black Durham*, 14.

12. Ibid., 20, 333–34.

13. See Greene, *Our Separate Ways*, chap. 7, on the role of this ideal in civil rights activism.

14. For example, "Some Children's Books Stereotype Sex Roles," *Carolina Times*, May 12, 1973, p. 4B.

15. On the centrality of gender in white southern identity in the twentieth century, see Cahn, *Sexual Reckonings*.

16. Robertson, *Christian Sisterhood*, 3.

17. This was a constant problem for the Indianapolis YWCA, as will be discussed in the next chapter. See Richard Fague, head of the United Fund, to Doris White, December 14, 1962, folder 4, box 3; and "Indianapolis YWCA Recommendations Passed by the Executive Committee," August 4, 1969, folder 9, box 2, both in Indianapolis YWCA papers.

18. "Agency Information Outline," June 25, 1962, p. 1, folder 5, box 22, Durham YWCA papers.

19. "Are You Satisfied to Be a Woman in Today's World?," attached to "1957 Who's Who of the Harriet Tubman YWCA," folder 5, box 33, Durham YWCA papers.

20. Although Joanne Meyerowitz discusses African American magazines such as *Ebony* featuring articles instructing women on how to be sexually appealing to their husbands, articles that could also be found in magazines geared to white audiences, she does not address whether *Ebony* and other black periodicals discussed the stifling nature of housewifery in the same way that magazines such as *Redbook* and *Ladies Home Journal* did. Since many more African American women worked outside the home, it is doubtful they would have done so, which

makes the Tubman branch's use of the survey even more intriguing. On *Ebony*'s exploration of "heterosexual appeal," see Meyerowitz, "Beyond the Feminine Mystique," 244.

21. The majority of the members profiled in the "Who's Who" to which the questionnaire was attached worked outside the home. "1957 Who's Who of the Harriet Tubman YWCA," folder 5, box 33, Durham YWCA papers.

22. YWCA of the U.S.A., "Sex Morality workbook," p. 1, folder 2, box 22, Durham YWCA papers.

23. For example, Branch Committee on Administration meeting minutes, May 9, 1967, p. 1, folder 14, box 34, Durham YWCA papers.

24. YWCA board of directors meeting minutes, October 26, 1967, p. 1, folder 9, box 34, Durham YWCA papers.

25. "Annual Report of Participation Statistics in the Community YWCA" for 1969–70, p. 19, folder 3, box 21, Durham YWCA papers.

26. Historian Sylvie Murray has argued that avoiding gender-specific or "maternalist" language was common for civic organizations in the post–World War II period, even when such organizations were made up largely or entirely of women. Murray, *Progressive Housewife*. Creating a way for women to be politically active that was not tied to their sex had been one of the driving goals of the LWV at its founding in the early 1920s and continued to resonate with its members.

27. Durham LWV board of directors minutes, May 10, 1966, p. 3, folder 26, box 1, Durham LWV papers.

28. Durham LWV board of directors meeting minutes, November 11, 1975, p. 1, folder 3, box 2, Durham LWV papers.

29. "Sorority Forms Service to Youth Project May 29," *Carolina Times*, June 5, 1965, p. 3A.

30. "Says 'Women Are the Builders of the Race,'" *Carolina Times*, April 9, 1966, p. 1B.

31. White, *Too Heavy a Load*, 196–203.

32. "National Housewives League in Session Here, July 14–18," *Carolina Times*, July 13, 1968, p. 1A; "Durham Links Celebrate Tenth Anniversary," *Carolina Times*, November 30, 1968, p. 8A.

33. "Mrs. Gail Bradley before the League of Women Voters of North Carolina," May 1973, folder 1, box 8, Winifred Gail Bradley Papers, David M. Rubenstein Rare Book and Manuscript Library, Duke University, hereafter cited as Gail Bradley papers.

34. See Gilna Nance, oral history, p. 2; and Connie Winstead, oral history, p. 2.

35. Mathews and de Hart, *Sex, Gender, and the Politics*, 111–18.

36. Gail Bradley to Nancy Brock and Jane Patterson, June 14, 1974, p. 2, folder 3, box 1, Gail Bradley papers.

37. PR Committee meeting minutes, May 1, 1974, folder 3, box 1, Gail Bradley papers, emphasis in original.

38. "Durham LWV Bulletin," March 1975, p. 4, folder 8, box 1, Durham LWV papers.

39. Durham LWV board of directors minutes, February 17, 1970, p. 3, folder 1, box 2, Durham LWV papers.

40. "Program for Action—1970–1973," p. 1, folder 3, box 22, Durham YWCA papers.

41. Muriel Smith, Program Director, to Dr. Rose Browne, YWCA president, July 1, 1971, p. 1, folder 18, box 11, Durham YWCA papers.

42. Report of the Association Review Committee, 1971, folder 18, box 11, Durham YWCA papers, emphasis in original.

43. Muriel Smith, Program Director, to Dr. Rose Browne, n.d. (ca. spring 1971), folder 18, box 11, Durham YWCA papers.

44. Ibid.; Program Committee Report, July 1, 1971, p. 2, folder 18, box 11, Durham YWCA papers.

45. Program Committee Report, July 1, 1971.

46. "Annual Report of Participation Statistics in the Community YWCA, 1971–1972," p. 19, folder 3, box 21, Durham YWCA papers.

47. Winstead, oral history, p. 1; YWCA board of directors meeting minutes, September 25, 1975, p. 2, folder 34, box 35, Durham YWCA papers.

48. Winstead, oral history, p. 1.

49. Ibid., pp. 1–2; Gilna Nance, oral history, June 1, 2011, p. 1.

50. Winstead, oral history, p. 1; Nance, oral history, p.1.

51. "Triangle Area Lesbian Feminists: An Introduction," folder 15, box 7, Durham YWCA papers. The Durham Women's Center was partially spun off from the YWCA in 1976; its activities after that date will be discussed in chapter 5.

52. Winstead, oral history, p. 2.

53. Nance, oral history, p. 2.

54. On the centrality of consciousness-raising as one's point of entry into the women's movement, see Evans, *Personal Politics*, 215; Douglas, *Where the Girls Are*, 169, 190; and Farrell, *Yours in Sisterhood*, 20, among others.

55. "Annual Report of Participation Statistics in the Community YWCA, 1972–1973," p. 20, folder 3, box 21, Durham YWCA papers.

56. "Women's Town Meeting Slated," *Carolina Times*, November 3, 1973, p. 4A.

57. These newspapers are held as a second accession of the Durham YWCA papers at Duke University. *New Carolina Woman*, folder 9, box 2; *Women's Rights Law Reporter*, folder 17, box 2; *Southern Feminist Connection*, folder 20, box 2; *Distaff*, folder 6, box 3, all in Durham YWCA papers, accession 91–128.

58. Ezekiel, *Feminism in the Heartland*, 26.

59. Board of directors meeting minutes, June 23, 1970, p. 2, folder 1, box 5, Indianapolis YWCA papers.

60. Muriel Smith to Dr. Rose Browne, July 1, 1971, p. 2, folder 18, box 11, Durham YWCA papers.

61. "Annual Report of Participation Statistics in the Community YWCA, 1972–1973," p. 21.

62. Gilmore, *Groundswell*, 50.

63. For more on African American women and feminism, see Roth, *Separate Roads to Feminism*; Springer, *Living for the Revolution*; Thompson, "Multiracial Feminism;" and Valk, *Radical Sisters*.

64. Geraldine Rickman, "Black Women: Race or Sex?," *Carolina Times*, November 16, 1974, p. 2A.

65. Gloria Rigsbee, "Pregnancy Planning and Health," *Carolina Times*, February 20, 1971, p. 3B.

66. Sara [Evans] Boyte, "Thoughts on the Purpose of Lollipop Power," 1970, folder 17, box 4, Boyte Family papers, Rare Books, Manuscripts, and Special Collections Library, Duke University.

67. Minutes, "Curriculum Committee: Thursday Night session," p. 1, folder 3, box 2331, series III, North Carolina AFL-CIO papers.

68. Curriculum Committee recommendations, p. 5, folder 9, box 2331, series III, North Carolina AFL-CIO papers.

69. Untitled clipping, *[Duke] Summer Chronicle*, July 23, 1971, p. 1, folder 8, box 2330, series III, North Carolina AFL-CIO papers.

70. "Some Children's Books Stereotype Sex Roles," *Carolina Times*, May 12, 1973, p. 4B.

71. NOW meeting minutes, December 3, 1973, p. 1, folder 1, box 1, Durham NOW papers, David M. Rubenstein Rare Book and Manuscripts Library, Duke University, hereafter cited as Durham NOW papers.

72. "Organization for Women Holds Meeting," *Carolina Times*, March 24, 1973, p. 5A.

73. Durham NOW newsletter, July 1973, p. 1, folder 5, box 4, Gail Bradley papers.

74. NOW meeting minutes, September 10, 1973, pp. 1–2, folder 1, box 1, Durham NOW papers.

75. NOW meeting minutes, September 9, 1975, folder 1, box 1, Durham NOW papers. Congress passed the Equal Credit Opportunity Act in 1974.

76. The last set of meeting minutes is from November 1975. Minutes, November 11, 1975, folder 1, box 1, Durham NOW papers.

77. Anderson, *Durham County*, 461.

78. Interview with Miriam Slifkin by Emily W. Madison, transcript, p. 15, October 17, 1994, November 6, 1994, and November 30, 1994, interview G-0150, in the Southern Oral History Program Collection 4007, Southern Historical Collection, Wilson Library, University of North Carolina at Chapel Hill.

79. Ibid., p. 16.

80. Ibid., p. 15.

81. On the coffeehouse, see YWCA Women's Center newsletter, April 1978, p. 1, folder 15, box 7, Durham YWCA papers.

82. On WEAL, see Rosen, *World Split Open*, 83, 89.

83. Report on Task Force Meeting with Jane Patterson, November 25, 1977, p. 3, folder 7, box 11, Gail Bradley papers.

84. "N.C. Coalition for Choice," WEAL newsletter, January 1979, p. 2, folder 7, box 11, Gail Bradley papers.

85. In addition to Bradley, the May 1977 membership roster shows former League presidents Sylvia Kerchoff and Ruth Mary Meyer, as well as former NOW member Amanda Smith. North Carolina WEAL membership list, May 1977, folder 7, box 11, Gail Bradley papers.

Chapter Three. Feminist Coalitions and the ERA

1. Lynn Schrum to "Dear Chapters," ca. spring 1974, p. 1, folder 2, box 2, Indiana NOW papers, William Henry Smith Memorial Library, Indiana Historical Society, hereafter cited as Indiana NOW papers. The letter's content as well as its location in the folder (between a memo dated "spring 1974" and another dated December 22, 1973) establish the fact that the letter was also written in the spring of 1974.

2. "Health," "IndiaNOWpolis Woman" newsletter, May 1974, p. 7, folder 1, box 2, "IndiaNOWpolis Woman" newsletter collection, William Henry Smith Memorial Library, Indiana Historical Society, hereafter cited as "IndiaNOWpolis Woman" collection.

3. "Rally for Right to Choose," Indianapolis NOW newsletter, April 1974, p. 1, folder 1, box 2, "IndiaNOWpolis Woman" collection.

4. Lynn Schrum to Paula Cole, December 22, 1973, p. 1, folder 2, box 2, Indiana NOW papers.

5. On HERA's dissolution, see Indiana Women's Political Caucus Policy Council meeting minutes, March 13, 1976, p. 1, folder 11, box 2, Indiana Women's Political Caucus papers, William Henry Smith Memorial Library, Indiana Historical Society, hereafter cited as IWPC papers.

6. HERA Policy Council meeting minutes, August 18, 1974, p. 2, folder 2, box 1, HERA papers.

7. "From Our ERA Coordinator," LWV Bulletin, August 1974, p. 9, folder 1, box 8, Indianapolis LWVpapers.

8. On the bridal fair picket, see "Bridal Fair Is Foul," Indianapolis NOW newsletter, March 1974, p. 1; on the bookstore, see "One Woman," Indianapolis NOW newsletter, July 1974, p. 7, both in folder 1, box 2, "IndiaNOWpolis Woman" collection.

9. "Image, Local," Indianapolis NOW newsletter, April 1974, p. 5, folder 1, box 2, "IndiaNOWpolis Woman" collection.

10. "Myra Ferris," IWL newsletter, March 1972, p. 6, folder 18, box 1, Indiana NOW papers.

11. "Conference," Indianapolis NOW newsletter, October 1974, p. 1, folder 1, box 2, "IndiaNOWpolis Woman" collection.

12. This is one of Stephanie Gilmore's central arguments in her recent book *Groundswell.*

13. "President's Message," September 1965 Bulletin, p. 2, folder 6, box 7, Indianapolis LWV papers.

14. Ibid.

15. "A Woman' Place Is . . ." League Bulletin, November 1967, p. 10, folder 7, box 7, Indianapolis LWV papers.

16. "Why Volunteer?," President's Message, Annual Report 1967, p. 3, folder 1, box 4, Indianapolis LWV papers.

17. Ibid., p. 4.

18. Flyer, "Women on the Move: A Forum on Employment," November 1966, folder 6, box 7, Indianapolis LWV papers.

19. This focus on employment was somewhat different from the NCJW's national leaders' vision of the "Women on the Move" program, which they saw primarily as a way to engage members with the problems of poor women. Chappell, *War on Welfare*, 33.

20. Flyer, "Women on the Move."

21. For the crime prevention work, see "Report of the Anti-Crime Crusade," 1962, p. 1, folder 3, box 3, Church Women United papers, William Henry Smith Memorial Library, Indiana Historical Society, hereafter cited as CWU papers; for the dropout program, see "Council to Consider School Drop-Outs and Other Problems," *Indiana Jewish Chronicle*, March 6, 1964, p. 1, folder 7, box 61, Indianapolis National Council of Jewish Women papers, Indiana Jewish Historical Society Collection, William Henry Smith Memorial Library, Indiana Historical Society, hereafter cited as Indianapolis NCJW papers.

22. Flyer, "Women on the Move."

23. Lorraine Nelson, "'Women on the Move' Forum Really Moves," *Indianapolis Star*, November 17, 1966, folder 7, box 61, Indianapolis NCJW papers.

24. 1965–66 Indianapolis NCJW Yearbook, p. 4, folder 4, box 60, Indianapolis NCJW papers.

25. Draft of Indianapolis NCJW History, 1974, p. 18, folder 8, box 61, Indianapolis NCJW papers.

26. Board of directors meeting minutes, March 23, 1965, p. 3, folder 7, box 2, Indianapolis YWCA papers.

27. "Women's Job Corps Pays Volunteers in Satisfaction," *Indianapolis Star*, May 9, 1965, p. 3, folder 7, box 61, Indianapolis NCJW papers.

28. Annual Report 1960–61, p. 9, folder 2, box 3, CWU papers.

29. Pamphlet, "Preparation for Christian Marriage," ca. 1966, p. 4, folder 9, box 3, CWU papers.

30. Weiss, *To Have and to Hold*, 116.

31. 1969 Yearbook, p. 16, folder 6, box 4, CWU papers.

32. Annual Report 1966, pp. 7–8, folder 9, box 3, CWU papers; Program for Mary McLeod Bethune memorial tea, April 25, 1971, folder 18, box 1, Indianapolis National Council of Negro Women papers, William Henry Smith Memorial Library, Indiana Historical Society.

33. List of denomination representatives, 1969, p. 8, folder 6, box 2, CWU papers; "Board of Directors 1963–64," p. 1, folder 6, box 2, Indianapolis YWCA papers.

34. "Assignment: Race," *Indiana Church Woman* newsletter, June 1962, p. 1, folder 4, box 3, CWU papers.

35. Indianapolis Churchwomen United Yearbook 1964, p. 22, folder 6, box 3, CWU papers.

36. *Indiana Church Woman,* January 1966, p. 3, folder 6, box 5, CWU papers.

37. The board of trustees was a group of businesspeople—predominantly men until the 1970s—who oversaw the YWCA's finances. The board of directors was an elected group of YWCA members and was therefore all women; it supervised the day-to-day operations of the organization. While League of Women Voters chapters and, in Indianapolis, Churchwomen United kept public offices, only the YWCAs owned entire buildings. Smaller groups like the AAUW and the NCJW generally did not maintain any facilities, instead keeping materials in officers' homes.

38. C. W. Long, United Fund Allocations, to Doris White, YWCA Executive Director, July 12, 1963, p. 2, folder 6, box 3, Indianapolis YWCA papers.

39. "Tentative Draft, Indianapolis YWCA," October 8, 1963, p. 3, folder 5, box 2, Indianapolis YWCA papers.

40. "This is the YWCA" (draft of speech for United Fund presentation), p. 1, folder 3, box 4, Indianapolis YWCA papers.

41. "Indianapolis YWCA Northeast Area Report, Sept. 1966–April 1967," p. 1, folder 2, box 6, Indianapolis YWCA papers.

42. "Indianapolis YWCA Northeast and Northwest Mothers' Morning Out Program Evaluation," 1965, p. 2, folder 1, box 4, Indianapolis YWCA papers.

43. Board of directors meeting minutes, March 23, 1965, pp. 2–3, folder 7, box 2, Indianapolis YWCA papers.

44. "We Appraise Ourselves" form, December 1, 1965, p. 5, folder 7, box 2, Indianapolis YWCA papers.

45. On African American women's role in the luncheons, see "Indianapolis YWCA Summary of Findings from March 1973 Action Audit Meetings," p. 3, folder 2, box 3, Indianapolis YWCA papers.

46. Program review of Breaking Barriers, June 17, 1969, p. 1, folder 3, box 6, Indianapolis YWCA papers.

47. "One Woman," Indianapolis NOW newsletter, July 1974.

48. In this context, I use "sustainable" to refer to the groups' stability as organizations. Both Indianapolis NOW and the Greater Indianapolis Women's Political Caucus remained in constant operation with fairly large memberships from their founding until at least the end of the 1970s; neither suffered the kind of stops and starts that marked the efforts of Durham NOW.

49. Radical women's groups functioned in this way in cities and towns throughout the country by occupying what historian Jo Freeman described as a "radical flank" that legitimated the claims of those activists who appeared less extreme in their demands. Freeman, *Politics of Women's Liberation*, 236.

50. See Echols, *Daring to Be Bad*, on radical feminism; and Rosen, *World Split Open*, chap. 3, on liberal feminism.

51. "From our ERA Coordinator," LWV Bulletin, August 1974.

52. In late 1974, the national Business and Professional Women's Club, one of the major pro-ERA organizations, considered Indiana as likely to ratify only if one more state was needed to pass the amendment. HERA Policy Council meeting minutes, December 14, 1974, p. 2, folder 2, box 1, HERA papers.

53. "Our History," YWCA website, http://www.ywca.org/site/pp.asp?c=djISI6PIKpG&b=281379, accessed Feb. 13, 2007.

54. "Association Review," September 20–21, 1972, pp. 3–5, 9, folder 1, box 3, Indianapolis YWCA papers.

55. Natalie Boehm, Doris Fletcher, and Jean Harr, "Indianapolis YWCA Summary of Findings from the March 1973 Action Audit Meetings" (draft), p. 1, folder 2, box 3, Indianapolis YWCA papers.

56. Ibid., p. 1.

57. Ibid., p. 2. While the suburban programs were called Mothers' Morning Out, the inner-city versions were referred to as Mothers' Clubs.

58. Boehm, Fletcher, and Harr, "Indianapolis YWCA Summary of Findings from Action Audit" (draft), p. 3.

59. Ibid., pp. 2, 4–5.

60. Ibid., p. 4.

61. "Indianapolis YWCA: Summary of Findings from Action Audit," p. 2, folder 2, box 3, Indianapolis YWCA papers.

62. Ibid., p. 3, emphasis in original.

63. Ibid., p. 2.

64. Indianapolis YWCA Program Report, 1971–72, June 22, 1972, p. 2, folder 1, box 3, Indianapolis YWCA papers.

65. Board of directors meeting minutes, February 22, 1972, p. 1, folder 1, box 3, Indianapolis YWCA papers.

66. Board of directors meeting minutes, March 28, 1972, p. 3, folder 1, box 3, Indianapolis YWCA papers.

67. Board of directors meeting minutes, November 26, 1974, p. 1, folder 3, box 3, Indianapolis YWCA papers.

68. "The YWCA of Indianapolis: Active in Today's World," p. 1, folder 5, box 5, Indianapolis YWCA papers.

69. "The YWCA of Indianapolis: A Look at the Future," p. 1, folder 5, box 5, Indianapolis YWCA.

70. See Deutsch, *Women and the City*; and Muncy, *Creating a Female Dominion*, among many others.

71. Pat Ulen and Betty Williams were both on the boards of the League and the YWCA in the early 1970s and served successive terms as YWCA presidents from 1972 to 1974. It was during their tenures that the YWCA wrote letters on the amendment's behalf. See, for example, YWCA board of directors meeting minutes, December 12, 1972, p. 3, folder 1, box 3, Indianapolis YWCA papers.

72. "Indianapolis YWCA Recommendations from Program Planning Committee, 1974–75," p. 6, folder 3, box 3, Indianapolis YWCA papers.

73. Donna Langfitt, "We Could Strike but There Is So Much to Do," LWV Bulletin, September 1970, p. 2, folder 9, box 7, Indianapolis LWV papers.

74. Ibid., p. 2

75. Legislative letter, February 1971, p. 3, folder 10, box 7, Indianapolis LWV papers.

76. Board of directors meeting minutes, March 3, 1971, p. 3, folder 1, box 3, Indianapolis LWV papers.

77. Board of directors meeting minutes, December 1, 1971, p. 4, folder 1, box 3, Indianapolis LWV papers.

78. Betty Williams, "President's Letter," LWV Bulletin, April 1972, p. 2, folder 11, box 7, Indianapolis LWV papers.

79. In the middle years of the decade, the group ran a "Let's Get Acquainted" column in the bulletin that featured short biographical sketches of new members. Every month at least one woman profiled had been drawn into the League through ERA work. See, for example, "Let's Get Acquainted," LWV Bulletin, May 1975, p. 4, folder 2, box 8, Indianapolis LWV papers.

80. "From the President's Desk," LWV Bulletin, November 1975, p. 4, folder 2, box 8, Indianapolis LWV papers.

81. Board of directors meeting minutes, September 5, 1973, p. 3, folder 2, box 3, Indianapolis LWV papers.

82. "From Our ERA Coordinator," LWV Bulletin, August 1974.

83. "Issues Workshop," LWV Bulletin, October 1974, p. 12, folder 1, box 8, Indianapolis LWV papers.

84. Flyer, "Libraries, Literature, and the Law," p. 1, folder 2, box 8, Indianapolis LWV papers.

85. "On Our Way Together," national program 1972, pp. 5–6, folder 7, box 2, CWU papers. On these developments within the national CWU office, see Hartmann, *Other Feminists*, chap. 4.

86. "New Generations Project," announcement, fall 1971, p. 1, folder 11, box 3, CWU papers.

87. "Editor's Needlepoint," Indianapolis CWU newsletter, October 1973, p. 2, folder 11, box 5, CWU papers.

88. Program, Forty-Fourth Missionary Education Institute, June 4, 1973, p. 2, folder 10, box 7, CWU papers.

89. Minutes, November 7, 1963, pp. 1–2, folder 2, box 1, Indianapolis Fortnightly Club papers, William Henry Smith Memorial Library, Indiana Historical Society, hereafter cited as Fortnightly Club papers.

90. Minutes, November 8, 1968, p. 1, folder 2, box 1, Fortnightly Club papers.

91. Minutes, November 12, 1969, p. 2, folder 2, box 1, Fortnightly Club papers.

92. Minutes, May 6, 1971, p. 1; October 7, 1971, pp. 1–2; November 11, 1971, p. 2, all in folder 2, box 1, Fortnightly Club papers.

93. Minutes, April 6, 1972, p. 2; February 1, 1973, pp. 1–2, both in folder 2, box 1, Fortnightly Club papers.

94. HERA Policy Council meeting, December 14, 1974, p. 1.

95. Excerpts from speech by Meg Mallory, October 27, 1974, p. 1, folder 13, box 1, HERA papers.

96. "Richard Lugar: A Star Library Biography," http://www2.indystar.com/library/factfiles/people/l/lugar_richard/lugar.html, accessed April 23, 2008.

97. One of Butters's first feminist articles, published on Mothers' Day 1970, was credited by Indianapolis Women's Liberation with greatly increasing its membership. See Karin Ohrn, "Women's Lib," *Indianapolis Free Press*, May 28, 1970, p. 2, reel 38, Underground Newspaper Collection, University of Virginia. On Butters's partisan affiliation, see Mayor's Commission on the Status of Women members (draft), n.d., p. 1, folder 18, box 1, IWPC papers.

98. "Image, Local," Indianapolis NOW newsletter, April 1974.

99. "Editor's Needlepoint," Indianapolis CWU newsletter, October 1973, p. 2, folder 11, box 5, CWU papers; board of directors meeting minutes, September 5, 1973, p. 3, folder 2, box 3, Indianapolis LWV papers.

100. HERAPolicy Council meeting minutes, January 12, 1975, p. 2, folder 3, box 1, HERA papers.

101. "Memorandum re: Indiana Women's Political Caucus," October 12, 1971, p. 2, folder 1, box 2, IWPC papers.

102. Rymph, *Republican Women*, 189–90.

103. Karin Ohrn, "Women's Lib," *Indianapolis Free Press*, May 28, 1970, p. 2, reel 38, Underground Newspaper Collection.

104. "Liberation and Amber Mist," *Indianapolis Free Press*, September 1, 1970, p. 15, reel 38, Underground Newspaper Collection.

105. Ibid.

106. There is no collection of IWL papers. The only surviving papers of the group are part of the Indiana NOW collection, corroborating my claim that IWL was absorbed by Indianapolis NOW sometime in 1973.

107. IWL Newsletter, April 1971, p. 4, folder 18, box 1, Indiana NOW papers.

108. Ibid., p. 9. Welfare reform was a frequent topic in the pages of the *Indianapolis Free Press.* Stories there reveal an active Indianapolis Welfare Rights Organization that held major actions, including hosting national WRO president George Wiley at a January 1971 rally. "Welfare Rights Action Day," *Indianapolis Free Press*, January 25, 1971, p. 3, reel 301, Underground Newspaper Collection.

109. IWL Newsletter, April 1971.

110. IWL newsletter, March 1972, p. 6, folder 18, box 1, Indiana NOW papers.

111. Ibid., pp. 2, 8.

112. On the "schism" that lesbianism caused within the Washington, D.C., feminist community, for example, see Evans, *Tidal Wave*, 102–4. On how that city's leading lesbian feminist groups, the Furies, saw their distinct role in the women's movement, see Valk, *Radical Sisters*, chap. 6.

113. Clipping, "Movement Given Substantial Support," *Indianapolis Star*, January 2, 1972, p. 1, in folder 1, box 4, IWPC papers.

114. Norma Card to Kathy Rand, July 2, 1972, p. 1, folder 17, box 1, Indiana NOW papers.

115. Betty Newcomb to national NOW office, April 3, 1972, folder 16, box 1, Indiana NOW papers; "August 26, Women's Day," Indianapolis NOW newsletter, August 1972, p. 2, folder 17, box 1, Indiana NOW papers.

116. See Echols, *Daring to Be Bad*; and Rosen, *World Split Open*, among many others.

117. "NOW President Discusses Rights," *Indianapolis News*, March 28, 1972, folder 17, box 1, Indiana NOW papers.

118. Betty Newcomb, state NOW coordinator, to "Dear NOW member," July 27, 1972, p. 4, folder 16, box 1, Indiana NOW papers.

119. IWL Newsletter, April 1971; IWL newsletter, March 1972, pp. 2, 6, both in folder 18, box 1, Indiana NOW papers.

120. "Indiana Civil Rights Commission Public Inquiry on Problems of Discrimination Based on Sex," November 14, 1972, p. 3, folder 17, box 1, Indiana NOW papers.

121. Card to Rand, July 2, 1972.

122. "Chapter Stuff," Indianapolis NOW newsletter, July 1974, p. 2, folder 1, box 2, "IndiaNOWpolis Woman" collection.

123. Indianapolis NOW newsletter, September 1974, p. 4, folder 1, box 2, "IndiaNOWpolis Woman" collection.

124. "Image, Local," Indianapolis NOW newsletter, April 1974.

125. "Health," Indianapolis NOW newsletter, February 1974, p. 5; "Health," Indianapolis NOW newsletter, May 1974, p. 7, both in folder 1, box 2, "IndiaNOWpolis Woman" collection.

126. "Bridal Fair Is Foul," Indianapolis NOW newsletter, March 1974. "The Politics of Housework" had also appeared in the *Indianapolis Free Press* in July 1970. "Politics of Housework," *Indianapolis Free Press*, July 9, 1970, p. 14, reel 38, Underground Newspaper Collection.

127. Card to Rand, July 2, 1972.

128. "Taking Action: Credit," Indianapolis NOW newsletter, January 1974, p. 4, folder 1, box 2, "IndiaNOWpolis Woman" collection.

129. "Priorities Picked," Indianapolis NOW newsletter, September 1974, p. 1, folder 1, box 2, "IndiaNOWpolis Woman" collection.

130. "Success!," Indianapolis NOW newsletter, October 1974, p. 3, folder 1, box 2, "IndiaNOWpolis Woman" collection.

131. "Employment," Indianapolis NOW newsletter, December 1974, p. 6; "Employment Task Force Report," Indianapolis NOW newsletter, October 1974, p. 3, both in folder 1, box 2, "IndiaNOWpolis Woman" collection.

132. Indianapolis NOW newsletter, December 1974, p. 3, folder 1, box 2, "IndiaNOWpolis Woman" collection.

133. "Conference," Indianapolis NOW newsletter, October 1974.

134. Schrum to "Dear Chapters," ca. spring 1974.

135. Ibid.

136. "First Priority: ERA," Indianapolis NOW newsletter, January 1975, p. 3, folder 2, box 2, "IndiaNOWpolis Woman" collection.

137. "Work on Sex," Indianapolis NOW newsletter, July 1975, p. 4, folder 2, box 2, "IndiaNOWpolis Woman" collection; "Fragments," Indianapolis NOW newsletter, December 1975, p. 2, folder 2, box 2, "IndiaNOWpolis Woman" collection.

138. "Fragments," Indianapolis NOW newsletter, December 1975, p. 2, folder 2, box 2, "IndiaNOWpolis Woman" collection.

139. On "Alice Doesn't Day," see Rosen, *World Split Open*, xxvii.

140. "Alice Doesn't," Indianapolis NOW newsletter, November 1975, p. 4, folder 2, box 2, "IndiaNOWpolis Woman" collection; Pat Persinger to Gene McPherson, October 30, 1975, p. 1, folder 1, box 2, Indiana NOW papers.

141. "Not Now, Later," Indianapolis NOW newsletter, June 1975, p. 1, folder 2, box 2, "IndiaNOWpolis Woman" collection.

142. Freeman, *Politics of Women's Liberation*, 161.

143. Memo, November 22, 1971, folder 1, box 1, IWPC papers.

144. Memorandum re: Indiana Women's Political Caucus, October 12, 1971, p. 1, folder 1, box 2, IWPC papers.

145. "Some Recommended Goals and Program Areas," March 6, 1972, p. 1–2, folder 7, box 1, IWPC papers.

146. "Conference on Changing Roles Planned," GIWPC newsletter, October 1973, p. 4, folder 26, box 1, IWPC papers.

147. Julia Carson to Virginia Dill McCarthy and Helen Pavicich, November 24, 1973, p. 1, folder 1, box 1, IWPC papers.

148. On the lack of a women's center, see untitled, unsigned document ("In February of this Bicentennial year . . .") 1976, p. 1, folder 8, box 5, Indiana NOW papers.

149. LWV Bulletin, October 1972, p. 1, folder 11, box 7, Indianapolis LWV papers.

150. "The Equal Rights Amendment: What Is It?," LWV Bulletin, October 1972, p. 8, folder 11, box 7, Indianapolis LWV papers.

151. Ibid.

152. "ERA Not Home Free Yet!," LWV Bulletin, March 1973, p. 9, folder 12, box 7, Indianapolis LWV papers.

153. An article in the LWV bulletin noted that the League was one of "at least twelve" women's organizations working on the amendment's behalf in 1973 but did not list the other groups. Ibid.

154. "Lobbying on Capitol Hill at This Time in Our History," pp. 5–6, folder 12, box 7, Indianapolis LWV papers.

155. "Betty's By-Line," LWV Bulletin, February 1973, p. 2, folder 12, box 7, Indianapolis LWV papers.

156. Williams' leadership may also have troubled some members. While she was a longtime League member (joining the Indianapolis chapter in 1964), she was also

a committed feminist. In the 1970s, she volunteered with a battered women's shelter in Indianapolis, and beginning in 1980 she spent a decade as a paid lobbyist for Planned Parenthood. While other League leaders were equally fervent supporters of the ERA, none of the others I interviewed were as deeply engaged with such a range of feminist issues outside the confines of the LWV. Betty Williams oral history questionnaire, June 8, 2011, p. 1.

157. "Equal Rights Amendment," LWV Bulletin, October 1973, p. 7, folder 12, box 7, Indianapolis LWV papers.

158. HERA Policy Council meeting minutes, June 30, 1974, folder 2, box 1, HERA papers.

159. HERA Policy Council memo, October 17, 1973, p. 1, folder 2, box 1, HERA papers.

160. HERA Policy Council memo, November 2, 1973, p. 1, folder 2, box 1, HERA papers.

161. Ibid.

162. Lynn Schrum to Paula Coale, December 22, 1973, p. 1, folder 2, box 2, Indiana NOW papers.

163. Schrum to "Dear Chapters," ca. spring 1974.

164. "Rally for the Right to Choose," Indianapolis NOW newsletter.

165. Scroggins, "Organizing on Their Own Terms," 46; Clipping, "Hoosiers in Profile: Virginia Dill McCarthy," *Indianapolis Star Magazine*, April 9, 1972, in folder 2, box 4, IWPC papers.

166. HERA Policy Council meeting minutes, June 30, 1974.

167. HERA Policy Council meeting minutes, August 18, 1974. The group had distributed a questionnaire to the membership at its June meeting, and it was from those results that it determined women's lib was a turnoff.

168. Audra Bailey to "Dear Indiana Legislator," November 21, 1974, p. 1, folder 2, box 1, HERA papers.

169. Ibid.

170. List of HERA Organizations, November 1975, folder 5, box 1, HERA papers.

171. "Special Newsletter and Call to the HERA Policy Council Meeting," January 6, 1975, p. 1, folder 3, box 1, HERA papers.

172. LWV Annual Report 1974–1975, p. 2, folder 5, box 4, Indianapolis LWV papers.

173. Collection Guide, Audra Sydney Bailey Papers, William Henry Smith Memorial Library, Indiana Historical Society.

174. Audra Bailey to Nominating Committee and Policy Council, April 12, 1975, p. 1, folder 3, box 1, HERA papers.

175. Virginia Dill McCarthy to Sen. Philip E. Gutman, February 14, 1975, p. 2, folder 11, box 1, HERA papers.

176. Mrs. Lewis (Betsy) Lurie, LWV president, to Sen. Philip E. Gutman, February 17, 1975, p. 1, folder 10, box 5, Indianapolis LWV papers.

177. Audra Bailey to Senators, April 9, 1975, p. 1, folder 4, box 1, HERA papers.

178. IWPC Policy Council meeting minutes, March 13, 1976.

179. Ibid.

180. Agenda for ERA Indiana meeting, November 18, 1976, p. 1, folder 8, box 6, IWPC papers.

181. ERA Steering Committee meeting minutes, November 18, 1976, p. 1; ERA Indiana Steering Committee meeting minutes, November 30, 1976, p. 1, both in folder 8, box 6, IWPC papers.

182. Ticket stub, "ERA Indiana Presents a Reception with Maureen Reagan," January 10, 1977, folder 11, box 6, IWPC papers.

183. "ERA Vigil Fact Sheet," p. 1, folder 11, box 6, IWPC papers, emphasis in original. See also Carole McKee, Indiana NOW ERA rally coordinator to "all supporters," December 2, 1976, pp. 1–2, folder 10, box 6, IWPC papers.

184. See Kathleen Ross to Molly Rucker, January 19, 1977, folder 11, box 6, IWPC papers.

185. Ruth Adams, campaign director, ERA Indiana, to "Unratified States," January 21, 1977, p. 1, folder 3, box 97, ERAmerica papers, Manuscript Division, Library of Congress, hereafter cited as ERAmerica papers.

Chapter Four. "Not by Tearing Down"

1. Meeting minutes, January 23, 1968, pp. 2–3, folder 30, box 2, Denver Fortnightly Club papers.

2. "Association Review Report," April 8, 1975, p. 2, folder 11, box 30, Denver YWCA papers.

3. Meeting minutes, March 16, 1966, p. 2, folder 27, box 2, Denver Fortnightly Club papers.

4. On feminist women in the leadership of the national Republican Party in the 1970s, see Rymph, *Republican Women*, chap. 7.

5. Barasko, *Governing NOW*, chapter four.

6. Freeman, *Room at a Time*, 22, 49.

7. Edwards, *Angels in the Machinery*, 105.

8. "Colorado Legislators Past and Present," http://www.state.co.us/gov_dir/leg_dir/lcsstaff/StaffInfo/LegislatorBiography.html, accessed March 10, 2008.

9. In 1967 only 4 percent of all state legislators nationwide were women. That same year Colorado had five women out of 102 legislators, meaning nearly 5 percent of its legislators were women. Richardson and Freeman, "Gender Differences in Constituency Service," 169; "Colorado Legislators Past and Present."

10. "House of Representatives by Year," http://www.leg.state.co.us/lcs/leghist.nsf?OpenDatabase, accessed March 10, 2008.

11. Mathews and de Hart, *Sex, Gender, and the Politics*, 57–62.

12. Ibid., 54.

13. Abbott, Leonard, and McComb, *Colorado*, 301.

14. Ibid., 314. On other post–World War II western boom towns that exhibited similar trends, such as Dallas and Seattle, see Carl Abbott, "The Metropolitan Re-

gion: Western Cities in the New Urban Era," in Nash and Etulian, *Twentieth Century West*, 87.

15. Abbott, Leonard, and McComb, *Colorado*, 316, 374. Love served very little of his third term because he resigned the governorship to become the "energy czar" in the Nixon administration. Ibid., 374.

16. On the persistence of individualism as an influential western ideal, see Etulian, "Prologue: The Twentieth Century West," in Nash and Etulian, *Twentieth Century West*, 25.

17. Colorado was first by only a few months; California liberalized its abortion laws in a similar way in June 1967. See Luker, *Abortion*, 87–91.

18. "Colorado Abortion Law Moves toward Passage," *Washington Post*, April 8, 1967, p. A2; Lisa Rykman, "Ground Zero on Abortion," *Rocky Mountain News*, April 24, 2007.

19. Fred Brown, "House Panel Hears Abortion Bill Views," *Denver Post*, March 10, 1967, p. 1.

20. "Abortion Mecca Predicted," *Denver Post*, March 10, 1967, p. 3.

21. Brown, "House Panel Hears Abortion Bill."

22. Leonard Larsen, "House Okays Abortion Bill's Final Version," *Denver Post*, April 9, 1967, p. 1.

23. Rymph, *Republican Women*, 189.

24. Ibid., 190. On Republican support of the ERA in the 1940s and 1950s, see Rupp and Taylor, *Survival in the Doldrums*, 59–64; and Harrison, *On Account of Sex*, chap. 2.

25. Rymph, *Republican Women*, chap. 7; Freeman, *Room at a Time*, ix.

26. "Colorado State Archives," http://www.colorado.gov/dpa/doit/archives/cap/blue.html, accessed March 10, 2008. In the wake of the President's Commission on the Status of Women called by President Kennedy, every state had such a commission—most one-time investigations of state law—at some point in the 1960s. Harrison, *On Account of Sex*, 172–73.

27. CCSW meeting minutes, April 24, 1976, p. 2, folder 11, box 3, Commissions on the Status of Women collection, Arthur and Elizabeth Schlesinger Library, Radcliffe Institute, Harvard University, hereafter cited as Commissions on the Status of Women collection.

28. "Women's Resource Center History," http://www.womens-resource.org/text/history.html, accessed February 22, 2008.

29. CCSW meeting minutes, April 24, 1976, pp. 4–6.

30. "Colorado Legislators Past and Present." Of the nine women elected to the Colorado legislature for the first time in 1974, seven were Democrats. It is impossible to disaggregate the reasons for this substantial Democratic swing, as Watergate, the women's movement, and other factors all played a part.

31. Mathews and de Hart, *Sex, Gender, and the Politics*, 167–68.

32. Board of directors meeting minutes, May 24, 1960, p. 1, folder 14, box 2, Denver YWCA papers.

33. Board of directors meeting minutes, October 25, 1960, p. 3, folder 16, box 2, Denver YWCA papers.

34. Young Adult Committee meeting minutes, April 20, 1960, p. 1, folder 1, box 21, Denver YWCA papers.

35. Young Adult Committee meeting minutes, May 8, 1964, p. 2, folder 1, box 21, Denver YWCA papers.

36. Board of directors meeting minutes, October 25, 1960, p. 1.

37. Board of directors meeting minutes, April 23, 1963, folder 16, box 2, Denver YWCA papers.

38. YWCA of America Sex Morality workbook, p. 1, folder 2, box 22, Durham YWCA papers.

39. Young Adult Committee meeting minutes, December 11, 1964, p. 2, folder 1, box 21, Denver YWCA papers. The Young Adult Committee designed programs for women under the age of forty.

40. Board of directors meeting minutes, November 22, 1996, p. 3, folder 22, box 2, Denver YWCA papers.

41. Board of directors meeting minutes, April 18, 1967, p. 1, folder 22, box 2, Denver YWCA papers.

42. By 1970 the national organization supported the repeal of abortion laws, but there was no national policy at this early date. The minutes of the Denver YWCA's discussion on the issue does not make its position clear. "Questions and Answers about Abortion," December 31, 1970, folder 35, box 4, Denver YWCA papers.

43. "AAUW of Denver Branch History, 1898–1973," p. 3, folder 18, box 5, series VIII; board of directors meeting minutes, February 12, 1957, p. 2, folder 23, box 8, series VIII, both in AAUW of Denver papers.

44. Board of directors meeting minutes, February 14, 1956, p. 2; board of directors meeting minutes, May 8, 1956, p. 2, both in folder 22, box 8, series VIII, AAUW of Denver papers.

45. Board of directors meeting minutes, August 14, 1956, p. 2, folder 23, box 8, series VIII, AAUW of Denver papers.

46. Board of directors meeting minutes, December 10, 1957, pp. 2–3, folder 24, box 8, series VIII, AAUW of Denver papers. The chapter's Status of Women committee also examined how women's changing roles affected the AAUW and conducted a "volunteerism survey" in 1965. Board of directors meeting minutes, August 3, 1965, p. 2, folder 29, box 8, series VIII, AAUW of Denver papers.

47. For example, "President's Message," September 1965 Bulletin, p. 2, folder 6, box 7, Indianapolis LWV papers; "A Woman's Place Is . . . ," League Bulletin, November 1967, p. 10, folder 7, box 7, Indianapolis LWV papers.

48. Annual Report 1965–66, p. 10, folder 2, box 2, Denver LWV papers.

49. Annual Report 1963–64, p. 3; public relations questionnaire, Annual Report 1967–68, p. 1, both in folder 2, box 2, Denver LWV papers.

50. Annual Report 1966–67, p. 2, folder 2, box 2, Denver LWV papers.

51. *Voter* newsletter, October 1966, p. 3, folder 8, box 2, Denver LWV papers.

52. Annual Report of Young Adult Committee, 1964–65, p. 1, folder 1, box 21, Denver YWCA papers. That same year, only 159 people took classes at the YWCA; YWCA Wives was by far the largest program the organization offered.

53. Board of directors meeting minutes, October 25, 1966, p. 3.

54. Board of directors meeting minutes, September 22, 1970, p. 4, folder 28, box 3, Denver YWCA papers.

55. Board of directors meeting minutes, February 28, 1967, p. 2, folder 22, box 2, Denver YWCA papers.

56. Board of directors meeting minutes, April 18, 1967; board of directors meeting minutes, October 26, 1971, p. 3, folder 28, box 3, both in Denver YWCA papers.

57. Special board of directors meeting minutes, June 15, 1970, p. 2, folder 28, box 3, Denver YWCA papers.

58. Fiftieth Anniversary of the Denver League of Women Voters, p. 1, folder 7, box 2, Denver LWV papers.

59. "Schomp, a Denver Jewel," *Denver Post*, November 24, 2000, p. B6.

60. "Women's Resource Center," Denver NOW newsletter, May 1976, p. 12, folder 23, carton 3, NOW chapter newsletter collection, Arthur and Elizabeth Schlesinger Library, Radcliffe Institute, Harvard University, hereafter cited as NOW chapter newsletter collection.

61. *Voter* newsletter, March 1972, p. 4, folder 8, box 2, Denver LWV papers.

62. "Vocal Point" newsletter, fall 1972, p. 1, folder 7, box 37, Denver YWCA papers.

63. "Legislature Okays Rights Amendment," *Denver Post*, April 25, 1972, p. 10; voter services briefing, September 19, 1972, p. 3, folder 7, box 1, Denver LWV papers.

64. See the YWCA's report on this organizational meeting, board of directors meeting minutes, January 26, 1971, p. 3, folder 28, box 3, Denver YWCA papers.

65. Participating organizations included the YWCA, the AAUW and the Denver Business and Professional Women's Club. See board of directors meeting minutes, October 26, 1971, Denver YWCA papers; board of directors meeting minutes, June 1, 1971, p. 1, folder 14, box 8, series VIII, AAUW papers; and BPW Newsletter 1971–72, p. 18, "Clipping File, Denver Societies and Clubs, Business and Professional Women's Club," Western History and Genealogy Division, Denver Public Library.

66. On NOW's work, see Denver NOW newsletter April 1971, p. 4; and Denver NOW newsletter, May 1972, p. 7, both in folder 23, carton 3, NOW chapter newsletter collection.

67. "Opening Up New Woman Power for a New Era by Opening Windows on Day Care," p. 1, folder 3, box 3, National Council of Jewish Women papers, Peryl H. and Ira M. Beck Memorial Archives, Penrose Library, University of Denver.

68. Board of directors meeting minutes, December 1, 1970, p. 1, folder 14, box 8, series VIII, AAUW of Denver papers.

69. Board of directors meeting minutes, February 2, 1971, p. 2, folder 14, box 8, series VIII, AAUW of Denver papers.

70. Board of directors meeting minutes, November 6, 1973, p. 2, folder 1, box 6, series VIII, AAUW of Denver papers.

71. Board of directors meeting minutes, October 2, 1973, pp. 1–2, folder 1, box 6, series VIII, AAUW of Denver papers. The AAUW president attended one of the first interest meetings for NOW, in August 1970, but there is no other mention of NOW in the AAUW papers until this call for cooperation in 1973. Board of directors meeting minutes, August 4, 1970, p. 2, folder 14, box 8, series VIII, AAUW of Denver papers.

72. "Spirit of Denver '76" Brach Program for 1975–76, p. 1, folder 30, box 7, series VIII, AAUW of Denver papers.

73. Flyer, "A New YWCA Offering: Timely! Vital!," January 29, 1970, folder 35, box 4, Denver YWCA papers. See also the winter 1971 program bulletin, folder 2, box 28, Denver YWCA papers.

74. Board of directors meeting minutes, April 27, 1971, p. 2, folder 28, box 3, Denver YWCA papers.

75. Board of directors meeting minutes, January 26, 1971, p. 2.

76. On other liberal religious organizations' support of abortion reform, see Luker, *Abortion*, 82–83.

77. 1975 Budget (drafted July 1974), p. 3, folder 35, box 4, Denver YWCA papers. The budget notes that the YWCA was reducing the clinic's rent, indicating that it was already in operation when the budget was drafted.

78. Denver NOW newsletter, March 1975, p. 8, folder 23, carton 3, NOW chapter newsletter collection.

79. Brochure on Better Jobs for Women, p. 3, folder 15, box 30, Denver YWCA papers.

80. Refunding Proposal for Better Jobs for Women, March 26, 1974, pp. 1–2, folder 35, box 4, Denver YWCA papers.

81. English and Spanish brochure, "Better Jobs for Women," p. 4, folder 15, box 30, Denver YWCA papers.

82. "Association Review Report," April 8, 1975.

83. Alex Habenicht, "Volunteers and Volunteering," February 1974, p. 1, folder 35, box 4, Denver YWCA papers.

84. Judy Schuenmeyer, "Report of the National Youth Conference," *Voter* newsletter, November 1969, p. 4, folder 8, box 2, Denver LWV papers.

85. President's letter, *Voter* newsletter, May 1970, pp. 1–2, folder 8, box 2, Denver LWV papers.

86. "Decisions Made at Annual Meeting," *Voter* newsletter, April 1971, p. 3, folder 8, box 2, Denver LWV papers.

87. President's letter, *Voter* newsletter, June 1971, p. 1, folder 8, box 2, Denver LWV papers.

88. "State Convention Report," *Voter* newsletter, June 1971, p. 5, folder 8, box 2, Denver LWV papers.

89. Cynthia Hayes, legislative wrap-up memo, June 1972, p. 2, folder 6, box 1, Denver LWV papers.

90. Minutes of program chairmen orientation meeting, May 10, 1971, p. 2, folder 5, box 2, Denver LWV papers.

91. Action briefing, September 13, 1971, p. 1, folder 5, box 2, Denver LWV papers.

92. *Voter* newsletter, September 1971, p. 4, folder 8, box 2, Denver LWV papers.

93. *Voter* newsletter, April 1972, p. 6, folder 8, box 2, Denver LWV papers. The National Women's Political Caucus was founded in 1971 by several prominent feminists including Gloria Steinem and Bella Abzug. Evans, *Tidal Wave*, 70–76.

94. *Voter* newsletter, March 1972, p. 4, folder 8, box 2, Denver LWV papers.

95. Ibid.

96. Clipping, "Modern Black Woman Is Topic," *Denver Post*, July 28, 1971, folder 29, box 1, Colorado Association of Colored Women's Clubs papers, Western History and Genealogy Division, Denver Public Library, hereafter cited as CACWC papers.

97. Eunice Norris, "Today's Black Woman and What She Desires," p. 1, folder 88, box 1, CACWC papers.

98. Sohndra Reid Edmonds, "Today's Black Woman and What She Desires," p. 1, folder 88, box 1, CACWC papers.

99. Lucy Margaret Walker, "Today's Black Woman and What She Desires," p. 2, folder 88, box 1, CACWC papers.

100. Renee Cousins, "Today's Black Woman and What She Desires," p. 2, folder 88, box 1, CACWC papers.

101. Rosalyn Y. Wheeler, "Today's Black Woman and What She Desires," pp. 1–2, folder 88, box 1, CACWC papers.

102. Interracial Integration Committee meeting minutes, March 15, 1955, p. 1, folder 6, box 22/23; "Study of the Place of the Welton Branch within the Denver YWCA," 1955, pp. 15–16, folder 7, box 22/23, Denver YWCA papers.

103. Branch Committee on Administration meeting minutes, June 10, 1958, p. 2, folder 6, box 24, Denver YWCA papers.

104. Program Planning Committee report, April 23, 1957, p. 1, folder 9, box 22/23, Denver YWCA papers.

105. Northeast area evaluation, July 31, 1964, pp. 2–3, folder 16, box 27, Denver YWCA papers.

106. "Our History," YWCA website, http://www.ywca.org/site/pp.asp?c=djISI6PIKpG&b=281379.

107. "Presentation to Be Made to the Board," October 1969, p. 1, folder 8, box 28, Denver YWCA papers, emphasis in original.

108. Minutes of the annual meeting, May 2, 1970, pp. 2–3, folder 2, box 21, Denver YWCA papers.

109. Board of directors meeting minutes, September 28, 1971, p. 1, folder 28, box 3, Denver YWCA papers. For more on the conference, see Roth, *Separate Roads to Feminism*, 145–49.

110. Agenda for Mexican-American Women's Conference, p. 1, folder 9, box 28, Denver YWCA papers.

111. Board of directors meeting minutes, May 25, 1971, p. 3, folder 28, box 3, Denver YWCA papers.

112. Board of directors meeting minutes, October 27, 1970, p. 1, folder 28, box 3,

Denver YWCA papers; meeting of Executive Committee, October 16, 1975, p. 1, folder 3, box 1, La Raza papers.

113. Board of directors meeting minutes, May 25, 1971, Denver YWCA papers; Mark Saiz to Don Pacheco and Sam Martinez, May 31, 1967, p. 2, folder 1, box 1, La Raza papers.

114. Board of directors meeting minutes, September 28, 1971, Denver YWCA papers; memo, March 31, 1970, p. 1, folder 1, box 1, La Raza papers.

115. Nominations to the board of directors, December 1971, p. 1, folder 2, box 1, La Raza papers.

116. By 1975 women held nine of the seventeen seats on the board. "Board Nominations for 1975," folder 3, box 1, La Raza papers.

117. Minutes of the annual meeting, May 2, 1970. On the national YWCA's adoption of the One Imperative to eliminate racism, see "Our History," YWCA website, http://www.ywca.org/site/pp.asp?c=djISI6PIKpG&b=281379.

118. Abbott, Leonard, and McComb, *Colorado*, 331.

119. Ibid., 330, 332.

120. "They Want an 8-Point Women's Bill of Rights NOW," *Rocky Mountain News*, August 27, 1970, in "Clipping File: Colorado: Women: Equal Rights, 1970," Western History and Genealogy Division, Denver Public Library.

121. Kathleen Cram, "'Remain on the Radical Edge,'" Denver NOW newsletter, August 1974, p. 6, folder 23, carton 3, NOW chapter newsletter collection.

122. "Open Forum," *Western Graphic*, October 8, 1971, p. 2, *Western Graphic 55–58*, Penrose Library, University of Denver.

123. Freeman, *Politics of Women's Liberation*, 85. Stephanie Gilmore uncovered a dynamic similar to the one outlined by Freeman in the NOW chapters she examined, especially Memphis NOW. Gilmore, *Groundswell*.

124. See "Board Elections: Candidate Profiles," Denver NOW newsletter, November 1971, p. 4; and Sally Crandall, "Profiles," Denver NOW newsletter, November 1972, p. 7, both in folder 23, carton 3, NOW chapter newsletter collection. None of NOW's leaders or active members appear to have belonged to other women's organizations; NOW served a new constituency of Denver women.

125. Barasko, *Governing NOW*, chap. 4; Gilmore, *Groundswell*.

126. "They're Talking about It: Bills That You Should Know About and Be Writing About," Denver NOW newsletter, July 1971, p. 4, folder 23, carton 3, NOW chapter newsletter collection.

127. "Get to Grass Roots Theme of Workshop," Denver NOW newsletter, September 1971, p. 3; and "Effort to Liberalize Abortion Law Fails," Denver NOW newsletter, March 1972, p. 3, both in folder 23, carton 3, NOW chapter newsletter collection.

128. "NOW Entertains, Informs Legislators at Buffet Dinner", Denver NOW newsletter, January 1973, p. 1, folder 23, carton 3, NOW chapter newsletter collection.

129. "NOW Honors the Winners," Denver NOW newsletter, September 1975, p. 1, folder 23, carton 3, NOW chapter newsletter collection.

130. "Effort to Liberalize Abortion Law Fails"; "Looking Ahead: NOW Goes 'Big-

Time,'" Denver NOW newsletter, January 1974, p. 1; "Republican Women Needed for State WPC," Denver NOW newsletter, March 1973, p. 1, all in folder 23, carton 3, NOW chapter newsletter collection.

131. "Caucus Started," Denver NOW newsletter, June 1973, p. 1, folder 23, carton 3, NOW chapter newsletter collection.

132. "Task Force Chairpersons [and officers], 1974," Denver NOW newsletter March 1974, p. 7; "Final Nominees Named; Voting in December," Denver NOW newsletter December 1973, pp. 1, 3, both in folder 23, carton 3, NOW chapter newsletter collection.

133. Rymph, *Republican Women*, 190.

134. "Consciousness = Self-Knowledge," Denver NOW newsletter, June 1972, folder 23, carton 3, NOW chapter newsletter collection.

135. Ibid.

136. "Meeting," Denver NOW newsletter, January 1974, p. 1; "Image, Role, and Identity: Concepts for Thought," Denver NOW newsletter, April 1974, p. 4; "C-R Groups Forming," Denver NOW newsletter, December 1975, p. 9; "C-R Task Force," Denver NOW newsletter, July 1976, p. 10, all in folder 23, carton 3, NOW chapter newsletter collection.

137. "Workshop Topic: Rape," Denver NOW newsletter, May 1972, p. 1, folder 23, carton 3, NOW chapter newsletter collection.

138. "Rape: A Personal Account"; "Rape: A Panel Discussion," both in Denver NOW newsletter, April 1973, p. 4, folder 23, carton 3, NOW chapter newsletter collection.

139. "Crisis Line Established," Denver NOW newsletter, July 1973, p. 3, folder 23, carton 3, NOW chapter newsletter collection.

140. "Coalition Plans Conference on Rape for March 2," Denver NOW newsletter, February 1974, p. 4, folder 23, carton 3, NOW chapter newsletter collection.

141. "Rape Task Force Merges with Coalition," Denver NOW newsletter, April 1974, p. 3, folder 23, carton 3, NOW chapter newsletter collection; "Association Review Report" April 8, 1975.

142. "Criminal Justice Committee Report," *Voter* newsletter, April 1974, p. 4, folder 8, box 2, Denver LWV papers.

143. "Rape Task Force Merges with Coalition."

144. "August Task Force Reports," Denver NOW newsletter, September 1974, p. 4, folder 23, carton 3, NOW chapter newsletter collection.

145. Judi Stutman, "Legislation on Sexual Assault," Denver NOW newsletter, July 1975, p. 7, folder 23, carton 3, NOW chapter newsletter collection.

146. Ezekiel, *Feminism in the Heartland*, 237.

147. On Indianapolis's Women Against Rape program, see "Image, Local," Indianapolis NOW newsletter, April 1974, p. 5, folder 1, box 2, "IndiaNOWpolis Woman" newsletter collection. The Durham YWCA ran a rape crisis hotline through its Women's Center. YWCA board of directors meeting minutes, September 25, 1975, p. 2, folder 34, box 35, Durham YWCA papers.

148. "NOW Acts," Denver NOW newsletter, March 1971, p. 1, folder 23, carton 3, NOW chapter newsletter collection.

149. "Mountain Bell Talks Big; Little Action Results," Denver NOW newsletter, January 1973, p. 1, folder 23, carton 3, NOW chapter newsletter collection.

150. "NOW Demonstrates Support for Western's Stewardesses," Denver NOW newsletter, November 1974, p. 6, folder 23, carton 3, NOW chapter newsletter collection. In addition to the picketing, the woman's union also sued the airline.

151. "Meeting," Denver NOW newsletter, March 1973, p. 1, folder 23, carton 3, NOW chapter newsletter collection.

152. "Local NOW Adopts Minority Women Resolutions," Denver NOW newsletter, April 1973, p. 1, folder 23, carton 3, NOW chapter newsletter collection.

153. "Minority Women State Goals," Denver NOW newsletter, May 1973, p. 3, folder 23, carton 3, NOW chapter newsletter collection.

154. "Minority Women's Task Force Decides to Go on Own," Denver NOW newsletter, March 1974, p. 4, folder 23, carton 3, NOW chapter newsletter collection.

155. Roth, *Separate Roads to Feminism*, 82–85, 92, 96–97; Springer, *Living for the Revolution*, 116.

156. "Minority Women's Task Force Pulling Out of NOW," *Denver Post*, March 27, 1974, p. 57. In making this decision, Denver NOW's black members were in line with many other feminists of color around the country. See Roth, *Separate Roads to Feminism*, chap. 5.

157. "Minority Women's Task Force Pulling Out of NOW."

158. "Minority Women's Task Force Decides to Go On Own."

159. "Meeting," Denver NOW newsletter, June 1974, p. 1, folder 23, carton 3, NOW chapter newsletter collection.

160. "Minority Women's Task Force Meets," Denver NOW newsletter, December 1975, p. 10, folder 23, carton 3, NOW chapter newsletter collection.

Chapter Five. Responses to Conservatism and the Evolution of Political Tactics

1. *Voter* newsletter, June 1978, p. 7, folder 8, box 2, Denver LWV papers.

2. "Public Relations," *Voter* newsletter, October 1977, p. 3, folder 8, box 2, Denver LWV papers.

3. Annual Report 1964–65, p. 15, folder 2, box 2, Denver LWV papers. This response was to the question, "Did you experience any attacks on League positions this year?" Including such a question on the annual report form is a clear indication that the national League was aware that its positions were sometimes controversial.

4. Zelizer, *Taxing America*, 160. Other works that examine consensus politics include Fraser and Gerstle, *Rise and Fall*; Hodgson, *America in Our Time*; Patterson, *Grand Expectations*; and Wall, *Inventing the "American Way."*

5. On the founding of the League, see Young, *In the Public Interest*.

6. On the political goals and tactics of social conservative women, see Critchlow,

Phyllis Schlafly and Grassroots Conservatism; Klatch, *Women of the New Right*; McGirr, *Suburban Warriors;* and Nickerson, *Mothers of Conservatism.*

7. Historians are just beginning to delve into the central role of gender politics in reshaping the American political order in these years. See Self, *All in the Family*; and Spruill, "Gender and America's Right Turn."

8. On the loaves of bread incident, see Mathews and de Hart, *Sex, Gender.*

9. Stephanie Gilmore finds a similar dynamic at work among members of Memphis's NOW chapter. Because Tennessee ratified the national amendment quickly, Memphis NOW did not give it much attention and was caught flat-footed when an organized drive to rescind ratification developed. Gilmore, *Groundswell*, 52–55.

10. *Voter* newsletter, February 1975, p. 5, folder 8, box 2, Denver LWV papers. Also see *Voter* newsletter, August 1975, p. 4, folder 8, box 2, Denver LWV papers; board of directors meeting minutes, September 25, 1975, p. 2, folder 29, box 4, Denver YWCA papers. On the League's continued activism after attempts to gain repeal through legislation failed, see *Voter* newsletter, December 1975/January 1976, pp. 5–6, folder 8, box 2, Denver LWV papers. For more on rescission nationally, see Berry, *Why ERA Failed*, 70–74.

11. "League Lobbies: ERA," *Voter* newsletter, December 1975/January 1976, p. 5.

12. Board of directors meeting minutes, February 25, 1975, p. 4, folder 29, box 4, Denver YWCA papers. See also "Anti-ERA Petition Submitted," Denver NOW newsletter, July 1976, p. 1, folder 23, carton 3, NOW chapter newsletter collection.

13. Board of directors meeting minutes, September 25, 1975.

14. "Anti-ERA Petition Submitted"; "The Fight against ERA," *Denver Post*, August 8, 1976, p. 6.

15. "ERA Colorado," Denver NOW newsletter, July 1976, p. 1, folder 3, carton 23, NOW chapter newsletter collection; Elizabeth King Brown, Denver YWCA director, to Mr. Munn, ERAmerica national office, August 19, 1976, folder 10, box 93, ERAmerica papers.

16. "Drive to Kill ERA in Colo. Meets Defeat," *Denver Post*, November 3, 1976, p. 56, in "Clipping File—ERA," Western History & Genealogy Division, Denver Public Library.

17. CCSW meeting minutes, April 24, 1976, p. 2, folder 11, box 3, Commissions on the Status of Women collection.

18. See, for instance, the YWCA's efforts to create a pro-ERA group in late 1972. "Vocal Point" newsletter, fall 1972, p. 1, folder 7, box 37, Denver YWCA papers.

19. "Phyllis and Janie to All NOW Members," Denver NOW newsletter, March 1976, p. 7; "Action Task Force Report," Denver NOW newsletter, May 1976, p. 6, both in folder 23, carton 3, NOW chapter newsletter collection.

20. "PSA's," Denver NOW newsletter, April 1976, p. 6, folder 23, carton 3, NOW chapter newsletter collection.

21. "Public Relations Task Force," Denver NOW newsletter, April 1976, p. 5, folder 23, carton 3, NOW chapter newsletter collection.

22. David L. Abrams, ERA Colorado Development Coordinator, to Beverly Baily, August 19, 1976, p. 2, folder 7, box 93, ERAmerica papers.

23. Sue Bollman was an active member of the Denver League of Women Voters, heading that group's ERA task force for several years. See, for example, "League Lobbies," *Voter* newsletter, February 1976, p. 6, box 2, folder 8, Denver LWV papers.

24. Sue Bollman and Barbara Dean to Shelia Greenwald, ERA America Executive Director, July 22, 1977, folder 7, box 93, ERAmerica papers.

25. Shelia Greenwald to Sue Bollman and Barbara Dean, August 8, 1977, folder 7, box 93, ERAmerica papers.

26. Ibid.

27. "Women's Resource Center," Denver NOW newsletter, May 1976, p. 12, folder 23, carton 3, NOW chapter newsletter collection.

28. Josie Heath and Betty Karowsky, Chairs of the CCSW, to "Dear Friend," August 24, 1979, folder 19, box 32, Denver YWCA papers.

29. Undated memo to "Dear Friends," folder 19, box 32, Denver YWCA papers.

30. Ibid.

31. "Interbranch Notes," AAUW newsletter, November 1978, p. 4, folder 6, box 6, series VIII, AAUW of Denver papers.

32. "Legislative Priorities 1979 for Denver Branch," AAUW newsletter, March 1979, p. 3, folder 6, box 6, series VIII, AAUW of Denver papers.

33. The legislature elected in 1976 had eighteen Republicans and seventeen Democrats in the senate, and thirty-four Republicans and thirty-one Democrats in the house. http://www.leg.state.co.us/lcs/leghist.nsf?OpenDatabase, accessed June 21, 2011.

34. "As Usual, CO Legislators Vow Efficiency, Hard Work," *Denver Post*, January 3, 1979, pp. 3, 22.

35. Mathews and de Hart, *Sex, Gender*, 185.

36. Ibid., 205.

37. In 1975 the organization changed its name from North Carolinians United for ERA to ERA United. For the sake of consistency and clarity, I refer to the group as NCUERA throughout the text.

38. NCUERA board of directors meeting minutes, March 13, 1977, p. 1, folder 1, box 2, Gail Bradley papers.

39. Ibid.

40. "Legislative Overview: Legislative 'Climate' in North Carolina," NCUERA Legislative Report, fall 1976, p. 4, folder 6, box 1, Gail Bradley papers.

41. What Happened?," ERA United newsletter, May 22, 1975, p. 1, folder 7, box 103, ERAmerica papers.

42. Wyatt-Brown, *Southern Honor*.

43. In their study of the ERA in North Carolina, Donald Mathews and Jane Sherron de Hart identify the state's pro-ERA forces as "for the most part white." Mathews and de Hart, *Sex, Gender*, 124.

44. What Happened?"

45. "Legislative Overview: Legislative 'Climate' in North Carolina."

46. Memo, Gail Bradley to Anita Miller, Equal Rights Amendment Project, Sacramento, March 15, 1976, p. 1, folder 6, box 1, Gail Bradley papers.

47. Memo to ERA United board members, June 1, 1976, p. 1, folder 6, box 1, Gail Bradley papers. The majority of NCUERA's "political advisors" and lobbyists throughout the ERA fight were men, another stark difference from the situation in Indiana, where Virginia Dill McCarthy took the lead on the amendment's behalf in the state legislature.

48. Clipping, "Tar Heel GOP Asking for More Trouble," *Raleigh News and Observer*, May 28, 1976, in folder 6, box 1, Gail Bradley papers.

49. Shelia Greenwald to Jane Patterson, July 21, 1977, p. 1, folder 3, box 104, ERAmerica papers.

50. Assessment report by Karolyn Kaye-Hervey, enclosed with Karolyn Kaye-Hervey to Shelia Greenwald, ERA America executive director, and Maria Bliss, NCUERA executive director, May 9, 1978, pp. 3–4, folder 8, box 103, ERAmerica papers.

51. Ruth Mary Meyer, LWV of N.C. President, to "Dear Friend," July 1978, p. 1, folder 17, box 4, Durham LWV papers.

52. "YWCA Membership," Women's Center newsletter, July 14, 1977, p. 3, folder 15, box 7, Durham YWCA papers. Gilna Nance was hired in the summer of 1974 to be the center's director, and in 1978 Suzi Woodward was serving in that role. Both women were on the YWCA payroll. Gilna Nance oral history; Suzi Woodward to "Dear Lawyer," January 30, 1978, p. 1, folder 15, box 7, Durham YWCA papers.

53. Gilna Nance to "Dear Milly," May 13, 1976, p. 2, folder 15, box 7, Durham YWCA papers.

54. Gilna Nance oral history. An article in the Women's Center newsletter also records the 1976 sale of the Central building but indicates that the group did not abandon the Central building until 1979. Presumably the group was renting it from the current owner in the intervening three years. Durham Women's Center newsletter, November 15, 1979, pp. 1 and 6, folder 7, box 15, Durham YWCA papers.

55. "YWCA membership," Women's Center newsletter, July 14, 1977.

56. Gilna Nance oral history, p. 1; YWCA Women's Center newsletter, May 1978, pp. 1–2, folder 15, box 7, Durham YWCA papers.

57. "President's Letter," Durham Women's Center newsletter, November 15, 1979, pp. 3–4, folder 15, box 7, Durham YWCA papers, parentheses in original.

58. See President Patricia Robert Harris, remarks to national convention, May 18, 1979, folder 7, box 7, Durham YWCA papers.

59. Board of directors meeting minutes, November 15, 1976, p. 2, folder 4, box 2, Durham LWV papers.

60. "President's Letter," Durham LWV newsletter, January 1978, p. 2, folder 11, box 1, Durham LWV papers.

61. Ibid.

62. Phyllis Noel, "Members Corner: Some Thoughts on the League," November

1979 newsletter, p. 2, folder 11, box 1, Durham LWV papers, abbreviation and emphasis in original.

63. Board of directors meeting minutes, November 8, 1979, p. 1, folder 5, box 2, Durham LWV papers.

64. In 1961 the "candidate meeting"—the League-hosted debate—had 100 percent attendance, a success Mrs. Byrnes, the Voters' Services chair, attributed to "the more secure position of the League in the community at [that] time." Board of directors meeting minutes, May 25, 1961, folder 23, box 1, Durham LWV papers.

65. "Goals for 80–81, Adopted by Durham LWV Board of Directors," Agenda for August 1980 board of directors meeting, p. 3, folder 5, box 2, Durham LWV papers.

66. In February 1978, the League organized a public discussion on President Carter's actions with regard to the Panama Canal. Board of directors meeting minutes, January 22, 1978, pp. 1–2, folder 5, box 2, Durham LWV papers.

67. "ERA Booth at Duke University, April 14. Give an Hour to ERA!," p. 8, Durham LWV newsletter, April 1978, folder 11, box 1, Durham LWV papers.

68. "Three New Committee Opportunities," p. 1, Durham LWV newsletter, March 1978, folder 11, box 1, Durham LWV papers.

69. "Women's Rights Committee," p. 3, Durham LWV newsletter, October 1978, folder 11, box 1, Durham LWV papers.

70. "Women's Rights Committee," p. 4, Durham LWV newsletter, December 1978, folder 11, box 1, Durham LWV papers.

71. Marion Nichol's Remembrance, in "A Voice for Change: The Years 1951–1995," p. 34, folder 7, box 1 (accession 2000–0268), Durham LWV papers. Nichol was the second consecutive Durham League member to serve as state president, following Ruth Mary Meyer, who held the office from 1975 to1979.

72. "Goals for 80–81, Adopted by Durham LWV Board of Directors," agenda for August 1980 board of directors meeting, p. 3, folder 5, box 2, Durham LWV papers.

73. On this evolution, see Spruill, "Gender and America's Right Turn," 71–89.

74. "Natural Resources: Environment," Annual Report 1978 (for 1977–78 program year), p. 1, folder 9, box 4, Indianapolis LWV papers.

75. The rider was first attached to the appropriations bill for Medicaid in 1976.

76. Board of directors meeting minutes, July 20, 1978, p. 1, folder 7, box 3, Indianapolis LWV papers.

77. Board of directors meeting minutes, April 25, 1978, p. 4, folder 7, box 3, Indianapolis LWV papers.

78. Board of directors meeting minutes, May 10, 1978, p. 1, folder 7, box 3, Indianapolis LWV papers.

79. Mary Lou Rothe, oral history questionnaire, June 3, 2011, p. 2.

80. Betty Williams, oral history questionnaire, June 8, 2011, p. 2.

81. Nancy Chesterton Smith, oral history questionnaire, May 27, 2011, p. 2.

82. Nancy C. Smith, "Impact on Issues: Proposed National Program '76–'78", April 1976, p. 2, folder 5, box 3, Indianapolis LWV papers.

83. Smith, oral history, p. 1.

84. Rothe, oral history, p. 2.

85. Ibid.

86. "At Last! Women's Shelter NOW," "IndiaNOWpolis Woman" newsletter, June 1979, p. 1; "Battered Wimmin," "IndiaNOWpolis Woman" newsletter, October 1979, p. 4, both in IndiaNOWpolis Woman newsletter collection.

87. Jill Chambers, "Bayh Bayh, Quayle!" "IndiaNOWpolis Woman" newsletter, December 1979, p. 4, IndiaNOWpolis Woman newsletter collection, emphasis in original.

88. Indianapolis LWV 1978 Annual Report, p. 10, folder 9, box 4, Indianapolis LWV papers.

Conclusion

1. See, for example, Echols, *Daring to Be Bad*, 287–92; Evans, *Tidal Wave*, chap. 6; Valk, *Radical Sisters*, 181–86.

2. Faludi, "Death of a Revolutionary," 57.

3. Gilmore, *Groundswell*, 19.

4. "The 1972 Virginia Slims American Women's Opinion Poll" (includes 1971 data), http://arc.irss.unc.edu/dvn/faces/study/StudyPage.xhtml?globalId=hdl:1902.29/H-2137&studyListingIndex=0_888a7ffac98ae0246e054aab53de; "The 1974 Virginia Slims America Women's Opinion Poll," http://arc.irss.unc.edu/dvn/faces/study/StudyPage.xhtml?globalId=hdl:1902.4/USRSPVASLIMS1974–0547&studyListingIndex=0_888a7ffac98ae0246e054aab53de; "The 1980 Virginia Slims American Women's Opinion Poll," http://arc.irss.unc.edu/dvn/faces/study/StudyPage.xhtml?globalId=hdl:1902.4/USRSPVASLIMS1979–0678&studyListingIndex=0_888a7ffac98ae0246e054aab53de, all in Odum Institute Dataverse, http://arc.irss.unc.edu/dvn/, University of North Carolina–Chapel Hill, accessed June 15, 2013.

5. "The Male-Female Ratio in College," *Forbes Magazine*, February 16, 2012, http://www.forbes.com/sites/ccap/2012/02/16/the-male-female-ratio-in-college/, accessed June 13, 2013.

6. "U.S. Firms: Ownership by Gender, Race, Ethnicity, and Veteran Status," U.S. Census Bureau, *2012 Statistical Abstract*, 507. http://www.census.gov/compendia/statab/2012/tables/12s0768.pdf, accessed June 13, 2013.

7. Annie-Rose Strasser, "Despite Growing Number of Female Lawyers and Doctors, Women's Pay Still Lags Behind," December 5, 2012, *ThinkProgress* website, http://thinkprogress.org/economy/2012/12/05/1284131/women-pay-gap-persists/?mobile=nc, accessed July 8, 2013.

8. Chappell, "Reagan's 'Gender Gap,'" 117.

9. Evans, *Tidal Wave*, 190.

10. Brigid Schulte, "Nearly 40 Percent of Mothers Are Now Family Breadwinners, Report Says," *Washington Post*, May 29, 2013.

11. The group's work on these issues is under the auspices of state-level areas of consensus, and both are grouped under the broad heading of "social justice."

"Positions of the League of Women Voters of Indiana," http://www.lwvin.org/Positions_LWV_Indiana.html, accessed June 13, 2013.

12. League of Orange-Durham-Chatham, "Positions for Action" http://odc.nc.lwvnet.org/ActionAlerts.html#action, accessed June 13, 2013

13. "Advocacy," Denver League of Women Voters website, http://www.lwvdenver.org/advocacy/index.html, accessed July 8, 2013.

14. YWCA of Indianapolis, "YWCA of Indianapolis to Officially Close this Spring," http://www.ywca.org/site/pp.asp?c=qkI3KgMTIrF&b=3841093, accessed June 13, 2013.

15. YWCA FAQ, http://www.ywca.org/site/c.cuIRJ7NTKrLaG/b.7515903/k.ADCE/FAQ.htm, accessed June 13, 2013.

BIBLIOGRAPHY

Primary Sources

Archival Collections

ATLANTA, GEORGIA

Special Collections and Archives, Georgia State University Library

North Carolina AFL-CIO papers

CAMBRIDGE, MASSACHUSETTS

Arthur and Elizabeth Schlesinger Library, Radcliffe Institute, Harvard University

Committees on the Status of Women Collection
NOW Chapter Newsletter Collection

CHAPEL HILL, NORTH CAROLINA

Wilson Library, University of North Carolina–Chapel Hill

Southern Oral History Program Collection

DENVER, COLORADO

Library of the Colorado Historical Society

Young Women's Christian Association of Denver papers
La Raza—Denver Chapter papers

Penrose Library, University of Denver

Peryl H. and Ira M. Beck Memorial Archive

Special Collections Division, Auraria Library, University of Colorado–Denver

American Association of University Women, Denver Chapter papers

Western History and Genealogy Division, Denver Public Library

Colorado State Association of Colored Women's Clubs papers
Delta Sigma Theta scrapbooks
Denver Fortnightly Club papers
League of Women Voters of Denver papers

DURHAM, NORTH CAROLINA

David M. Rubenstein Rare Book & Manuscript Library, Duke University

Winifred Gail Bradley papers
Sara Evans papers
League of Women Voters of Durham papers
Young Women's Christian Association of Durham papers

INDIANAPOLIS, INDIANA

William Henry Smith Memorial Library, Indiana Historical Society

Churchwomen United of Indiana papers
Hoosiers for the ERA papers
League of Women Voters of Indianapolis papers
National Council of Jewish Women papers
National Council of Negro Women papers
Young Women's Christian Association of Indianapolis papers

WASHINGTON, D.C.

Manuscript Division, Library of Congress

ERAmerica papers

Newspapers

Carolina Times
Denver Post
Durham Morning Herald
Durham Sun
Indianapolis Star
Rocky Mountain News
Western Graphic
Underground Newspaper Collection, University of Virginia

Oral Histories

Carol Kirk, questionnaire administered by author, May 20, 2011.
Gilna Nance, questionnaire administered by author, June 1, 2011.
Mary Lou Rothe, questionnaire administered by author, June 3, 2011.
Nancy Chesterton Smith, questionnaire administered by author, May 27, 2011.
Betty Williams, questionnaire administered by author, June 8, 2011.
Connie Winstead, questionnaires administered by author, May 28 and August 23, 2011.

Websites

"Colorado Legislators Past and Present," http://www.state.co.us/gov_dir/leg_dir/lcsstaff/StaffInfo/LegislatorBiography.html

Odum Institute, University of North Carolina–Chapel Hill
http://www.irss.unc.edu/odum/home2.jsp

Secondary Sources

Abbott, Carl, Stephen J. Leonard, and David McComb. *Colorado: A History of the Centennial State*. Niwot, Colo.: University Press of Colorado, 1994.

Anderson, Jean. *Durham County: A History of Durham County, North Carolina*. Durham, N.C.: Duke University Press, 1990.

Barasko, Maryann. *Governing NOW: Grassroots Activism in the National Organization for Women*. Ithaca, N.Y.: Cornell University Press, 2004.

Bartley, Numan V. *The New South, 1945–1980*. Baton Rouge: Louisiana State University Press, 1995.

Baxandall, Rosalyn, and Elizabeth Ewen. *Picture Windows: How the Suburbs Happened*. New York: Basic Books, 2000.

Berry, Mary Frances. *Why ERA Failed: Politics, Women's Rights, and Amending the Constitution*. Bloomington: Indiana University Press, 1986.

Brienes, Winifred. *The Trouble between Us: An Uneasy History of White and Black Women in the Feminist Movement*. New York: Oxford, 2006.

Browder, Dorothea. "A 'Christian Solution to the Labor Situation': How Workingwomen Reshaped the YWCA's Religious Mission and Politics." *Journal of Women's History* 19, no. 2 (Summer 2007): 85–110.

Brown, Leslie. *Upbuilding Black Durham: Gender, Class, and Black Community Development in the Jim Crow South*. Chapel Hill: University of North Carolina Press, 2008.

Busby, Michelle. "The Price of Integration: The Charlotte YWCA in the 1960s." In *Men and Women Adrift: The YMCA and the YWCA in the City*, edited by Nina Mjagkij and Margaret Spratt, 206–30. New York: New York University Press, 1997

Cahn, Susan K. *Sexual Reckonings: Southern Girls in a Troubling Age*. Cambridge, Mass.: Harvard University Press, 2007.

Cazenave, Noel A. *Impossible Democracy: The Unlikely Success of the War on Poverty Community Action Programs*. Albany: State University of New York Press, 2007.

Chappell, Marisa. "Reagan's 'Gender Gap' and the Limitations of Free Market Feminism." *Journal of Policy History* 24, no. 1 (Winter 2012): 115–34.

———. "Rethinking Women's Politics in the 1970s: The League of Women Voters and the National Organization for Women Confront Poverty." *Journal of Women's History* 13, no. 4 (Winter 2002): 155–79.

———. *The War on Welfare: Family, Poverty, and Politics in Modern America*. Philadelphia: University of Pennsylvania Press, 2010.

Clotfelter, Charles T. *After Brown: The Rise and Retreat of School Desegregation*. Princeton, N.J.: Princeton University Press, 2004.

Cobble, Dorothy Sue. *The Other Women's Movement: Workplace Justice and Social Rights in Modern America.* Princeton, N.J.: Princeton University Press, 2004.

Critchlow, Donald T. *Phyllis Schlafly and Grassroots Conservatism: A Woman's Crusade.* Princeton, N.J.: Princeton University Press, 2005.

Deutsch, Sarah. *Women and the City: Gender, Space, and Power in Boston, 1870–1940.* New York: Oxford University Press, 2000.

Dorsett, Lyle W. *The Queen City: A History of Denver.* Boulder, Colo.: Pruett, 1977.

Douglas, Susan J. *Where the Girls Are: Growing Up Female with the Mass Media.* New York: Three Rivers Press, 1994.

Echols, Alice. *Daring to Be Bad: Radical Feminism in America 1967–1975.* Minneapolis: University of Minnesota Press, 1989.

Edwards, Rebecca. *Angels in the Machinery: Gender in American Party Politics from the Civil War to the Progressive Era.* New York: Oxford University Press, 1997.

Enke, Anne. *Finding the Movement: Sexuality, Contested Space, and Feminist Activism.* Durham, N.C.: Duke University Press, 2007.

Evans, Sara M. *Personal Politics: The Roots of Women's Liberation in the Civil Rights Movement and the New Left.* New York: Vintage, 1979.

———. *Tidal Wave: How Women Changed America at Century's End.* New York: Free Press, 2003.

Ezekiel, Judith. *Feminism in the Heartland.* Columbus: Ohio University Press, 2002.

Faludi, Susan. "Death of a Revolutionary." *New Yorker*, April 15, 2013.

Farrell, Amy Erdman. *Yours in Sisterhood:* Ms. *Magazine and the Promise of Popular Feminism.* Chapel Hill: University of North Carolina Press, 1998.

Fergus, Devin. *Liberalism, Black Power, and the Making of American Politics, 1965–1980.* Athens: University of Georgia Press, 2009.

Fraser, Steve, and Gary Gerstle, eds. *The Rise and Fall of the New Deal Order, 1930–1980.* Princeton, N.J.: Princeton University Press, 1989.

Freeman, Jo. *The Politics of Women's Liberation: A Case Study of an Emerging Social Movement and Its Relation to Public Policy.* New York: David McKay, 1975.

———. *A Room at a Time: How Women Entered Party Politics.* Boulder, Colo.: Rowman and Littlefield, 2000.

Gere, Anne Ruggles. *Intimate Practices: Literacy and Cultural Work in U.S. Women's Clubs, 1880–1920.* Urbana: University of Illinois Press, 1997.

Gerhard, Jane E. *The Dinner Party: Judy Chicago and the Power of Popular Feminism.* Athens: University of Georgia Press, 2013.

Gilmore, Stephanie. "The Dynamics of Second-Wave Feminist Activism in Memphis, 1971–1982: Rethinking the Liberal/Radical Divide." *NWSA Journal* 15, no. 1 (Spring 2003): 94–117.

———, ed. *Feminist Coalitions: Historical Perspectives on Second-Wave Feminism in the United States.* Urbana: University of Illinois Press, 2008.

———. *Groundswell: Grassroots Feminist Activism in Postwar America.* New York: Routledge, 2012.

Greene, Christina. *Our Separate Ways: Women and the Black Freedom Movement in Durham, North Carolina*. Chapel Hill: University of North Carolina Press, 2005.

Harrison, Cynthia. *On Account of Sex: The Politics of Women's Issues 1945–1968*. Berkeley: University of California Press, 1988.

Hartmann, Susan M. *The Other Feminists: Activists in the Liberal Establishment*. New Haven, Conn.: Yale University Press, 1998.

Hewitt, Nancy A., ed. *No Permanent Waves: Recasting Histories of U.S. Feminism*. New Brunswick, N.J.: Rutgers University Press, 2010.

Higginbotham, Evelyn Brooks. *Righteous Discontent: The Women's Movement in the Black Baptist Church, 1880–1920*. Cambridge, Mass.: Harvard University Press, 1993.

Hodgson, Godfrey. *America in Our Time: From World War II to Nixon, What Happened and Why*. New York: Vintage, 1976.

Klatch, Rebecca E. *Women of the New Right*. Philadelphia: Temple University Press, 1987.

Leary, Edward A. *Indianapolis: The Story of a City*. New York: Bobbs-Merrill, 1971.

Luker, Kristin. *Abortion and the Politics of Motherhood*. Berkeley: University of California Press, 1985.

Mathews, Donald, and Jane Sherron de Hart. *Sex, Gender, and the Politics of ERA: A State and the Nation*. New York: Oxford University Press, 1990.

McGirr, Lisa. *Suburban Warriors: The Origins of the New American Right*. Princeton, N.J.: Princeton University Press, 2001.

Meyerowitz, Joanne. "Beyond the Feminine Mystique: A Reassessment of Postwar Mass Culture, 1946–1958." In *Not June Cleaver: Women and Gender in Postwar America, 1945–1960*, edited by Joanne Meyerowitz, 229–62. Philadelphia: Temple University Press, 1994.

Muncy, Robyn. *Creating a Female Dominion in American Reform, 1890–1935*. New York: Oxford University Press, 1991.

Murray, Sylvie. *The Progressive Housewife: Community Activism in Suburban Queens, 1945–1965*. Philadelphia: University of Pennsylvania Press, 2003.

Nadasen, Premilla. *Welfare Warriors: The Welfare Rights Movement in America*. New York: Routledge, 2005.

Naples, Nancy A. *Grassroots Warriors: Activist Mothering, Community Work, and the War on Poverty*. New York: Routledge, 1998.

Nash, Gerald D., and Richard W. Etulian, eds. *The Twentieth Century West: Historical Interpretations*. Albuquerque: University of New Mexico Press, 1989.

Nickerson, Michelle. *Mothers of Conservatism: Women and the Postwar Right*. Princeton, N.J.: Princeton University Press, 2012.

Orleck, Annelise. "The War on Poverty from the Grassroots Up." In *The War on Poverty: A New Grassroots History, 1964–1980*, edited by Annelise Orleck and Lisa Gayle Hazirjian, 1–28. Athens: University of Georgia Press, 2011.

Patterson, James T. *Grand Expectations: The United States 1945–1974*. New York: Oxford University Press, 1996.

Pierce, Richard. *Polite Protest: The Political Economy of Race in Indianapolis, 1920–1970*. Bloomington: Indiana University Press, 2005.

Richardson, Lilliard E., Jr., and Patricia K. Freeman. "Gender Differences in Constituency Service among State Legislators." *Political Research Quarterly* 48, no. 1 (March 1995): 169–79.

Robertson, Nancy Marie. *Christian Sisterhood, Race Relations, and the YWCA, 1906–1946*. Urbana: University of Illinois Press, 2007.

Rosen, Ruth. *The World Split Open: How the Modern Women's Movement Changed America*. New York: Penguin, 2000.

Roth, Benita. *Separate Roads to Feminism: Black, Chicana, and White Feminist Movements in America's Second Wave*. New York: Cambridge University Press, 2004.

Rupp, Lelia J., and Verta Taylor. *Survival in the Doldrums: The American Women's Rights Movement, 1945–1960*. New York: Oxford University Press, 1987.

Rymph, Catherine E. *Republican Women: Feminism and Conservatism from Suffrage through the Rise of the New Right*. Chapel Hill: University of North Carolina Press, 2006.

Schuyler, Lorraine Gates. *The Weight of Their Votes: Southern Women and Political Leverage in the 1920s*. Chapel Hill: University of North Carolina Press, 2006.

Scroggins, Eloise E. "Organizing on Their Own Terms: Women and the Equal Rights Amendment in Indiana." Master's thesis, Indiana University–Purdue University Indianapolis, 2003.

Self, Robert O. *All in the Family: The Realignment of American Democracy since 1960*. New York: Hill and Wang, 2012.

Springer, Kimberly. *Living for the Revolution: Black Feminist Organizations, 1968–1980*. Durham, N.C.: Duke University Press, 2005.

Spruill, Marjorie. "Gender and America's Right Turn." In *Rightward Bound: Making America Conservative in the 1970s*, edited by Bruce J. Schulman and Julian E. Zelizer, 71–89. Cambridge, Mass.: Harvard University Press, 2008.

Thompson, Becky. "Multiracial Feminism: Rethinking the Chronology of Second Wave Feminism." *Feminist Studies* 28, no. 2 (Summer 2002): 337–60.

Valk, Anne M. *Radical Sisters: Second-Wave Feminism and Black Liberation in Washington, D.C.* Urbana: University of Illinois Press, 2008.

Wall, Wendy L. *Inventing the "American Way": The Politics of Consensus from the New Deal to the Civil Rights Movement*. New York: Oxford University Press, 2008.

Weiss, Jessica. *To Have and to Hold: Marriage, the Baby Boom, and Social Change*. Chicago: University of Chicago Press, 2000.

Wheeler, Marjorie Spruill. *New Women of the New South*. New York: Oxford University Press, 1993.

White, Deborah Gray. *Too Heavy a Load: Black Women in Defense of Themselves, 1894–1994*. New York: Norton, 1999.

Willrich, Michael. *Pox: An American History*. New York: Penguin, 2011.

Wyatt-Brown, Bertram. *Southern Honor: Ethics and Behavior in the Old South.* New York: Oxford University Press, 2007.

Young, Louise M. *In the Public Interest: The League of Women Voters, 1920–1970.* New York: Greenwood Press, 1989.

Zelizer, Julian. *Taxing America: Wilbur D. Mills, Congress, and the State, 1945–1975.* New York: Cambridge University Press, 1998.

INDEX